Choptank River

• East New Market

Cambridge

Sharptown

DELAWARE

Vienna

Mardella

Meekins Creek

Hebron

• Golden Hill

Rockawalking

Quantico

Salisbury
Tony Tank

Fishing Creek

Langrells
Island

Tyaskin

Fruitland

• Crapo

Elliott
Island

Nanticoke River

White
Haven

Head of
the Creek

OOPER
SLAND

Hoopersville

Wicomoco River

Mount Vernon

Perryhawkin
Princess Anne

Venton

Dames Quarter

Chance

Oriole

DEAL
ISLAND

Wenona

HOLLANDS
ISLAND

Fairmount

Teague Creek

CHESAPEAKE

Pocomoke City

Annemessex River

Marion

Rehobeth

Kizze's Point

SMITH
ISLAND

Ward's Crossing

Ewell

Hopewell

Shelltown

Rhodes
Point

Tylerton Calvar

Crisfield

JANE'S
ISLAND

Jenkins Creek

Lawsonia

Mariners

Sedges

Byrdtown

Pocomoke River

Great Point

Shanks

Saxis

VIRGINIA

BAY

TANGIER
ISLAND

0   6   12

miles

CORTESI

A Faraway Time and Place

Lore of the Eastern Shore

George Carey

A Faraway
Time and Place

Lore of the Eastern Shore

Robert B. Luce, Inc.

Washington-New York

For H.P.B.

Scholar, Seaman,
Mentor, Friend.

At the wharf, Rock Point, Maryland

Preface

The power of tradition and the art of oral storytelling, though diminished by the thrust of the mass media, are by no means dead on the Eastern Shore of Chesapeake Bay. This book, I hope, will bear that fact out. Yet if in a phrase we can call folklore the traditions of a specific group of people which are unconsciously passed along by imitation or word of mouth, then it might well be contended that folklore can never truly thrive on the pages of any book. Indeed, anyone who has listened to an Eastern Shore waterman, standing on the town wharf among his peers, deliver a tale in the rich local dialect may find these printed texts somewhat of a falling off. The compilation of this book has been pointed toward the collection and preservation of some of the oral stories and traditions that I have encountered in my field-work over the past four years. Certainly it is clear that the people themselves show little interest in their own folklore; understandably, it is carved too naturally into the fabric of their lives to even warrant investigation.

To say that this book represents the folklore of all the cultures of the Eastern Shore would be very misleading. The emphasis has been rather on one group, the white watermen, and on one small area, namely the region between the Nanticoke and the Pocomoke Rivers. But it is really quite foolish to try and impose too strict boundaries on folklore. If nothing else, it is ubiquitous. Tales that I have found active in Crisfield, others have discovered in Rock Hall, St. Michaels, Annapolis, as well as in Europe and Asia.

Obviously when one stresses one particular group, he slights others. The lower Eastern Shore of the Chesapeake is, after all, as much a farming culture as it is a maritime one. Almost as many people there follow the plow as follow the water. Also, a segment of the population is black and their remarkable folk culture deserves, and will no doubt soon receive, book-length treatment.

This book is not strictly speaking a book of folklore texts. When a story defied exact transcription I have tampered with it and put it into my own words. But when a tale is given as a direct quote I have endeavored to render it in the exact words of the storyteller, though I did not feel equipped to try and catch all subtle nuances of the regional dialect speech. In certain stories where I felt aspersion might be cast on particular individuals, I have taken the liberty of changing names.

Most of the material given here I gathered myself. In some instances, however, I have drawn on the contributions of students, and I am of course grateful to those students who took the time and energy to prepare good collections of folklore for the Maryland Folklore Archive in College Park. All the material in this book, both mine and that of students, is presently housed in that Archive. After each text of a story a number will appear. This number, if checked in the Appendix, will cite either the name and address of the storyteller or else will refer one to a collection in the Archive. (Many collectors requested that all names be withheld.) For example, an item listed as (ES 69-14) refers to a text that can be found in the 14th collection from the Eastern Shore turned over to the Archive in 1969.

As with any endeavor of this sort, one leans heavily on the favors of others. I am grateful to Richard M. Dorson, Rae Korson, Morris Freedman, Connie Jugans, Esther Birdsall, my editors Joseph Binns and Wendy Cortesi, the English Department at the University of Maryland, and to the Maryland University College system which provided me with courses to teach on the Eastern Shore of Maryland and thereby brought me closer to the culture through my students. Also, I am deeply indebted to The American Council of Learned Societies, the American Philosophical Society, and the University of Maryland General Research Board whose generous grants-in-aid enabled me to carry out my fieldwork with limited financial burdens. And last but not least, to my cheery wife go the deepest thanks. She has endured my absenses, withstood my moodiness, read and criticized manuscript, and all under the duress of maintaining a home, holding down a teaching position, and rearing a small urchin.

Contents

Introduction

Strangely enough, the idea for this book came to me in Bloomington, Indiana, of all places. During 1966, I was in the Midwest finishing up my Ph.D. dissertation. Always anxious to escape the rigors of that situation, my usual Sunday ritual was to buy a *New York Times* and lose myself in the travel section. One of those Sunday mornings I stumbled upon a piece about an engaging place, engaging for the folklorist at any rate. Smith Island, Maryland, the article explained, was a "marshy archipelago" lying eight miles off the Maryland coast in the middle of Chesapeake Bay. It was isolated; its people drew their living from the wildlife which the bay provided; its speech patterns dated back to the 17th century when the island was discovered; its religion: iron-bound Methodism. It was, according to the *Times* writer, "one of the last American frontiers."

Folk communities like this, I had been told, tended to be conservative and to preserve tradition. And, as I had been searching for a place to do some fieldwork and study, Smith Island's location dovetailed nicely with my plans to teach folklore at the University of Maryland the following year. Moreover, I knew that no one previously had conducted folklore field research on the Chesapeake Bay's Eastern Shore.

Once in Maryland I began some probing. I looked at maps and charts, read some books about the Eastern Shore, and took several investigative trips to view the area and get a sense of the people. The more probing I did, the better things looked. Long fingers of marshland snaked out into the Bay from the Eastern Shore, divided and criss-crossed by rivers and creeks. At the ends of these long peninsulas stood small villages populated primarily by watermen and their families, all cut off from the hustle of Routes US 50 and 13 which split the Eastern Shore in two. Beyond the long land fingers lay the islands themselves, Smith Island in Maryland and Tangier Island in Virginia. And the towns on the mainland suggested folk speech and naming: Dames Quarter, Crapo, Fishing Creek, Chance, Shelltown, Calvary.

During the academic year I pressed my students into service. I sent them back to their hometown communities to see what sorts of oral traditions they might unearth. Several residents from the Eastern Shore returned with fertile collections. One young man in particular secured such a rich variety of traditional stories from the area around Crisfield that I decided the lower Eastern Shore of Maryland (what Mencken used to refer to as "trans-Choptankian") held the kind of folk culture I was after. Thus, on the 5th of July, 1967, armed with a notebook and a tape recorder, I left College Park, headed east, and two and one half hours later I was in Crisfield, once labelled "The Seafood Capitol of the World." It is no longer; like many ports along the Maine coast, it is a bypassed pocket of culture, a dead town in the eyes of some, but alive with the oral traditions and the deep-set pattern of life that make a folklorist's pulse quicken.

As suggested, only sketchy folklore collecting has been carried out on the Eastern Shore, and that all too often by untrained folklorists. Such a meaty sounding title as *Land of Legendary Lore,* published at the turn of the century when picturesque books on "charming" places were common, turns out to be little more than an uneven local history of Talbot County with one chapter on folklore entitled, "Weird Tales that are Told." Similarly, a volume called *Recollection of a Long Life on the Eastern Shore* provides the reader with little but nostalgia concerning the writer's upbringing and the family's paternalistic attitude towards their slaves. More recently, Hulbert Footner's *Rivers of the Eastern Shore* comes closer to sampling the folk culture, although he too fastened his main attention on the quaint and picturesque. Footner, during his travels up and down these marshland rivers, evidently did have an ear open for folk speech and the traditional spoken tale. He rightly terms Crisfield a place where "salty yarns" roll off the tongues of raconteurs, and he retells several tales

12

which I collected versions of twenty-three years later.

A number of quite recent publications have dealt with the folk culture and life style of those who follow the maritime trade on the Chesapeake Bay. William Tawes's *God, Man, Salt Water and the Eastern Shore* recollects his childhood days around Jenkins Creek just below Crisfield. The book, though too personal at times and frequently impeded by rambling philosophical comments, does depict the traditional flavor of life in a small fishing community on the lower Eastern Shore. A splendid book and much more acute and sensitive in its approach to folklife and traditional methods of fishing and oystering on the Bay is Varley Lang's *Follow the Water.* Lang is not a native but he is a waterman nonetheless, and he knows the trade and the men who follow the water. His understanding of the watermen's conservative nature and independent temperament complements his extensive knowledge of their traditional methods for securing a living from the Bay. Interspersed with the explanations and descriptions of fishing practices one also finds well chosen examples of the waterman's speech patterns, humor and lore.

Writers like Tawes and Lang, without being actively aware of it, have produced literature of great value to the student of folk culture. In their attempts to explain their trade or recollect their past they have described their culture, not as professional scholars, but as men who know their group from the inside out. Novelists likewise frequently produce pieces of fiction which unconsciously reveal a good deal about their culture. Gilbert Bryon, lifelong resident of the Eastern Shore, captures the sense of folklife as he remembered it growing up on the Chester River. In *The Lord's Oysters,* he reveals his sensitivity towards proverbial folk speech, his awareness of traditional weather lore, and his sympathy and understanding of the waterman's habits. Superstition, traditional children's games, ghost yarns and tall tales are all woven naturally into the fabric of his story which is told from the wide-eyed viewpoint of the child. Similarly, R. Nels's novel, *The Unpolished Diamond* sets twentieth century Tangier Island characters in the period of 1812 and unwinds a love story of war and woe. Interestingly enough, the book, written under a pseudonym, was suppressed on the lower Eastern Shore after its publication in 1930, as island inhabitants felt it was uncomplimentary to their young girls.

Clearly, though, Nels had done his homework, for all the names of characters ring true (common surnames such as Riggin, Sterling, Dize, Crockett, and Lawson), and the description of the folk milieu appears to be accurate. In a passage much like Twain's description of the raftmen's storytelling session in *Life on the Mississippi,* the author recounts a yarning episode on the Bay in which a group of watermen trade ghost stories and songs aboard ship. In another instance Nels explains that,

> every afternoon and evening, except on Sundays, a large percentage of the Island's male population congregated at Harve Peters' store and smoked and gossiped and drank and cajoled. On this particular day the Islanders had exhausted sundry topics ranging from the last time a ghost was seen on Tangier to the possible outcome of the war. (p. 254)

While most books on the Eastern Shore incorporate folk material unconsciously, there is some indication that a few individuals have actively sought folklore *per se* in that region. As early as 1889 Fanny Bergen published an article in the *Journal of American Folklore* which cited a number of black superstitions found on the Eastern Shore, but she made little comment other than that they existed. Bullock and Whitney canvassed for folklore through the mails to produce their *Folk-lore from Maryland.* A good portion of it came from the Eastern Shore, but it is impossible to tell from the context of the book precisely where or from whom the traditions came. More recently, John Burrison, a professionally trained folklorist, uncovered Captain George Allan Wheatley on Tangier Island and recorded a number of his songs and anecdotes. Other than this, the folklorist has left the Eastern Shore pretty much alone.

This thin sheaf of writing, then, provided my only introduction to Eastern Shore folk culture as I turned my car off Route 13 and headed down that long flat finger of land to Crisfield. Much of the town of Crisfield (pop. 5000) sits on oyster shells. During the years of the great oyster harvests between 1880 and

1920 the town actually grew physically in size as more and more oyster shells piled up and watermen constantly moved their shanties further and further out into the Little Annamessex River to be at the water's edge. The town itself clusters around two centers: the waterfront and the main village. Crab houses line the harbor on either side of the main wharf. A new modern marina flourishes on the inner harbor. In the village proper, a drab main street cuts between a series of two story buildings: stores, a restaurant, a barber shop, a filling station, and a dispensary. Then the main street runs out of town southward between a procession of traditional I-houses (one room deep, two rooms wide) to the outlying communities of Lawsonia, Calvary, Jenkins Creek, and Mariners. Black communities are interspersed with white ones, as Crisfield has no single black settlement which is confined to a particular area. Though once oriented totally to the seafood business, Crisfield has recently begun to branch out in other directions. A rubber factory and a knife-making plant suggest a drift towards industrialization and the inevitable influx of people whose habits and background are not those of the watermen.

Since I knew no one in the town, I thought my best approach might be at the office of the local newspaper, *The Crisfield Times*. There I sat across the desk from a tall aristocratic Eastern Shoreman named Quinn whose family had owned and run the weekly for several generations. I was collecting old stories and customs for a book; did he know who might help me out? Yes, and he gave me a couple of names. I might do just as well, he continued, to simply hang around the bench down on the wharf and listen to some of the old timers who spent the better part of their day there. Did the black people still sing in the crab houses while they were picking crabs? Not like they used to although some still do. But we don't need anybody like you around here stirring up those people. I explained that was the farthest thing from my mind and departed in search of some of the people Quinn had mentioned.

As any fieldworker in folklore knows, much of the proffered information that one receives leads down blind alleys. People who are touted as "good talkers" or "fellas who can really tell you something" frequently turn out to be bereft of any traditional material or presently so absorbed with religion that they have forgotten all the old yarns they used to know. My first few days in Crisfield were just that unpropitious. Calling at the homes of different old people in the town, I was continually put off ("Oh, if you'd only come down here twenty-five years ago"), and each visit simply turned out to be more disappointing than the last. Finally, I took Quinn's advice and went down to the "liar's bench" on the town wharf. In the space of one afternoon, sitting between two old watermen while others passed back and forth, I collected more than one hundred traditional stories, anecdotes, and beliefs.

Off and on for the next two and a half years I spent summers and free time in the winter months garnering waterman's folklore in the area below Cambridge, Maryland. I spent time on Smith Island and Tangier. I wandered the waterfronts and frequented the stores of Deal Island, Chance and Dames Quarter. I went out with the crabmen when they crab potted and joined the proggers when they sought clams along the shores. I shipped with the crew of dredge boats to witness their methods and better understand their folk culture. I talked with those who ran the crab houses and those who worked in them. I interviewed men who worked on the Bay at the turn of the century and conversed with others who had previously been blue water sailors.

Collecting folklore from such a wide variety of people over an extended period of time invariably produces odd incidents for the collector. During the summer of 1968 several people in the Crisfield area suggested I go and talk with Captain Charles McMann. He was old, had followed the water all his life, and was now retired and had plenty of time to talk. Surely he would tell me something. I knocked at the door of his house one afternoon and his wife let me in. No, her husband was out right now, but if I would come back the following day he would be glad to talk with me and she would let him know. Twenty four hours later I stood before the same door and knocked again. No answer. After a few moments a neighbor approached me from the other side of the street.

"Are you looking for Charlie McMann?"

"Yes, I was supposed to see him this afternoon."

16

"Well," she explained, "I don't think you'll be able to; he died of a heart attack last night."

Not all my experiences were quite so traumatic. Most of them were more amusing, at least in retrospect. Later that same summer I went out to Smith Island for a week. Before I left I parked my car in a local lot not far from the main wharf. I locked most of my valuables in the trunk but left some clothing on the back seat. When I returned from the island a week later, the driver's vent window had been smashed and the car broken into. All the clothes were gone except for what I thought was a nice madras sports jacket which lay in the back seat. On top of it sat the traditional *grumus merdae* or burglar's calling card, not the usual feces, but a used prophylactic. While seeking tradition in one place, I had been victimized by it in another in what is one of the oldest traditional rites of thieves.

There were other amusing incidentalia. Though the folklorist employs the benefits of modern technology, they are not always impervious. Tape recorders often become snarled in their own tape, always in the midst of a splendid recording session. A camera loaded with pictures of informants has a tendency to sink when dropped into Chesapeake Bay. Motor cars break down. Much to my chagrin I learned that tape recorder microphones are highly sensitive to wind, and I continually had to twist myself into the most contorted positions while recording on the town wharf in Crisfield. The prevailing southwest wind blows right in your face.

And indoor wind is no mean hazard either. One evening I made an arrangement to meet an older waterman at his Calvary home for a recording session. His daughter had been a student of mine and I was anxious to retrieve on tape some of the tales she had collected from her father. The situation looked perfect when I arrived. No one else was in the house, and it was a peaceful though extremely sultry evening. I had no sooner recorded one excellent tale than my host wanted to know if I wasn't awfully hot. I innocently replied that yes, it was a pretty stuffy evening. With that he jumped up, crossed the room, and drew back the curtain on a gigantic fan. Within seconds the wind in the room was gusting to twenty knots in the puffs and the high whine of the fan made a mockery of the recording session.

Then too there were the unpleasant moments, moments when my mission was misunderstood and my entire project castigated. Late in the summer of 1968, I went out to Smith Island to try and piece together some information on a local hero by the name of "Lickin' Billy" Bradshaw. Smith Island where Bradshaw made his home lies about nine miles due west of Crisfield and about twelve miles east of the mouth of the Potomac River. Captain John Smith, that doughty Englishman, reputedly cruised the waters near the island and left his name on the land. But what was doubtless a sizeable, well-wooded, and potentially arable island three centuries ago has since been considerably eroded by the relentless chewing of the tides and winds of Chesapeake Bay. As one approaches the main part of the island up through the narrow shallow channel, low flat marshes peal off to the right and left as far as the eye can see, good for little but gunning ducks. The channel curves and bends around; outside the dredged part, the bottom is clearly visible less than two feet below the surface. The boat's engine slows, then backs down, and the vessel nudges in along the town pier of Ewell.

Ewell is the largest of Smith Island's three communities. South about a mile and a half lies Rhodes Point, and south and a bit to the east, across a sluice of water lies Tylerton. The island's total population: near one thousand souls. Though the three villages possess individual characteristics, there is a pleasant sameness about them that strikes the newcomer. White frame houses abut the main street separated by neatly cropped lawns. Bright flowers adorn prim little gardens in the spring and early summer. Down the side lanes stand equally fresh-looking homes, but no lane runs too far, for the community is just a cluster of buildings with the water at its front, and the marsh at its back. Like the other villages, Ewell has its local store where the residents wander in to shop, gulp a soft drink, or simply absorb the latest news. Rough hewn benches line the walls of the store and the mind's eye skins back the generations to imagine the leathery hides of watermen whose backsides warmed that wood while they spouted accounts of their daily activities.

Along the waterfronts of these three small villages, the resi-

18

due of a maritime existence catches even the insensitive observer. Piles of chicken wire crab pots lie randomly about. Oyster shells cover the bottom beneath every dock or float that juts out into the harbor. A ways holds a vessel drawn up for minor repairs. There is little to suggest a profession other than following the water.

But specifically, I had come out to this seafaring island to find out something more about this legendary folk hero, Lickin' Billy, who had been dead since 1916 but whose deeds still lingered on the tongues of the people in the region. In Crisfield I had collected a number of tales about Bradshaw's feats of strength and his antics in church, but I wanted more intimate information from members of his family. His two grandsons, I was informed, lived in Rhodes Point. Local residents directed me to the home of Bain Bradshaw. Bain turned out to be a man of great compassion and generosity. He met me at the door and enthusiastically ushered me into his tidy front living room. Of course he remembered his grandfather, one of the strongest men on the island. No, he didn't care if I recorded some stories about the old man. On went the recorder and the tales began to fall from Bain's lips, one after the other. But not for long. Out of the kitchen marched a thunder cloud in the guise of Mrs. Bradshaw. Large and seemingly indominable, she was trailed by an equally husky female friend from Tangier Island. Who was I? What was I doing on the island? Why did I want to record her husband's voice? Why was I so interested in finding out about people who had been dead more than fifty years? And on and on. Dodging the barbs, I tried to explain my purpose as well as I could. No use. The Tangier friend chimed in. She had seen the likes of me before. There was some ulterior motive in my being there; I wanted something out of them. Gradually as the conversation continued, the two women became less hostile and slowly the reason for their suspicion and hostility surfaced. Several years before a young man had come onto the island selling aluminum siding for houses. He convinced a number of islanders to make a $200 down payment as investment for the work to be done. Then he stepped aboard the ferry and was never seen again. And there had been other instances when naive island residents had been fleeced by slippery operators. Mark Twain's Duke and King worked other regions besides the Mississippi River.

Even Bain and his wife had been the victims of a dreadful scheme. Not long before they had taken into their hearts and their home a pleasant young man whom Bain had met in Crisfield. He came out to the island with Bain, slept in the family's bed, ate the family's food, and, against his will, Bain had consented to take him fishing on Sunday. Before he departed, the young man asked Bain if he would be good enough to sell him some ducks. Unwittingly, he obliged. Less than a week later Bain Bradshaw was arrested and carted off the island to appear in a Baltimore court where he was heavily fined. The innocent man the Bradshaws took under their roof was a game warden, and in the words of the local folk, "a no good son-of-a-bitch."

If the folklorist can be almost literally cast out from the homes of his informants, he can also ironically be mistaken for one of the group he is working with. In March of 1969, just one week before the end of the oyster season, I went aboard a dredge boat in Annapolis, once more to flavor their life and do some collecting. When I did this sort of thing, I usually dropped my college professor role. I let my beard grow a day or so, wore hip boots, soiled pants and jacket, and tried to appear salty. After that particular day on the water, as I was walking up through the town of Annapolis, I passed a middle aged man on the street. "Well," he remarked, "you've only got one more week to go." I nodded. To the untrained eye I had been accepted as a member of the group I was studying. It was time to go home and write the book. And so I did.

Folklife on the Eastern Shore

Some folklorists contend that a folk group is any group of people with at least one thing in common. College professors might be considered a folk group, for instance. So might bridge builders, or Black Panthers, or Hasidic Jews, or even a gathering of five year olds. Obviously, then, one individual can be the member of more than one folk group. Professionally a man may be

20

a lawyer. At work, during the day, he partakes of that group's customs and rituals and stories, but in the early evening, he may repair to the Lions Club and thus indulge in the activities and practices of that group. Finally, he will doubtless return home to the patterns and traditions of the smallest folk unit, the family itself.

In the fluid world of the suburb and the city, people move casually from one group pattern to another without being strictly conscious of it. But when one moves into a rural situation the folk group becomes more easily defined. This is due in part to the built-in closeness that isolation fosters. Surely the Eastern Shore provides such isolation. Until 1952 when the Bay Bridge was completed, the Shore was practically insular. From Washington one either had to ferry across the Bay to get there, or take the long trip up through Baltimore and down the peninsula.

Yet even with new highways cutting their concrete paths across the table top of the Eastern Shore, there are parts of the region that still remain noticeably remote, not just because of their inaccessibility but also because of the kind of self-imposed isolation that Eastern Shoremen indulge in. They do not take to outsiders. They do not like tourists, or city slickers, or folklorists coming into their domain and staring at them. In Maine they tell the story of the young female tourist, decked out in her best summer finery, who approaches a lobsterman on the wharf one day while he is mending his traps. After much scrutinizing she shakes her head and says, "My lord, Maine is sure full of a lot of queer people."

The old man looks up from his work and replies, "Yes, mam, but they all leave by Labor Day."

Though I have never heard a version of this story told in the Eastern Shore, I am sure it has been uttered there in some form or other. Certainly the tale illustrates the Shoreman's attitude: an observable suspicion of outsiders as "queer" people. But at the same time it is this self-imposed isolation from the outside that keeps the small fishing villages conservative, that preserves their way of life, and that nourishes their folklore.

Other factors are also at work to keep these small communities unified and thick-skinned. In places like Smith Island, Wen-

21

ona, Fairmount, and Wingate, there is but one thing to do: follow the water. It is done with a vengeance. In the winter it is dredging or tonging; in the summer crab potting, crab scraping or fishing. With the water consuming almost the entire working force of these small towns, it is not surprising that the general bent of conversation turns on the occupation. When I asked a Jenkins Creek store keeper what the men usually talked about when they sat around in the store, he answered, "Nothing. Just boats and engines, engines and boats, crabbin' and oysters."

Religion also acts as a cohesive force to draw these communities closer together. Ever since Joshua Thomas, the parson of the islands, helped to spread the gospel of Methodism among the people of the lower Eastern Shore in the early part of the 19th century, the tenets of that faith have pervaded the lives of watermen and their families with unmistakable results. The walls of many island homes display Christian memorabilia; crucifixes and signs proclaiming that "Jesus Saves" and "God is Love" which adorn the rooms and suggest the transitory nature of life. Bibles are prominent fixtures. Aboard dredge boats, even among the most rugged appearing crew, there is a reverence for "the word of God," and a solemn grace preludes every meal eaten on board ship.

The annual camp meeting, long a fixture in the Methodist firmament, still occurs in various places on the Shore. Smith Island still holds one, but from all accounts it is a far cry from the camp meetings that took place more than half a century ago. Back then it really was a "camp meeting", as men from all over sailed their vessels out to the island and literally camped there for the duration of the meeting. The talent then was home grown with local preachers and laymen voicing "the word", and local heroes leading the marching. Today, much of this has been altered. Watermen now power their crafts out to the island for the day and return home at night. A special ferry boat leaves Crisfield to carry the faithful to the island, but it too returns after the services are concluded. A professional group is called in to run the meeting. They set up the schedule, provide the preacher, the instrumentalists, and the vocalists. Though the religious fervor is still there, the catered professionalism has diluted much of the

22

traditional quality of the camp meeting as it occurred in Joshua Thomas's day and after.

Although the annual camp meeting is the high point of the religious year on Smith Island, church business as usual is continually occupied with faith. The three island communities, Ewell, Rhodes Point, and Tylerton each have a church, but they have to share one preacher who conducts services in a different church each Sunday. Apparently a generation ago, however, the island preacher used to conduct three different services every Sunday, one in each community. Such a procedure, obviously taxing on the parson, frequently gave rise to humorous situations. On one occasion, an island woman had the flu rather badly, so the preacher chose as his text, "And Miss Liza was so sick with the fever." When he reached Tylerton, a local waterman who had sat through the other two services jumped up just after the preacher had begun with the same text again. "My God," he complained, "ain't that woman dead yet?"

But the real specter of death itself is never treated lightly in these devout and isolated communities. The sight of the ferry boat being loaded at the Crisfield wharf with the undertaker's accoutrements—the oblong box and the purple vestments— evokes wonder and contemplation. Someone out there on the islands has gone to his or her reward. Either old age or the Bay has done its work.

Once, when I was staying in Tylerton, an old waterman perished while crab netting in his skiff. He had been an epileptic and had presumably been taken with a fit and fallen overboard. Someone noticed his empty skiff washed ashore in the marsh; later they found the body nearby. For the next several days in the village, all talk centered on the drowned man. He had been warned, everybody said, not to go out on the water alone knowing his propensity for fits. But he had been on the water all his life and he could never be at ease ashore. When a man stopped being active, stopped doing the only thing he knew, there was nothing left for him but death. It was just as well he went this way, they claimed; he was doing something he enjoyed: keeping busy on the water. The funeral was solemn, simple, and reverent.

The waterman divides his year into two parts. Late May

23

through mid-September and mid-October through mid-March. In late May the crabs begin to come into the Bay and by the middle of July the annual harvest is well under way. Though the average crab potter puts in a good eight or more hours of work a day, his hours differ considerably from a typical factory worker or IBM employee. He rises around three o'clock in the morning, breakfasts, and heads for his boat. As he points his power driven forty-foot craft out the harbor, there is a hint of grey in the east, and by the time he reaches his first string of pots, he can just see. He works at this time of day, not because he likes to rise early necessarily, but because the hours near dawn usually breed calm water on the Bay, and no man enjoys hauling his pots while his boat lurches and pitches beneath him.

The day is long, monotonous, and as the sun begins to climb, inevitably hot and humid. The crabber works with the same rhythmical precision, pulling in the chickenwire pot, dumping the crabs into barrels, throwing back what is not takable, rebaiting the pot and pushing it back overboard. Over and over again. One hundred pots, maybe more. He may have a partner or his young son to help him, but more often than not he works alone. By noon he is done. He returns to Crisfield, sells his catch, buys bait for the following day, puts up his boat, and then either goes home or to the local store or tavern to catch the news.

Such a pattern of life obviously creates a great deal of spare time. The hours between one in the afternoon and nine in the evening form a large gap. Several generations ago this time was almost wholly consumed at the local store. "I remember," a Tangier Island watermen told me, "sitting in that store of a Saturday night, both sides there lined up with men, lined up talking. It was a pleasure to hear them talk. And now everyone of them's gone but me."

Though some of the old people have died off, the island of Tangier has with obvious exceptions remained very much the same. Like Smith Island it lies almost equidistant between the mouth of the Potomac and Crisfield. Knowing the nature of the Bay and its affinity to swallow up the land, it seems obvious that at one time Smith Island, which lies but a few miles north in Maryland, and Tangier in Virginia were a single piece of land.

24

Today water definitely separates the two, but a look at a chart of the region would convince all but the extremely foolish that a trip between the two islands even in a shoal draft vessel would be an ill-starred venture.

Approaching Tangier from Crisfield, one comes on the island from the northeast, and during the summer months that usually means right into the teeth of a warm twenty-five knot southwest wind. All the land on the Eastern Shore is low slung without the prominent headlands one finds in New England, and as a result the vessel is practically on the beach before the land is visible. Bearing down on Tangier, the first thing one spies, appropriately, in this tight little Methodist stronghold, is the spire of the church. The ferry enters the channel to the harbor and gradually threads its way between a string of anchored work boats; a laughing gull wheels over the roofs of a cluster of crab shanties that line the northern entrance of the harbor; a waterman in a skiff leaning on a dipnet hails a friend for a tow.

The watermen of Tangier appear to care little for the appearance of their harborside. Alongside the wharf, floating debris of every description drifts in and out among the pilings: pop bottles, Clorox containers, rubber boots, socks, tires. But the qualms of the initial impression are quickly dispelled as one walks down through the main street of the village of Tangier. As with Smith Island, the freshly scrubbed look is everywhere apparent. The houses, with the exception of an occasional trailer, are mostly white and wood framed. Though the picturesque picket fences that once enclosed the various plots of land have given way to the more functional steel fencing, the lawns they enclose are neat, green, and well manicured. Family burial plots adorn some front yards and the white protrusion of the cement tombs suggests the immediacy of the water table. At the height of the day, women and children crowd the street, and the rush and roar of motor scooters dashing by makes walking hazardous at times.

Tangier Island's population is about the same as Smith Island: one thousand souls, but unlike its Maryland neighbor, the island has but one official community, the village of Tangier itself. Still, the residents have pinned on the land such names as Meat-soup, or Upards, or King's Ridges', though it is highly doubtful that the people in Richmond know anything about it. Each grouping of homes has its own local store where the watermen congregate, but with the advent of the media, the role of the store as the ultimate source of news has greatly diminished. Many storekeepers who used to keep their establishments open until ten or eleven at night now close early as everyone drifts home to get the news from Walter Cronkite. Yet there is still much time to converse, and many of the old stories even now get passed from lip to lip at these stores.

As the season shifts from summer to winter, the waterman alters his life style and his boat. A few minor changes in the rig and instead of a crabbing boat he has one he can tong oysters with. Men from Tangier and Smith Island as well as those from Crisfield take their converted vessels over into the Potomac River where they tong the river bottoms with long scissor-like rakes, scraping up oysters. During the week they live aboard their boats and on weekends come home, either by boat or by car. Tongers, like crabbers, usually work alone or with a single partner. Their day begins at dawn, as in the summer, but it does not end until close to dusk when they head back for the harbor to sell their daily catch either to "buy boats" or to trucks that come down to the wharfside.

More romantic than the tonger perhaps, is the waterman who works aboard a Chesapeake Bay dredge boat. He is the last remnant of a residue fleet of sailing vessels in the United States which are required by law to take their catch under sail. He signs on with a group of five or six other crew members aboard a shoal draft sloop-rigged vessel termed, by outsiders, a skipjack, and by the watermen themselves, a bateau. If he doesn't quit or go on a bender, he works the long cold winter months, Monday to Friday, culling out the good oysters from the bad as the dredge scoops them from the bottom of the Bay. Like the old whaling sailor, he is paid off in shares, and the amount of oysters determines his weekly wages. It can run anywhere from $50 to $400 to nothing, depending on the weather.

Like others who follow the water, the crew member of a dredge boat begins his day early. Well before daylight the boat stirs into life as the cook rises to begin preparing breakfast. Just at daybreak, the bateau, pushed by a gasoline-powered yawl boat, leaves the evening anchorage (Annapolis, Tilghman's Island or Cambridge), and heads with other boats in the fleet to the oystering ground. Once there, the yawl boat is hauled up into the davits, the crew hoists the sails, the work day begins. Back and forth the vessel moves over the oyster bank or "rock", as the sails are continually reefed and unreefed to make the vessel move at the optimum speed so the dredge on the bottom can gather oysters most effectively. At nine in the morning there is a coffee break; at noon there is lunch. If the wind drops without sign of revival, the dredge boat heads back to harbor. Otherwise, the captain and crew remain on the oyster rock until about an hour before sundown, when once more the yawl boat is lowered from the davits and the bateau is pushed back to her evening port. Like tongers, the dredge boat captains sell their daily catch to truckers or buy boats, before rafting for the night alongside several boats from the fleet. The crew clean the vessel, wash themselves, and then have supper.

An uncommon comfort pervades the after cabin of a working bateau at the end of a day on the water. An oil-burning stove heats the cabin; a plain board swings down from the overhead to provide the dinner table; the crew sits around, having peeled off their heavy jackets and foul weather gear, while a meal of fish and potatoes and tomatoes and buns and greens appears. Talk diminishes. There is time for thought, and food.

In the days of the great oyster catches when oysters were plentiful but cheap, the dredge boats stayed out on the oyster rocks or in convenient nearby harbors for almost the entire season. They left in October and did not return home until Christmas. Then they left again until March. The buy boats came to the fleet instead of the fleet going to the buyers. These buy boats, usually large schooners or pungy boats, then transported the oysters to the most profitable market: Baltimore or Norfolk or Crisfield. With the advent of the gasoline engine, of course, this all changed. Today the watermen who work a dredge boat no longer undergo the long separations from their families that their forebearers did. Every Friday afternoon the entire crew leave the vessel, crawl into their cars and drive home for the weekend. It is

27

much less romantic, but more sensible system.

Dinner is over; conversation revives. The cook clears the dishes and the dinner table goes back up to the overhead. A black face appears in the hatchway. A crew member aboard the captain's brother's boat has rafted alongside. There is banter; a couple of yarns spun, and then a portion of the other boat's crew come into the cabin. More talk. Then the table comes down from the overhead again, and a card game begins.

Certainly from the folklorist's point of view, the cuddy of a Chesapeake Bay bateau provides an incisive look at the folk milieu. Like the wharfside liars' bench in Crisfield and the local store in most small Eastern Shore towns, the atmosphere that persists in a skipjack cabin after a day's work is as conducive to traditional folk repartee as anything I have ever come across.

If one seeks a pattern of life with infinite variety, he will not find it in the fishing communities of the Eastern Shore. Rather he will find the beat of life slowed by convention and tradition. Though places such as Smith Island and Deal Island no longer exhibit the self-sufficient qualities they once had, there are still indications that these were once very independent communities.

Take, for example, Deal Island. It is not an island in the sense that either Tangier or Smith is. It lies connected by a short bridge to the mainland but a scant twenty miles by road from the county seat of Princess Anne. Today that road is blacktop and in reasonably good shape, but once it was dirt, and the trek with a horse and wagon to Princess Anne was not something one undertook unless he really had something to do. And so, in effect, Deal Island provided the same kind of isolation that the offshore islands did, for it was much easier and more practical to go places by water, much simpler to raise one's own food at home, or take it out of the Bay and bring it home for the table. With limited access to the outside, watermen had to rely on their own ingenuity; they made their own fishing gear with the materials at hand; they built their own boats, cut their own sails, fashioned their own oyster tongs, and lived frugally, always close to the water which dictated their very lifestyle.

Wenona, the small waterman's community at the southern end of Deal Island, typifies the independence of the Eastern Shore watermen. The town boasts its own sailmaker in Albert Brown whose father passed the business on to him. While much of his business today comes from yachting clientele, Brown still, on occasion, pieces together a suit of canvas sails for an oystering skipjack. The tools of his trade are the same ones used by sailmakers for generations. Likewise, both Smith Island and Tangier support a local boatbuilder who turns out two or three work boats a year. But Island folk no longer need depend on their gardens for produce as they once did. Nor do they require land to raise their own cattle and other livestock. They now lean heavily upon the island ferries that run from the mainland each day, or on the blacktop roads that lead up across the marshes to the towns of Princess Anne, Salisbury, and Cambridge.

Every once in a while one can glimpse the entire course of a traditional lifestyle suggested in the artifacts that an individual has left behind. I had this startling experience one cold March afternoon outside Crisfield. I was down there with another folklorist, Henry Glassie, to gather pictures of the material culture of the Eastern Shore, the traditional house styles, boat designs, tools and the like. Out in the marsh we approached a deserted crab shanty. From the exterior it looked like any other shanty that dots the creeks and rivers. It abutted the water and had a small docking inlet where the waterman once moored his skiff. A handmade rocking chair sat on the small porch outside, and scattered in the marsh grass around the shanty lay a number of crab floats. Once inside Glassie noted immediately that the building design was identical to the *crogglofft,* a shanty type of building used by fishermen along the southwest coast of England, where the ancestors of many Eastern Shoremen come from.

In the loft over the bedroom and spread throughout the building we discovered the traditional implements which once allowed this waterman, whoever he was, to take his living from the Bay. Four eel pots, hand woven from oak strips of wood, cluttered a corner of the shack. The handle of an eel gig, an instrument shaped like Neptune's trident, stuck out from the loft. So did the handles or shaves of a pair of hand tongs and a pair of nippers. Two tow smacks or "live boxes" were pushed into the back of the loft. In the days of sail they had been towed behind

29

the boat and used for keeping peeler crabs in the water. On a corner of the shanty lay a long coil of rope, obviously, what had once been a trotline, traditionally used as a means of catching crabs. In another section of the main room of the shanty there were some hand carved duck decoys and the remains of an old ship model that the waterman had evidently whittled in his spare time.

Suddenly the place, despite its seemingly shabby nature, came alive. What had seemed mere litter began to suggest, in essence, an entire way of life. This waterman had fashioned his own quarters in an unconsciously traditional way, and then had followed the water in the same pattern as his father and grandfather had doubtless done before him. As the seasons changed, so did the seafood and game he sought. He altered his tools to fit his needs and shaped his day according to the weather. And probably, after a long summer day on the water, he returned to his shanty, sat in his homemade rocking chair looking at the Bay as the evening southwester cooled off the land and traded stories and anecdotes with a group of his friends.

Storytellers and the Narrative Style

Every narrator tells a story his own way. He may employ certain traditional characteristics such as an opening and closing formula ("I stepped on the tin and the tin bent, and that's the way the story went") or proverbial expressions or rhymes and jingles, but his method of delivery will usually be individual. It is the very nature of oral tradition that each storyteller hears a tale and then adapts it to fit his own style and the requirements of his immediate audience. Obviously a good raconteur will not spin a particular yarn the same way for me as he does, say, for his wife or his best friend. He will add, subtract, adjust, delete an obscenity, add a moral, do anything, in fact, to achieve the best response from his listeners.

Almost every community, or every group, for that matter, has what the folklorist calls "an active bearer of tradition." He is the person, male or female, who is known in the area as the best

30

singer, tale teller, riddler, or local historian. He is expected to perform his specialty at the request of the audience, most of whom the folklorist would term "passive bearers" (those who are familiar with traditional material, but do not actively pass it along). Most active bearers possess incredible memories; yet this is not surprising, for, knowing they are to be called upon to perform, they consciously store up tales, songs, riddles or history. Captain Alex Kellam of Crisfield is the perfect example of such an active bearer.

Early in my stay in Crisfield I had been advised about Kellam. "He can certainly tell you something, "I was informed, "but you don't want to believe everything he says." I met him the first day I sat down on the Crisfield liar's bench. He walked up, well dressed in a tie, hat and coat, and immediately started spilling out stories, one after another, as I rapidly jotted down the gist of them in my notebook. Intelligent despite only an eighth grade education, Kellam delivered his narratives articulately in a deep voice which issued from a powerful frame. At sixty, he is the picture of health, agile on his feet, alert, lean and hard, not at all "pussy" as the local people phrase it. "I guess the greatest compliment I ever got," he confided to me one day, "was when this fellow told me, he said, 'Kellam, even when you're feeling bad, you can still make people laugh." And he has the equipment to do it. When growing up on Smith Island he explained how he used to hang around the local store and listen to the "old head" talk. "It was sort of a hobby with me, remembering all those stories I used to hear then, and I haven't forgotten very many of them even now."

As a young man Kellam did what other island boys did, he followed the water. He worked for a number of seasons aboard the dredge boat, *Ruby Ford,* taking oysters out of the Potomac River; but in his early thirties he moved ashore to Crisfield. He traveled around a bit for a while, working in a Baltimore shipyard during the war and doing some semi-pro boxing here and there. When he came back to Crisfield he held several jobs before settling down as a life insurance salesman. Today he has a large clientele and a good business. His job allows him a good deal of spare time in the mornings and early afternoons, which in summer

31

months he spends lingering around the wharf in Crisfield. Once a week he journeys to Salisbury on business and there mingles in an office atmosphere. On his day off, Thursday, he goes sport fishing with his friend Charleton Marshall. Kellam's reputation as a fisherman even surpasses his reputation as a storyteller. Even such notables as Johnny Unitas and Bobby Boyd of the Baltimore Colts have accompanied him, for he knows where the fish are and how to catch them.

As a raconteur, Kellam furnishes the listener with all the storytelling drama imaginable. He acts out his tales with facial grimaces, changes of voice tone, dialectical innovations, and hand and body gestures. He sticks closely to the short humorous anecdotal story that turns on a punch line.

Kellam confessed to me his distaste for storytellers who edged with their narratives and failed to come to the point quickly. Kellam fuses the traditional stories he remembers hearing on the island with jokes that he hears at the office in Salisbury or at the local club where he goes to bowl. But clearly he achieves his utmost delight in recounting the narratives he heard as a young man. These are the tales that spring quickest to his mind and are most often retold. I found Kellam at his best when surrounded on the Crisfield wharf by older watermen whose casual remarks and personal anecdotes continually pricked his memory and launched him into one story after another.

In marked contrast to Alex Kellam are the older raconteurs whose performance is not as dramatic and whose narratives are not tailored quite so neatly to the short anecdotal style. Captain George Alan Wheatley, for example. In his mid-nineties, Wheatley lives on Tangier Island and undisputedly deserves the titles of island seer, local historian, and narrator. When I asked about people who knew a lot about the old times on the island, I was immediately dispatched to Wheatley's home where he lives by himself whiling away his days waiting for someone to come in and talk to him. Wheatley has lived on the island ever since his father moved over from the Western Shore of the Bay when he was a small boy. He followed the only trade available.

I started right out on the water [he told me]. I've drudged

on California Rock with cranks for twenty-five cents a day, eight dollars a month . . . Well, when I got married, that was in '98, I weren't a-getting but thirty-five dollars a month, and I married a woman with two children. In 1903 I bought me my own bateau, that's what they called them then, bateaux, and I got ready and got some men together and we went to Richmond to get some niggers to go dredging. We took out a third for the boat and all hands shared equal of what was left. And the most money I've ever got for a bushel of oysters, and I've seen many a one, was a dollar and thirty cents.

Wheatley followed the water in one way or another until he sold his skiff and his crab net at eighty-three and came ashore to nurse his sick wife. Presently, as the island's oldest living inhabitant, he has been elevated to the role of active bearer, a role it is doubtful that he played a generation ago. But his mind is sound and his memory still remarkably acute, particularly for episodes that occurred in the last century, and thus younger islanders regard their older neighbor as the repository for what they consider to be Tangier's history and lore.

Wheatley's repertoire includes a mixed bag of belief tales, legends, oral history, jests, anecdotes and tall tales. The modern joke is conspicuously missing. With an old man's deft recall he loads his accounts with details that furnish the listener with a catalogue of people, places, events and a good general sense of the waterman's life as it existed over the last three generations. Personalities emerge with all their human shortcomings and physical attributes; harbors and oystering rocks appear in minutest detail; gales and tides and memorable catches and hard times on the water engage the audience's imagination through the force of Wheatley's description.

Yet it is clear that as a storyteller, this older Tangierman is not innovative like Kellam. He possesses a relatively fixed repertoire which over the past ten years has probably expanded little; this, due to old age immobility and faltering commerce with the outside world, but also in part to Wheatleys' great admiration for the days and ways of those he refers to as the "old people." As a boy he recalled sitting in the local store in the evening listening

33

to the old people converse. He evidently absorbed richly at these gatherings and his present role allows him to cough back up what he heard. He does this with an almost mechanical fidelity. One requests strong man stories and is immediately rewarded with an entire cycle, told each time virtually the same way and in the same sequence as if one tale triggered another in a formulaic pattern. The delivery, unlike Kellam's, is downbeat. Wheatley achieves emphasis, not so much by vocal pyrotechnics as by simply engaging his listener with his eyes, leaning forward in his seat, and thrusting home the key point of his tale. He employs gestures and imitative sounds, but not with the imagination or the profusion that Kellam does. Wheatley's qualities as a narrator lie in his memory for detail, an almost total recall which stretches well back into the nineteenth century and draws forth stories and folklife sketches that no book has ever recorded.

Other raconteurs display yet different traits. Men for instance like Gorman Tull and Otis Evans and Dewey Landon. Landon, until very recently, ran a small store down by the wharf in Crisfield called the Harborside Shop. Here he catered to the whims of tourists, selling everything from driftwood that he picked up along the shores of the Bay to old bottles to defunct sewing machines. He opened his shop around noon after a morning's beachcombing and was available with his constant banter until six in the evening. Though Landon's forbears came originally from Smith Island, he grew up on the mainland, following the water in a number of different ways. Now in his early seventies, he is a man of firm opinions and he is as outspoken about them as he is firm. This adamant quality spills over into his storytelling. Most of his yarning is of the tall tale variety, yet he urges upon the listener the validity of his stories with intensity. A good lie about a chicken that laid an egg with a perfect double domino for a yolk cannot be refuted, according to Landon, because he has people in his family beside himself who witnessed the marvel. Most of his stories center on his own exploits; by making the experience personal, he attempts to close the credibility gap in his listener's mind and thereby have him swallow a "whopper."

Otis Evans and Gorman Tull both came originally from Smith Island and now, like so many other island people, live in Crisfield. For years, Evans ran a buy boat, carrying fish to Wash-

34

ington where he sold it. Young looking for his seventy plus years, Captain Evans has been slowed recently by a bad coronary. He has given up the water, a decision which now allows him to spend a good part of every summer day on the liar's bench in Crisfield, observing the activity he was once so much a part of. For him, storytelling is a fond way of reminiscing, and the tales he tells invariably deal with real people in believable situations. Though many of his yarns turn on humorous situations and he tells them with an obvious twinkle in his eye, there is no hint of the tall tale in his repetoire. Rather, Evans injects an historical sense into much of his narration. He recalls dates and names with apparent precision, and the articulate flow of his speech (I was informed that he had done some public speaking from time to time) lends credence to his narratives. Practical in his outlook and obviously successful in business when he followed the water, Evans expressed a considerable knowledge of the watermen's various beliefs, but he seldom admitted believing any of them himself. Instead, popular beliefs frequently became the vehicle for a narrative; a tale, for instance, about an islander he knew who had a blue wheelbarrow painted red so he wouldn't have to carry anything blue aboard his boat.

Gorman Tull, on the other hand, spun personal ghost yarns about haunted ships and spectral sights while all the time maintaining he didn't believe in such things. I met Tull very much by accident while on Smith Island. He had come over to the Island to do some carpentry work on a boat in Tylerton and one evening while I sat in the local store drinking a coke, he plopped himself down beside me on the bench, turned and said, "Now you won't believe this, but . . . " and immediately launched into two extended narratives of vessels tormented by spectral occurrences. The tales were extensive, rich in detail, fraught with intended pauses for effect, recaptured conversation, and alive with the local idiom. Later I was able to get these several stories on tape in Tull's home, but they lacked the spontaneity and the totality with which I first heard them. Sitting on Gorman Tull's front porch in Crisfield with a recorder on my lap was not the same as sitting beside him in the local store of the town where he grew up.

Presently in his late seventies, Tull has led a colorful career.

35

For a time, he followed the water on coasting schooners running the coast of North America. He has crabbed, oystered, built boats and houses, and, like Kellam, even done some semi-pro boxing. Wiry of frame yet incredibly strong, Tull recently underwent several operations on his urinary tract. Once, while discussing one of these operations, I suggested that as a man, he had had a pretty rough life. "Oh, no," he countered immediately, "I've had one of the best lives a man could ever wish to spend," and it was as sincere a remark as anyone could utter.

As with many older watermen who believe that to stop going is to die, Tull keeps himself busy building sixteen foot flat bottomed skiffs which he sells for $200. It bothers his wife to see him labor in the hot sun, but she knows better than to make him sit still. He talks easily while he works, telling old stories, recounting the past, and philosophizing on the present. His speech bristles with proverbial phrases. A piece of wood was "as green as parse's monkey" and once, after shucking the last of a small pile of oysters he had in his boat, he turned to me and said, "Now, that is what the carpenter killed his wife with, his awl." As an individual, Tull provides much that one could term exemplary in the life of an average waterman on the Eastern Shore. He has worked hard at many things, succeeded at most of them, but best of all perhaps, he expresses a rich fulfillment in looking back over a life of more than seventy-five years. As a storyteller he also exudes sheer delight in the simple process of recounting a yarn. His wife confessed to me that her husband enjoyed nothing so much as telling stories to his grandchildren. And, indeed, there is about his style a simplistic quality that would appeal to young audiences. Tull told me only one personal account that might be termed obscene, and like other older raconteurs, the modern joke failed to surface in his repetoire.

Not all the folklore that appears in this book came from watermen. Many informants followed trades other than the water, but their repertoires indicate the waterfront as the source of many of their stories. Ronald Purnell is as representative of this group of storytellers as any. Purnell has lived in Crisfield almost all his life and his ancestors are Eastern Shore people of long-standing. With a partner he runs a small foundry down near the

36

wharf in the village where he makes the tongs and other iron implements used by the watermen. Purnell's speech and general information portray a man of some learning, mostly home acquired through constant reading. His attitudes towards current events, though generally conservative following the trend on the Eastern Shore, do display a refinement unobserved among many of his peers. He is informed, interesting, almost genteel.

Although, for many of the storytellers on the Eastern Shore the oral tale has entertainment as its essential purpose, for Purnell the narrative performs a more immediate function. He employs tales to illustrate a point, but it moral, legal, or political. Purnell is more the conversationalist than the raconteur, and his ramblings frequently invoke philosophical observations capped with a story to drive his idea home. A remark about the hypocrisy of preachers draws forth a string of anecdotes on local parsons; a monologue about politics produces a traditional tale about a Virgina politician who drank more than he should. Humorous accounts of antics in the courtroom spring from ruminations on the legal system. And so it goes, from one topic to another with an illustrative tale for almost every subject covered.

The illustrative anecdote will frequently lead storytellers into a more general frame of reference. Purnell invariably claims that the event took place "in a town around here" or "somewhere up there in Pennsylvania" and the time and people are often introduced as, "There was this fella one time and ... " Yet, in a different vein, if prodded, Purnell can recall traditional tales heard in the waterfront restaurants where he takes his noontime meal. Clearly too, Purnell fancies himself, justifiably, a local historian. He draws, with easy recollection, lucid descriptions of Crisfield in the old days; how the town actually came to be built on oyster shells; how it received its name, and who its local luminaries and characters were. Purnell furnishes his listeners with a variety of information, yet one is never sure whether his knowledge or his narratives stem from oral tradition or his eclectic reading. Even he himself seldom knows the sources.

Most of the material that follows in this collection reflects

37

the anecdotal type of storytelling prominent along the eastern seaboard. A number of recent studies have revealed that the general trend in narrative style has been away from the long-winded tale, the extended tall story, for instance, in which the listener is drawn along step by step by a straight-faced narrator until at the end he realizes that he has been utterly taken in. Storytelling now depends more on short joke-constructed anecdotes which hinge wholly on the delivery of the final punch line. And it is not surprising, for time today has been noticeably telescoped.

Richard Lunt, in a monograph on a Maine raconteur by the name of Jones Tracy*, noted the essential differences between the yarn spinners who lived a generation or more ago, and those who presently furnish jests for area listeners. Sixty years ago, Jones Tracy enjoyed a lively reputation around Mount Desert, Maine, as a peerless oral storyteller. He mouthed his windies in an elaborate style, embellishing his accounts with infinite detail and often running his stories on for an hour or more. Today in the Mount Desert region, Tracy's reputation still flourishes though he has been dead almost thirty years; his stories still linger on the lips of present day raconteurs, although cut and pared away to anecdotal form. The reason for this obvious deterioration, Lunt observes, is the simple matter of time. A trip to the hunting lodge, which in Tracy's time took two days by horse, is now performed in a matter of minutes by plane. Time no longer hangs so heavy for either storyteller or listener and, according to Lunt, the narrator who misses the message and fails to conform to the short anecdotal style soon finds his audience sadly depleted.

I think the same sort of shift in the oral narrative exists along the lower Eastern Shore, and for much the same reasons. The trip from Crisfield to Smith Island, which in the days of sail might consume an entire day or even more, presently is accomplished by a diesel-driven ferry in less than an hour. And time at the local store is no longer as infinite as it used to be: it is sandwiched between television programs. The quilting bees and sewing

*Richard Lunt's monograph can be found in Volume X of *Northeast Folklore*.

bees, once a stock characteristic of the self-sufficient island and Bay communities where time and talk passed slowly, have given way to the mechanized looms of the haberdashers. With everything so accelerated by a mechanized society, it seems the storyteller too must accelerate or lose his position. Men like Alex Kellam, who still retain a constant band of listeners, consciously tailor their yarns to fit the modern pattern. But other narrators, like Ron Purnell, who fuse their tales with long conversational interludes and philosophical qualifications, appear to have lost most of their listeners. Purnell's foundry is hardly the gathering place I understand it once used to be.

Perhaps the best way to explain differences in narrative styles is to take one widely told tale and see how individual raconteurs handle it. This tale, which for lack of a better title I will call "The Lead Line," was first told to me by a man named Simmon Tilghman, a local Crisfield businessman. Our conversation, as recorded on tape, went like this:

Well, now, what was this other story?

This is a much better story, and they say it's the truth. Now this is a good one if you want to record this. Do you have the recorder running?

Yessir.

Well, on Old Island (we call it Old Island and I think the State has it now—it's really Jane's Island) there were at one time twelve or fourteen dwelling houses and a great big general store. The general store was two stories high and the upper story was used for classrooms, and old man Michael Sommers taught navigation there. And at one time he had two pupils, Captain Len Tawes who was to sea all his life, and a man by the name of Ward whose first name I've forgotten, but he come around Ward's Crossing and his mother was named Sarah Ann Ward and she had the largest flower garden in the county. She had over an acre of plants, nothing but flowers. And they called her Sarey Ann Ward. Her name was Sarah but they shortened it to Sarey Ann Ward.

And old man Michael Sommers taught these two students in navigation at the same time, and after they completed their course with him they went to Baltimore to try and get a command, and they went to a man who had a fleet of vessels running fruit from the West Indies and he said, "Boys, I have one on the ways building and it will be ready in a short time, but," he says, "I can't give it to you cause you're too young."

Well, they pleaded so hard, you know, that he said, "I'll tell you what I'll do: you go back to Crisfield and get Mr. Sommers to agree to make the first trip with you and I'll let you have my new boat."

So they came back and saw Mr. Sommers and he said, "Well, boys, I've retired from the sea and I don't want to go back on the sea again, but I'll tell you what I'll do: if Uncle Hance Lawson will keep store for me I'll make the trip with you, but you'll have to come to Old Island and get me."

So he contacted Mr. Lawson and he told them that he would keep his store. So old man Michael Sommers wrote a letter to this ship owner in Baltimore and they went back and he said, "Well, boys, I'm going to be good to my word. I'm going to let you have her."

So Captain Len went as Captain and the Ward man went as his first mate and they shipped a crew and came down to Old Island and they picked up Mr. Sommers. But while they were here, the Ward boy went up to Ward's Crossing to see his mother and when he left she gave him a potted plant which I'm sure he wasn't too enthusiastic about, but that was all she had. So he took it aboard and put it in the forepeake and they went to sea and down and loaded with fruit and they had a very uneventful trip down. The weather was good, and on the way back the weather was right fair so they got to the Capes and when they did it was so foggy that they couldn't see the forepeake standing at the wheel. And of course, there were about fifteen or twenty other vessels that anchored just inside the Capes because of the fog 'cause they couldn't see their way up the Bay.

The old man Michael Sommers, standing on the deck

looking around and he said, "Well, boys, it's pretty thick and we could kill a week laying here waiting for the fog to lift. Let's go on up to Baltimore. You boys hold her like I tell you and heave your lead every twenty minutes or half hour and bring the sample down to the cabin and I'll tell you how to hold her.

(You know how the lead is, don't you? The bottom is hollowed out and it has wax in it.)

So they started and the old man went down in the cabin and laid down on a locker with a pillow under his head and he was reading a book, and every time they'd throw the lead they'd just take him a sample of the earth and he'd look at it and tell them just how to hold the boat, hold it a couple of more points to the westward. So finally the Ward man became worried and he said, "I don't know whether the old man knows what he's doing or not. If we pile this vessel up on the shore somewheres and lose her, we never will get another command."

Well, Captain Len said, "I don't know; I'm sure he knows what he's doing." Still, the Ward man worried; finally he said, "I'm going to find out." So the next time they threw the lead he grabbed the draw bucket and dipped up some water from overboard and ran down into the forepeake and got his potted plant and he shook the dirt out of that thing and moistened some of the earth out of this plant and packed it in there and he carried it down to old man Michael. And he had a little table right by the locker, you know, with a tin waiter on it and they were dumping those dirt samples in this waiter, so they dumped the sample in the old man Michael looked at it and raised up about half way off the locker and ran his finger through it and he said, "Boys, heave to, you're right in the middle of Sarey Ann's flower garden."

That's a wonderful story. Where did you hear it?

It was told to me by a man named Cox here in town who is very good at such things like that and he usually tells the truth, and he said it was a positive fact. It really happened.

41

Was that Captain Len Tawes?

Yes, Captain Len Tawes who wrote the book.

Not long after I gathered this story, a student of mine collected another version of the tale from a storekeeper in Mount Vernon, Mayland, by the name of William Murray.

There's a man down to Crisfield named Fletcher Cox told me this story. I don't know if it's true or what, but it's supposed to be connected with Captain Tawes who was a great commercial waterman. He had several ships and after he got through following the water he run a store, and he didn't have any cash registers. He just kept his money in nail kegs and they just had half dollars in those days and all he sold was stuff to go with the waterman's needs such as oilskins and gum boots and crab nets and whatnot. And after he kept store for a number of years he got so old and he couldn't move out so he started a navigation school up above the store and he taught people down there to Crisfield how to sail ships.

So one year in particular there were these two boys and they wanted to go to Baltimore and get a ship. So they went to Baltimore and there wasn't nothing but one ship available, and that ship was a small sailing vessel and it was on the ways, and the man wouldn't turn it over to them unless they could get Captain Tawes to make one initial trip with them. And so they came back to Crisfield from Baltimore and told Captain Tawes that the man wouldn't let them have the vessel unless he would make the first trip. So finally he agreed, and they went to Puerta Rica and loaded with fruit, oranges and bananas and grapefruit, and they started back from Puerta Rica and they got into the Capes and there came an awful calm and all these vessels anchored except this one man and he said, "Well, we have to keep her going or these people are going to lose their fruit."

So they kept her on going up the Bay and every once in a while there was thick fog, and every once in a while he asked for a lead line and they'd throw a lead line out and

42

the Captain would read it. He never got out of the cabin he was so old, and they'd carry the lead line down to him and he'd read it.

And after a time these boys got scared. They thought they were going to run ashore and lose all their cargo, so they said to themselves, "We'll find out what he knows."

So when the next time came when they threw out the lead line, they took some dirt from a flower pot that the old Captain's wife had sent along (she thought he might never come back so she sent some flower pots along for the trip). So they took some dirt out of this flower pot and put it on the lead line and brought it down to the old man and said, "Where are we now?"

He felt that, looked it all over, felt it, and he said, "Well, I'll tell you, I'm not sure, but I think we're in the midst of old Betsy's flower garden."

Two informants suggesting a source for the story led me to seek out Fletcher Cox. I found him at his home outside Crisfield and for four hours one afternoon I sat in the shed behind his house and recorded his extended yarns. Very much in the old style of storytelling, he unwinds his tales slowly and meticulously leaning heavily on names and minute detail. It took him more than twenty minutes to uncork this version of the "The Lead Line."

Now, my grandfather, old man Michael Sommers, he had made his money when navigators were scarce. At that time, one hundred years ago, a good navigator could go all over the world. And then they were going in square riggers; no steamships then. And at that time a navigator could take a ship anywhere in the world, and they made good money. And they made runs to China and Japan and all round the South Sea Island, and after he retired from doing that, he had a store on Old Island, Jane's Island they call it, and he built a store on that. And at that time there were no roads out there and people went there by boat. And all up and around Fairmount and Deal Island there wasn't any store worth a damn so they'd come down there to the island by boat. It was a lot quicker than going on an old cart road with a horse, riding. And he had this big store and all the dredge boats they'd come in there and anchor at night.

Well, while he was at that store, he started a school and he had about ten fellows and he taught them navigation. And he had two fellows from Crisfield, Captain Len Tawes and Captain Ben Tawes, and then he had some other guy by the name of Culver. Then he had a lot from around Virginia. They come up there and took navigation from him.

Now the yarn they used to tell about that, it was Captain Len Tawes told this a long time ago, and he said it was the truth and he wasn't exaggerating it. So Captain Len said that Captain Michael got them out there on the Bay, out of sight of land and he said, "Come on boys, take the sun and your latitude and tell me where you're at." And so they did and he said, "I think you boys are O.K. and I can turn you loose and you can go anywhere you want." And so he give them their papers.

So, he said they went to Baltimore and they figured they could get a ship. They'd both go, one would go as Captain and the other as mate. So when they got to Baltimore, there was this fellow, Langhammer; he was a big fruit buyer and he owned ships. And he run down to the West Indies and South America and he didn't go across, but he run fruit mostly for the West Indies. And so they went to Langhammer to see if they could get a ship. And they showed him their papers, you know. Well Langhammer said, "I know Michael wouldn't have sent you if you weren't right, but you're young. You're young. I got a brand new boat that just come off the ways and I'd like for you guys to go as mate or something like that for two or three trips until you know more about it." But they kept after him to let them have the boat, so he finally said, "I'll tell you what I'm going to do: you're young and you've never been to sea, but if you can get old Michael to make one trip with you I'll let you have the boat."

Well, Captain Len said they got in the canoe in Baltimore and came on back to Old Island and came in there and old man Michael said, "How did you make out?"

"Well, we went to Langhammer and he told us the only way he'd let us have the boat was for you to make a trip with us. Go to the West Indies and load fruit."

Michael said, "Well I'm retired, I can't go to sea anymore. I've got this store here and I'm teaching and it's really impossible. But," he said, "if I can get old man Hance Lawson to take the store, I'll make the trip."

"Well," they said, "you'll have to give us the papers to take back to Langhammer."

Old man Michael gave him the papers and told Langhammer to let them have the boat, and they come on down the Bay to Old Island and they picked him up and he made the trip with them.

And they went on out and Michael said, "O.K. boys, take your sun and get your courses and all, and let me look at them." So they did and they were all right and they had a good trip and they got to the West Indies and they loaded with fruit. And they said there were a lot of more boats laying there loading fruit, come from Baltimore and New York and different places. And there were two of Langhammer's boats loading there. And after they got loaded, they all put out practically together, and old man Michael stayed down in the cabin most of the time. And he said, "Send your chart down to me and your log and let me read that. You're doing all right."

Well, just before they got to the Bay, it set in foggy and you couldn't see a thing. All them boats they got inside of Cape Henry on the anchoring ground and they anchored. Didn't want to start up the Bay—no buoys in the Bay or nothing. And they couldn't see a thing. But old man Michael, he said, "We're going up the Bay; this fog is going to last three days and they're going to lose their fruit. We're going on up the Bay and our fruit will be in good shape."

Now after they got by Old Point he said, "Boys, get me your lead line and bring me down a sample from the bottom." And there was just a light breeze a-going and they were going right up the Bay. "Bring me down a sounding every half hour, twenty minutes would be better, but don't make it over half an hour before you bring me down another sample."

He went back down there in the cabin. They throwed the lead line over and it come up about several handfuls of mud and they passed it down to him and he looked at it and he said, "All right, boys, you're doing all right, but change your course now about three or four points to the westward. You're right near the channel, but you're a little bit on the eastern side of it. Change about three more points to the westward and that will put right in the middle of the channel in the next half hour."

Well, they done that and come the night and the fog was so thick they said you had to feel the man that was next to you. And they were steering with a light over the compass so they could see that, and this fellow Ward says, "Uncle, he doesn't know where we are. We're going to run this boat aground and we'll never get another one. Langhammer nor nobody else will ever give us another boat. He don't know where he's at, foggy as it is."

Well, Captain Len said, "We ain't run ashore yet, and everytime you've thrown the line you've had some water."

So he carried a sample down and he come back up on deck and Uncle Michael said, "Now, hold right on that course for the next half an hour."

So they talked and Ward said, "Damned if I ain't going to find out what you know."

His mother was a great flower arranger and she lived right up here to what they call Ward's Crossing and she had the best flower garden in Somerset County. Her name was Betsy Ann Ward. And she knowed she'd never get to see him no more and she give him a flower in a pot to take aboard to remember her by. And so he said, "Len, I'm going to see how much he knows; you know that flower that mother gave me and I brought aboard? I'm going to throw that flower overboard and I'm going to wet that dirt from overboard and put it in there and send it down to him.

46

(It's the truth. I've heard them both tell it. Course Captain Ward got drownded, but Captain Len lived to be an old man, and I've heard him tell it a hundred times.)

He put this in there, dipped the lead line overboard and he dumped it out on the platter and sent it down to the old man. And he mushed it like mud, you know. Well Michael said, "Seems to me we're going all right." And he looked at this, looked all around, went through it and says, "Henry, run up just as quick as you can and tell Len to heave her hard to. You're right in the middle of Betsy Ann's flower garden."

On the lips of other raconteurs the story retains its basic structure, but there is little doubt that the process of deterioration has begun to take place. An ex-Tangierman named Rob Williams recounted the tale, putting a local character in the lead role:

This sailboat captain, his name was Richard Fenn, and he hired two fellows to go to Baltimore with him. He was a good captain, no booze, didn't want no booze on the boat. You had to know the water. They said, "We're going to fool him." (You've heard tell of lead lines, ain't you? Well, you know they've got a little hole in the center and then you get the smell of it and from the bottom you can tell where you're at.) They went out to his grandmothers I think it was to the toilet and dropped it down in the hole and they carried it aboard with them.

Well, they were going up the Bay and he said, "Boys, where we at?"

They said, "We don't know."

He said, "Sound the bottom, let's smell of it."

Well, they out with that lead they'd dropped down that toilet, they found the bottom; he smelled of it and said, "Lookee here, if you don't get this boat about, damned if we ain't going to run aground on a shithouse."

Where did you hear that story?

Oh, I knew that one a long time. I used to hear them talk about it home on the island one time.

In a very similar fashion, Alex Kellam, as is his style, takes the story and pins it on a local Smith Island captain, paring away all unnecessary detail so as to emerge with a slim anecdote which hinges on the final line.

You were telling about the guy who could only tell by the lead line where he was. Who was that?

I think his name was Ben Fudge. Benjamin Evans, but they called him Ben Fudge. Not knowing navigation (I don't suppose his was all memory), but they said they were going to Baltimore on this trip and said they would take their chickens right aboard and their geese and have them whenever they needed them, wanted them. And so he was telling them that he could tell them exactly where they were by the smell of the mud from the lead line. So they started off and when they got off Bear's island, they dropped the lead line.

He said, "You're right off Holland's Bar, about twenty miles off of here."

They said, "Damn it, right."

So they went up there till they got off of Barren Island, and they took another sounding. He said, "Right off Hooper's Strait, right off of Barren Island Light."

On up the Bay about eight or ten times and finally one of them said, "Damn if we don't see what the hell he does this time." So one of them took that lead line and smeared it round in the chicken coop, you know.

" 'Bout time for another sounding."

So they passed the lead down to him and he took it. "Godamn, if I didn't know we were right off of Thomas's Point, I'd swear I was right home in the back yard."

In a version of the story told by Crisfield crabhouse owner, Roy Milbourne, the tale loses even more of its particularities as actual characters drop away and the link to authenticity appears only in the name of the cabbage patch.

There is an old saying and this is true: people can tell where

48

they are by looking at the material collected in the bottom of a lead line. A lead line has a hole or sink in the bottom that gathers material from the bottom. These old fellows that followed the water, they knew the types of bottom in mostly all areas. Having no radar or modern equipment, they had to depend on their knowledge of the river or sound the bottom. We had one old fellow that claimed he could tell where he was by tasting this material from the bottom, so one day his crew decided to trick him. So when they were getting ready to go on a trip one day, one of the crew members gathered some mud from a neighbor's cabbage patch. And on the trip it got foggy so the captain told one of the men to get out the lead line, throw it overboard and bring him a sample of the bottom to taste. Instead of a sample of the river's bottom, they brought him a sample of Sol Bradshaw's cabbage patch. And when he'd finished tasting it, he yelled out, "Keep her off, bring her around, we going to run aground on Sol Bradshaw's cabbage patch!"

Finally, in Dewey Landon's rendition of the yarn, we find the narrative stripped of all definite associations with places or people and spun off with more emphasis on the scatalogical ending than on any precise fact.

They claim there was an old captain going up and down the Bay here, and no matter what, he could taste the bottom and tell you where you was at. He done it so much, he knew the different tastes of the bottom. And one of them, he went and dumped, and he shoved the lead line down in it and went and [the Captain] tasted it and he said, "I'll tell you one thing, if we don't get this boat turned around, we're going to run into a shithouse."

Much the same sort of variation occurs with many of the tales that follow. I have given in the text only what I felt was the best or the most complete version of the narrative. Comparative study can be valuable, for it tells us not only something about each narrator and his style and thereby something about his personality, but also something about the culture and the oral process. Folklore still thrives on the Eastern Shore because of the conservative nature of its people, its semi-isolation, and the remarkable tenacity of the folk memory. It is perhaps the folk memory, more than anything else, that has in one way kept many of these tales intact. At the same time it is each narrator's individuality that has altered them. But above all it is the essence of the waterman's culture and attitude that has shaped the type of story told; the same essence, no doubt that has made many a liberal legislator in Annapolis scratch his head with wonder as he ponders the words of an old jingle:

Fishermen on Deal Island, Maryland

Heroes: Saints, Strong Men, and Rogues

Few communities lack a folk hero. He is the figure who, during his lifetime, drew attention because of a particular characteristic: strength, cunning, fearlessness, piety. While alive, tales emerge about him which exemplify that feature of his personality which catches the folk imagination. After the local figure is dead, narrators still perpetuate his memory, spinning the old yarns about him, usually considerably embroidered for effect, and adding traditional floating stories to the cycle of tales. With time and retelling, the truth often gets stretched to extraordinary lengths and traditional tall tale patterns gradually replace fact.

Isolated Eastern Shore communities prove splendid spawning grounds for such hero tale cycles. Local stores and village liars' benches, where time hangs heavy, breed accounts of men who followed the water in an earlier time, a time when, as one Crisfield waterman commented, "things were done by main strength and ignorance." And the tales that spring to life at these gatherings form a vital part of community life. One woman who lived on Smith Island pointed out that these heroes, be they saints, strong men or rogues, live on in the watermen's yarning not only to preserve their fame, but also to inspire the young.

Saints

I doubt there is a Methodist living between Deal Island and Tangier who has not heard of Joshua Thomas. Those in the region who profess the faith frequently refer to Adam Wallace's 1861 study, *The Parson of the Islands,* which recounts Thomas' life as a home-spun preacher on the lower Eastern Shore.

While Adam Wallace's book intrigues the faithful, it is also of interest to the folklorist, for the author drew much of his information for the biography from oral sources. Some of the stories have persisted in oral circulation to this day.

Parts of the book also stem from a manuscript prepared by Reverend Levin M. Prettyman from personal interviews with Thomas before 1815. In Thomas' own words we receive the story of his conversion to the Methodist faith along with the now locally famous story of his confrontation with the British on Tangier Island during the War of 1812:

> Before they left Tangier, they sent word to me to be ready to hold a public meeting, and exhort the soldiers on the camp ground. I did not like to refuse, and yet I was very unwilling to perform this duty. . . .
>
> I stood on a little platform erected at the end of the camp nearest the shore, all the men facing me with their hats off and held by the right hand under the left arm. An officer stood on my right and one on my left, and the sentries were stationed a little distance to the rear.
>
> As I looked around on my congregation, I never had such feelings in my life; but I felt determined to give them the faithful warning, even if those officers, with their keen glittering swords, could *cut me in pieces* for speaking the truth.
>
> After singing and prayer, I began to feel better in the mind, and more at liberty. Soon all fear and embarrassment were taken away from me, and I proceeded in my exhortation as freely as ever I did, in any place, or before any people. . . .
>
> I told them it was given me from the Almighty that they *could not* take Baltimore, and would *not succeed in their expedition.* . . .
>
> When the battle was over, we saw them coming, and I went down to meet the first that landed. I felt great distress, for fear many of those I knew had been killed, and lest some of *our own people* (the citizens of Baltimore) had met their death. My worst fears were far short of reality.
>
> The first officers I met, I asked them if they had taken

Baltimore? They looked at me and said, 'No, but hundreds of our brave men have been slain, and our best General is killed. It turned out as you told us the Sunday before we left: we have had a bloody battle, and all the time we were fighting *we thought of you,* and what you told us. You seemed to be standing right before us, still warning us against our attempt to take Baltimore.'

As one begins to examine the life of Joshua Thomas, certain analogies with Christ emerge. Like Christ, Thomas was a fisherman as well as a fisher of souls. He gathered a large following but always preached humility. He sailed about Tangier Sound in a log canoe called the *Methodist,* and when he died in 1853, people actually sought pieces of the boat as relics. One Crisfield resident confided: "Now after he died, people got to getting pieces of that boat, and my uncle's grandfather, he had a piece of her; kept it on the mantel someplace." Moreover, Joshua Thomas had the power to heal the sick:

One time Joshua Thomas went to the home of a man who had been bedridden for years and asked him to take him somewhere on his boat the following morning, and this man looked at him and said, 'Reverend Thomas, you must be crazy, I haven't been out of this bed for years.'

Reverend Thomas said, 'If you could get up would you take me?'

The man looked at him for a moment, laughed, and said, 'Yes, if I can get up I'll take you.'

Thomas said, 'Good, meet me at the dock at nine o'clock in the morning.' The next morning that man got out of bed for the first time in years and kept his appointment with Joshua Thomas. Now that was a miracle. (5)

On another occasion, when Joshua Thomas needed to go to the Western Shore, he healed a Smith Island man so he might transport him.

Ham Bradshaw, he was a waterman. He lived on Smith

Island and Joshua Thomas lived on Tangier. There was this important meeting that was going to take place at Leonard-town, or some place there in the Potomac River. Captain Ham, he was lame and couldn't walk very well, he told Joshua Thomas that he wanted to go to this meeting but he was afraid to go 'cause of his condition. Joshua Thomas told him, said, 'Ham, if I go home and pray for your lameness, if you're able to go in the morning, will you carry me to this meeting?'

Ham said, 'I certainly will.'

So next morning, Joshua Thomas gets up and sets out for Smith Island in his boat. Before he got there, Ham Bradshaw had his sails all ready. Now, boy, that's what you call the power of prayer. (5)

Thomas also appears to have used his miraculous powers to illustrate moral judgements. He preached against greed and marvelously dried up a profitable fishing hole when his parishioners began squabbling over it.

Many years ago one of the best fishing places in Tangier Sound was a certain spot right off Deal Island and it was called "The Fishing Hole." Anyhow, lots of people went there for fish all the time. Even in the winter time, when everything was froze up with ice you could go there, break an air hole, get your fishing pole and line, and catch as many fish as you wanted.

One day the people in the area got to quarreling about this fishing ground and Joshua Thomas was very disappointed in the way the community behaved. Instead of being thankful, they were ungrateful, and so he prayed to God that no more fish would ever be caught there. And to this day, not a fish has ever been caught there. (5)

If Joshua Thomas providentially punished the greedy and ungrateful, he also secured sustenance for the needy in mysterious ways.

Well, we were speaking about Joshua Thomas, what a

good man he was. Well, we had another native on Deal Island that was a very sick man. He couldn't eat anything but fish and he just craved a piece of fish. And the doctor said to him, he said, 'You can't get no fish now, because you haven't any way to catch them because you haven't got no crabs.'

And this man named Joshua Thomas told the brother of the sick man to go down under a stump on Little Island and he would look in the hollow of a root at a certain place there and he would find one crab, and he would take that and go down to the south end of Little Deal Island and he would throw his line out, and he said he would get one bite and that would be a rockfish.

Well, that fellow did that and sure enough, it was just like Joshua Thomas said. He went there and got that crab and caught that rockfish and brought it back to his brother. (6)

Though the majority of stories circulating about Reverend Thomas treat his religious fervor and his astonishing deeds, there is some indication that humorous tales have become attached to him, as in this version of a well-known jest.

Now I was told this by Mrs. Anderson who used to run the boarding house on Deal Island. She said Joshua Thomas had these false teeth, and he lost them overboard one time. Everyone came around to help to see if they could find them. One young boy dove over to see if he could find them. Some of the men there used their tongs to see if they could get the teeth that way. Nobody had any luck.

Finally there was this woman that came along. She said she'd get them. So she went home and pretty soon she came back with this thing in her apron which had a long piece of string tied to it. She threw that overboard and it wasn't long before she brought up those teeth. They all asked her how she'd done it.

She said, 'There's only one way to catch a Methodist's teeth: with a piece of fried chicken.' (7)

55

More recent than Joshua Thomas, but equally endowed with reverence and miraculous powers, was another Tangier Island preacher, Reverend Charles P. Swain. Swain presided as parson on the island in the early part of the twentieth century, and the Swain Memorial Church bears testimony to his activity in raising money to build it. It appears, according to Gladstone Dize of Tangier who told the tale, that Swain actually stilled the waters to achieve his goal.

Now when they were trying to raise money for that church, Reverend Swain said he would not even begin to have the church built until all the money was raised. So he sent out some men to oyster over on the northwest side of the island and told them if they went there they'd have good luck and bring in a good catch and make some money. And they went up there like he said, and the water was calm and the breeze was just right and they made one of the best catches of the season. But those fellows who were working down on the southeast part of the island, they had to quit and come home 'cause it was blowing so hard and storming.

Swain evidentally possessed a personal magnetism which enabled him to make men more generous than they ever knew they could be. Captain Al Wheatley recalled: "Oh, he was a wonderful man, that Swain. He got up there and he ripped right out and he said, 'I won't eat a mouthful, sleep a wink, nor drink a drop till the debt for that church's paid.' And he turned to me and he said, 'You'll give me twenty-five dollars, won't you Alan?' And I said, 'Yeah,' and I weren't but making fifty cents working on the water then."

Reverend Swain, like Joshua Thomas, convinced his followers just by the sheer strength of his faith. He produced astonishing results through the simple force of prayer, as was the case with Harrison Crockett's drowned body.

Now about them two men out there on the island that got drownded. Tub Crockett was the name of one of the fellows, and Harrison Crockett was the other one. They went oystering in February on a boat with sail on her, and they were on their way home to Tangier and she capsized and both of them got drownded. Well, they found Tub Crockett's body on the Western Shore; he drifted all the way across the Bay. But they couldn't find the other fellow's body, and they didn't find it until the next summer. Well, that fellow's wife went to Mr. Swain and he said, 'Don't you worry, Mrs. Crockett, your husband will be found.' And he prayed to have her husband come home.

Well, after it got hot, he raised from the bottom and he was coming up with the flood tide, and they said that if the fellows out fishing their crab pots hadn't found him, he would have floated right up to her landing, and that would have been up a long little river. And they said he'd of come to her backyard. Now, somebody like that should have faith. (8)

Swain also convinced Wes Charnis of the power of faith.

Now this happened at what we call the camp meeting time. There were some fellows who brought a sugar barrel of beer out here and they landed their boat down the shore there. Well, Mr. Swain found out about it and he and two other men went down there. This other fellow, Wes Charnis, had a canoe pulled up there, and they used to keep ballast in them canoes so the rudder wouldn't come out of the water. And Wes had put that ballast in a little pile up there on the bank.

So Swain and them two fellows took that sugar barrel of beer and busted every one of them bottles over that ballast. And when Wes Charnis went down there, he went right back to the preacher, and he said, 'You've ruined my ballast.'

Swain said, 'That ballast will be all right when you want to get it.'

'Yes,' he said, 'but I can't move it. It's covered up with glass and I'll cut myself.'

Swain said, 'It'll be all right when you want to get it.'

And after awhile he painted his canoe and launched her. He went to get his ballast and he couldn't find a sprig of glass nowhere, not one sprig.

Oh, you talk about a good man, that Swain, he was a good preacher. (3)

Not long after this, Wes Charnis, who had never been much of a church man, went to the Sunday service. Swain spoke to him, "Well, Mr. Charnis, how about changing your mind?" When he said he didn't think he would, Swain whispered something in his ear and he replied, "Hold on, Mr. Swain, I'm ready."

Strong Men

Where miraculous deeds made heroes out of preachers on the Eastern Shore, so the waterman's culture nurtured other heroics based on feats of strength. The mark of a real man was not how smart he was or how affluent, but how easily he could lift a hundred and ninety-six pound barrel of flour. A Negro named Bob who lived on Tangier Island for a time gained a good deal of respect when he lifted a barrel with one hand by simply holding on to the rim at the top. His employer couldn't believe it; he thought•the barrel held crackers, but when he went over and tried to lift it, he failed to get it off the ground.

Bob used to work for the shell pile factory which Captain Pat ran and Captain Pat used to tote a pistol in his pocket for him in case he got out of hand. And one time they had a nigger cook in there for the crew, and this cook thought he was a better man than Bob was. And this one evening he called them all into supper and when Bob come into the table—everything was neat and clean—he said, 'Did the white folks eat?'

He said, 'Sit down, it don't matter whether they eat or not.'

And Bob said, 'No, we don't eat till the white folks eat.' And one word brought on another. And the cook, he was standing in the cookhouse door. Bob smacked him over four barrels full of oil into a tank of oil and they had to hold him up till it drained off.

'Now,' he says, 'if you ever cross my path again, I'll hit you.' (3)

Another Tangierman by the name of George Baker likewise acquired a reputation as a rugged individual. On a trip to the Patuxent River he displayed his strength catching a barrel of water.

One of the crew was mustering up some buckets to take to the well to tote water back to the boat and George Baker said, 'What are you doing, Bill?'

He said, 'I'm getting buckets for the water.'

George Baker said, 'We don't need buckets,' and he carried the barrel up to the well. And they didn't have scuttles in them then, just bungs. And he drove that bung in it and he rolled it down to the edge of the hill and the drop was nearly twelve feet to the beach. And George Baker, he got down under that and he said, 'OK Bill, roll her,' and Bill was scared to roll it down to him. And George Baker said to him, 'Look you little son-of-a-bitch, if I come up on that hill, you'll roll it down to me.'

So he said, 'Get under it.'

And when he caught that his bones creaked and it sunk right in his arms and he walked right down to the yawl boat and put it in the yawl boat.

Now he had right much power. (3)

Baker also used to run oysters to Baltimore with a man named Ligea Crockett. At that time the Baltimore dock space was limited and often boats had to raft alongside one another to unload their oysters. Usually, the inside vessel would unload and then slip out to let the next boat in. One time, however, the captain of the outside boat refused to let Crockett out until he had passed his oysters across Crockett's deck. George Baker came to the waist of the ship, rolled up his sleeves and spoke:

"Now, the first son-of-her that passes this deck with a basket of oysters, I'll lay this fist up against him. You can't get nary a man in Baltimore to pass an oyster across this deck, and if you think you can I'll put that fist against him and break his head from his body."

No one moved. Finally the captain of the other boat spoke: "Well, slack your lines boys; we'll get out of their way."(3)

Another strong man who generated a cycle of stories in the area around Fairmount, Maryland was George Davey.

Like other strong men, George Davey achieved his fame by his ability to lift things. On a trip to Baltimore, the boat he was aboard needed flour. Davey walked to the store and ordered two barrels. When the storekeeper told him the dray would be back presently to transport his flour to the wharf, Davey said he couldn't wait, took a barrel under each arm and walked down to his vessel. More impressive still, one Fairmount waterman claimed his father had seen George Davey lift and carry the mast for a sixty foot pungy boat, and the mast was more than a foot in diameter and seventy-five feet long. Not surprisingly the traditional tale of the strong man lifting the stone also got pinned on Davey.

> One time when they were building the rip-raps down there to Old Point, they had this big stone down in the hold of the boat, and there was two men, and they couldn't heist it out with throat halyards. George Davey jumped down in the hold and he put that stone up on the deck and it was so heavy that it mashed the deck down. And they say he carried that stone home to Fairmount and put it down for a doorstop, and that's still there.
>
> Oh, he was a man. (3)

Once a local man acquired the reputation for brute strength, stories about him spun off and the process of oral tradition carried them to other creek and island communities. When the bullies of these nearby towns heard of a new strong man, because there was no one to match them at home, they went looking for a fresh challenge. Several ventured to Fairmount seeking George Davey.

> They said there was this fella from the Western Shore. Oh, he was such a strong man. And he come over here to see George Davey. Wanted to fight him. So they told him where George Davey lived and he went down there where his home was, and he went into the house and inquired for him. They said, 'He's down in the swamp, making a boat, making a log canoe.'
>
> Well this fella said, 'I'm looking for him right now.'
>
> They said, 'Well, he's down in the woods making that boat.'
>
> So this fellow went down there and he looked around and he saw George Davey coming up there through the swamp carrying that boat on his back. That fellow just turned around and left. (9)

On another occasion, the challenger came from Saxis Island down in Virginia.

> Now this one time there was a fellow came here after George Davey. He came from over there to Saxis Island. (I know that place, I've drudged there many a time.) And this fellow told George Davey he wanted to fight with him. So he said, 'Yes, but let's get a drink first.'
>
> Fellow got his in a glass. George Davey picked up the barrel and got a drink out of it. That fellow walked right out of there after that. (9)

When George Davey was not around to accommodate a challenger, his sister took his place.

> Well, one time there was a man come down there to Fairmount wanted to fight with George Davey, you know. And so his sister met him to the door and said George Davey was gone what did he want, and he told her.
>
> 'Look,' she says, 'he's not here but when he's gone I take his place.'

And she sleeved up her sleeves, and that fellow give it
to her away. [Left] (3)

If Eastern Shore narrators reflect a recognizable admiration
for brute strength in their stories, their tales also display respect
for fair play. This widely told yarn is also hung on George Davey.

Well now, another funny thing: this was down to Fairmount, and this man come to George Davey and he wanted
him to lug his boat for him down to the water. Said he'd
give him five dollars to do it. So he went down there and got
a rope around it and pulled it overboard, and when he come
back to get his money, the fellow said, 'I ain't got the money
now.' He took that boat and pulled it right back up again.
(10)

The same tale is told on "Old Man Smack" down on Col-
bourne Creek. The boat he pulled overboard and then back, five
men had not been able to budge. And when the narrative moves
inland to the Salisbury region, the account is attached to a strong
man named Ross Henry, and the boat becomes a car.
Other communities on the Eastern Shore spawned equally
remarkable characters. Old man Hasty on Smith Island didn't
have much of a voice. He always spoke in a mumble. But he had
power. He picked up and carried off a huge anchor and chain
that two younger men failed to move a single inch. On Elliotts
Island, Danny R. had a reputation for endurance and stoicism as
well as strength. He never wore a coat even in the fiercest
weather, and one day while walking up the road barefoot, he
stepped on a rusty nail; he reached down, pulled it out and said,
"Damn if that wouldn't do something to a tire." Near Cambridge,
Hargis Prince held the watermen's respect as a man of great
power. He hefted flour barrels with the best, single-handed and
without even working up a sweat. But he married a woman
thirty years his junior, and after that he couldn't get an empty
barrel off the ground.
Yet perhaps most representative of the folk heroes of the

lower Eastern Shore is "Lickin' " Billy Bradshaw of Smith Island. Though he died in 1917, and the simple headstone in the Rhodes Point graveyard attests to a long life of eighty-three years, tales about him still flourish, not only on Smith Island itself, but in many of the neighboring island communities and creek towns. The tales depict a man of prodigious strength, simple faith, and comic tendencies.

William Bradshaw was a giant. He stood close to seven feet and had a neck on him like a bull. His hands were so large and powerful that he could take a hard clam into his palm and bust it open simply by squeezing. His tremendous size made clothing a problem. Nothing fit him. He wore size fourteen brogan shoes, and even then he never could lace them up. "Oh yes," recalled Alex Kellam who grew up in Rhodes Point, "I remember Lickin' Bill. I was real small when he died, though. He had a goatee that used to come down to his waist; practically all the older men in that day wore mustaches. I'd say he was about six-eight or ten, and he weighed two hundred and seventy-five pounds. 'Course, there was no tailoring in them days, and they said it was an awkward looking thing to see him going to church with his pants legs just below his knees and his coat sleeves up to his elbows."

If his size and dress were part of the tradition that sprang up around William Bradshaw, so too was his nickname, "Lickin'." One supposes that he might have acquired it because of the men he had licked in a fight, but the people of the island propose a different etymology. Thomas Tyler of Tylerton said his grandfather told it to him this way:

Lickin' used to have a habit. Everytime he got his mind on something he would have to lick it before he'd be satisfied. If he was out drudging oysters, and he'd have that urge, he'd tell them to lower the sails and he'd go up to the top of the mast and he'd have to lick that block up there. And another time he was coming up Tyler's Creek and he had this notion to lick the boom, and the crew had to pull it in to give him to lick.

A lick in waterman's lingo denotes a pass of the tongs or dredge over the oyster bed. It is a good lick when they come up full, a bad lick when they don't. For the waterman himself, the word has a sense about it, though he would never be able to define it. It springs from the occupation and the culture, and seems somehow inseparable from it. Watermen enjoy saying "lick," just as they like to utter Bradshaw's nickname. "Old Man Lickin' " or "Lickin' Billy" or more simply, "Lickin'," are the names storytellers use when referring to him, and they seem to relish pronouncing the words. Lickin' Bill's character seems to represent those characteristics (strength, reverence, and wit) so respected among Eastern Shore watermen, that are also symbolized by his nickname.

Tales of Lickin' Billy's incredible strength spring easily to the lips of Eastern Shore raconteurs. One of Bradshaw's own grandsons living in Rhodes Point recalled with considerable pleasure how the men used to hang around the local store waiting for his grandfather to come by. Then they would play a game. Lickin' would hold a broom handle out at arm's length and they would tie weights on the end until the handle broke in two. The younger Bradshaw also recounted his grandfather's method (albeit unintentional) for killing hogs.

> Let's see, there was another yarn. They used to kill hogs around here, and he [Lickin' Bill] was a hog killer, and he'd always knock them over the head with an axe. Well, he got in front of that hog and when he went to go down on him, the axe come off from the handle, you know, and he hit him with the handle: killed him right there. Killed him with one hand and the handle; that's all he used. (11)

Lickin' Billy often pitted his strength against other animals too. In the old days when sheep were common on Smith Island, once a year they had to be corralled for shearing.

> A long time ago on the island, the people used to keep sheep, away from Rhodes Point, right across the creek and the canal leading up there was called Sheep Pen Gut. They

64

still call it that today. And every spring they would bring the sheep to that big sandy place right on the edge of Sheep Pen Gut and shear them. Well, one time one of the rams got unruly and old man Lickin' got aggravated and he went out there and he caught him and started leading him towards the pen, but the ram bucked him all the way. So he took him by the horn and lifted him right off the ground. The horn broke right off in Lickin' Bill's hand. The ram took off and Lickin' held up the horn and said, 'Yes indeedy, I got a piece of him.' (1)

In another version of the story, Lickin' Bill grabs the ram by the horn, says, "If the horn stays on, the gentleman's going into the pen," and casually lifts the ram over the fence and in.

If Lickin' knew how to deal with animals, he also understood how to handle men in a fight. His reputation as the bully of Smith Island preceded him wherever he went and local strong boys continually tried to prod him into fights. More often than not he was equal to the task.

Once when Lickin' Bill went over to the Eastern Shore of Virginia to barter for sweet potatoes, they walked up to the country store that night. And the word got around that this big man from Smith Island was there. Well, they asked him if he was the bully of Smith Island, and they goaded him until they got him to fight. So when they went out of the store, and these three men jumped him, Lickin' hit one, and he grabbed the other and he must have thrown him fifteen or twenty feet end over end, and the other fella ran, and as he went by Lickin' kicked at him and his big brogan shoe—wasn't laced, you know—come off and hit the corner of the store and busted the weather boarding plank on it. Yes sir. (1)

On another occasion, he encountered a professional wrestler on Tangier Island.

Now Lickin', he went down to Tangier Island for the

65

camp meeting. All those islands had camp meetings then. And there was this fellow there from the mainland, and he was a professional wrestler. And this was on a Sunday.

So the Tangiermen found out Lickin' Bill was there and they went looking for him. When they found him they said, 'They tell us you're the bully of Smith Island and we challenge you to a wrestling.'

Now since it was Sunday, Lickin' wasn't too anxious and he had his good clothes on too. But he told them that the only way he'd wrestle would be to go down to the cowpen and do it there.

Now the way they used to do it in that day would be they'd get alongside of each other and one would make his break and the other would defend and try to keep from going down. Then the other would have his turn—side-holts they called it.

So they drew straws to see who would have the first break. Well, the challenger drew the straw and he went first. When he applied pressure on Lickin'—and he was a powerful man—he buried Lickin' Bill up to his knees in the cow dung.

Lickin' said, 'Yes indeedy, Captain, you didn't do it.' So Lickin' grabbed him by the back of the neck and the seat of his pants and threw him head first right into the cow dung. And you see, Lickin' was still the champion. (1)

Though Lickin' Bill usually bettered most of his opponents, there was at least one time when he realized that he had met his match.

Lickin' Bill, John Hoffman, and another man were over to Deal Island and they were sitting there between the morning and evening meeting, you know. Well, this big old fellow was sitting in front of them with his arms folded and his hat pulled down over his eyes.

Old man Lickin' says to John Hoffman, 'John, tip that man's hat.' (He was looking for a fight.) John Hoffman reached over there and tipped it. This fellow righted it and

66

didn't pay any attention. John Hoffman tipped it again. Nothing. Righted it and folded his arms.

Old man Lickin' said, 'Tip her good this time, John.' So he grabbed that hat and he pulled it right down over that fellow's ears.

He took that hat and pulled it up, stood up, and said, 'Gentlemen, I don't know who you are nor where you came from, but I'm Jobus T. Webster of Deal's Island, and I'm not afraid of the face of any man nor the ass of any woman, and I'll give you five dollars to do that again.'

Lickin' Bill said, 'Ahem, yes indeedy, boys, leave him alone.' (1)

A number of tales circulating about Bradshaw turn on his comic aspects. His witty remarks and somewhat idiosyncratic life-style produced a humor that greatly appealed to island story-tellers. As a tremendous man, Bradshaw possessed a vicious appetite. It often came upon him at odd hours and produced amusing results.

Now Norfolk Spot was Lickin' Bill's favorite fish, but they had been very scarce that summer. So when he come over to Crisfield one day he was able to buy a mess. He carried them home and salted them up so as to have them the next morning for breakfast.

That night around two o'clock he got them on his mind and he told his wife Atline, 'Atline, I'm going down and cook those fish and eat them.' So he got the fire going and he put the skillet on and he hollered up, 'Atline, where's the flour?'

She said, 'William, it's in the cupboard on the top shelf in a paper bag.' So he got it out and rolled the fish in it and put them in the skillet.

Pretty soon they begun to snap and crack and raise the devil and she called down, 'William, where did you get that bag?'

He said, 'On the top shelf.'

She said, 'My good Lord have mercy, that's the lime.'

He said, 'Yes indeedy, I've limed the horses.' (1)

Many of the stories told on Lickin' Bill combine his comic side with his simple but abiding religious faith. He was an ardent Methodist and his zealous attitude made him a leader in the church as well as the community. "I want to live life," he reportedly told his friends, "so that I can look back on a life well-spent in the service of my dear Lord and Master." With such displays of devotion, it is hardly surprising that Lickin' Bill was often selected to lead the marching at the annual camp meeting, and to act as a kind of lay preacher at certain church services. When called upon to talk to the congregation about the lesson for the day, he always preferred to address his remarks to the children present. One Sunday the lesson was on turning the other cheek. After Lickin' Bill had finished explaining the significance of the matter he faced his favorite audience and said, "Now little boys and girls, what would you do if someone hit you on the right side of your face?"

One young boy jumped up and shouted, "Why I'd swack him right back."

During a similar question and answer session, Bradshaw hid his ignorance with a clever remark.

Now Lickin' was called upon every Sunday to say something in church. And of course he always had a way of referring to the little boys and girls. So this one Sunday, the lesson was on the children of Israel crossing the Jordan River, and so he said, 'Little boys and girls, what did the children of Israel do when they crossed the Jordan River?'

Well, they didn't know. But Lickin' Bill didn't know either. Nobody said anything. In fact, nobody said a word for about thirty seconds. Pretty soon Lickin' Bill cleared his throat and said, 'Yes indeedy, boys and girls, *there* was a time.' (1)

One of the most widely told stories on the lower Eastern Shore is also attached to Lickin' Bill in a tale which characteristically depicts the inseparability of the waterman's profession and his religion.

Well, there was a man over on the island there and he had been a preacher and they said he was a right good one. So he got after the camp meeting committee to let him preach the opening sermon. He thought he deserved that honor, you know. So the committee got together and they said, 'Well, boys, he done a lot of good work, been a big help to us around here, he's a hard worker, let's let him preach the opening sermon."

And so he picked his text and he got up there and he began. 'And they casted forth seven anchors, and waited for the break of day.' Well, everything left him. He just went blank. So he walked backwards and forwards there a couple of times and he stopped and he pointed down his finger and he said, 'And they casted forth seven anchors and waited for the break of day.' Still didn't come. It was a blank. So he made a couple more passes and he stopped and he pointed and he said, 'And they casted forth seven anchors and waited for the break of day.'

Old man Lickin' Bill jumped up and said, 'Brother, that's twenty-one anchors. That'll hold any vessel in Tangier Sound.' (1)

The great age of sail during the nineteenth century has often been spoken of as a time of "wooden ships and iron men." And so too, on the Chesapeake Bay it took men of incredible physical endurance to withstand not only the hard taskmasters who captained the vessels, but also the misery of the cold weather. Some individuals simply became accustomed to it, as did one waterman shipwrecked north of Tangier Island.

There was this ship froze in the ice and drug ashore up there off of Shank's. Uncle Ligia Spence lived up there then with his wife. And the next day the captain and two men walked ashore on the ice. And Uncle Ligia asked them to come in the house to get warm. It was way below zero. But this one fellow stayed outside with his sleeves rolled up, and when Uncle Ligia asked the captain to tell that man to come in by the fire, he said, 'Oh no, don't worry about him.

He can take the cold. He sounded all last night in his shirt sleeves, bareheaded.'

And so the next day Uncle Ligia went out there on board that boat and there was that man with the jib bonnet flapped over him laying there in the shade fast asleep, and the temperature still way below zero. (3)

There were other characteristics that watermen displayed which helped them survive the rigors of their existence; such things as simple stoicism and the ability to face possible death with a sense of humor. These were characteristics clearly inherited from their English ancestors whose penchant for understatement is well-known. A personal account from a man who used to live on Smith Island reveals this uncanny humor under pressure.

My partner and I, we were young men, and we kept a store over on Rhodes Point. And there's a little channel that come in there from the Bay. But one winter we had a seven week freeze and everything was blocked right up. After a while, though, the tide cut a channel that come by our oyster house. The boys over there, they'd do anything to make a dollar and so they went out tonging for oysters, and they caught quite a bunch. And we brought them back, shucked them and canned them, thinking we could get them to market pretty soon. But the freeze held on and held on, and finally it started to break up.

Well, we wanted to get those oysters ashore to sell them. So we skidded them by hand down to the Sound shore and got them into three boats. We had a twenty-foot power boat with a gasoline engine, and then we had an eighteen-foot skiff astern, loaded with oysters, and we had a little double-ended skiff with nothing into it.

We started out and we were doing fine until we got right plum in the middle of Tangier Sound where the tide run strong. All at once the ice started to close in on us. We didn't know what to do, but we had to do something quick so we stuck the nose of the boat into the ice and I jumped on there with the line.

Well, we stayed there and we stayed there and time was going on and the day was getting on to about two o'clock. And pretty soon it begun to cloud up, big dark clouds up there in the northwest and they begun to come down towards us. And Noahy Jeems, who was with us, he looked up there and he said, 'Boys, by the looks of it, it's going to come northwest, and it looks like we're going to get our names in the paper tomorrow, but we ain't gonna be there to read them.'

And right after that the ice opened up, and we were able to bring one of those little skiffs right in here to the wharf in Crisfield. (4)

Rogues

On Smith Island the town of Rhodes Point used to be known as Rogues Point, pronounced "Pint" by the islanders. Similarly, a look at early maps and charts of the area reveals that Deal Island once was called Devil's Island, later spelled Deil's Island, deil being an older form of the word for devil. And near Deal Island there is a small settlement, known today as Dames Quarter, but listed by early cartographers as Damned Quarter or Quarter of the Damned. To go from Devil's Island to Damned Quarter, one had to pass through a town called Chance. It is not hard to speculate why.

How the names came to be bestowed, however, is another matter. The earlier nomenclature dates back to the eighteenth century and surely suggests the rough breed of rogues and devils that peopled the region then. Eastern Shoremen kept the image alive into the nineteenth and early part of the twentieth century when the oystermen frequently tangled with the law in what was, off and on, literally a shooting war. One writer who grew up along the Potomac in southern Maryland described the import that the name "Eastern Shorener" held for many.

When the Bay dredge boat started invading the Potomac in the 1880's, the oyster wars soon spread to the river.

71

Like the sons of all river families, the writer during his boy-hood, was nurtured on the stories of the terrible 'Eastern Shoreners,' a term which included all foreign dredgers, whether they were from Virginia, the Eastern Shore of Maryland, or from Baltimore. By and large they were a tough bunch of characters as is attested by reading county newspapers covering the past eighty years. During the dredg-ing season, in practically every year of this period there have been reports of armed clashes between our rivermen and the tidewater police on the one side and the 'Eastern Shoreners' on the other, with fatalities reported frequently.*

This image is reinforced in the story of the small girl from the Western Shore who asks her parents to please take her down to the Bay so she can see the Eastern Shore watermen. When she gets to the wharf and peers down at the crews sitting around on their dredge boats, she turns to her parents and exclaims, "They are men," presuming, of course, that she expected to see some species of sea monster.

Even the Eastern Shoremen themselves recite tales of ram-pages over on the Western Shore. Alex Kellam recalled:

Now I've heard Edgar Tyler say there was this place over there to Rock Point in the mouth of the Wicomico River in the Potomac and they used to have a glass cage in there where they gambled. Well, Captain Ed Hasty, Captain Wells Evans, Captain Charlie Middleton, Captain Barry Mid-dleton and old man Jack Hall—he was a right rough charac-ter—they went in there one time. And Jack Hall had this big bolo knife stuck right down in his artic; Captain Wells had this big horse pistol, they used to call them.

And when they went in there they went up to the bar and they got their drinks. And this glass cage was filled up with niggers playing cards. Jack Hall looked over there and said, 'Boys, I think it's about time we get rid of some of them

*This description of the "Eastern Shorners" comes from Edwin Beitzell's book, *Life on the Potomac* (1968), p. 79.

sons-of-bitches.' So he walked out in the middle of the floor and he reached down there and pulled the bolo knife out of his artic and he stepped up there and he said, 'Niggers, bring forth your razors 'cause this is going to be a cutting shooting game.'

'Damn,' they said. They begun to pile out of there heading for the door. The man who was running the bar said, 'You can't do that.'

Jack Hall went back there, looked at that fellow, and said, 'If you say one more word, I'll cut your head off even with your shoulders.' and they took over that place the balance of that day. Damned if that gang wouldn't do it. They were rough. They were all big, powerful men, every damn one of them. (1)

No question, life on the Bay from about 1870 to about 1920 was hard indeed. Oysters were plentiful but prices were low. Old oyster rocks were quickly depleted and new ones constantly had to be uncovered to keep the captain and the crew in bread and clothes. It was a difficult and dangerous time, and it bred difficult and dangerous men. They were reckless and fearless. Many of them cared little for the value of human life. To them a human life was a body they shipped aboard their boat in Baltimore or Norfolk. They collected their crews from shipping clerks in those ports, and the men had invariably been plucked, drunk or drugged, from any of a number of waterfront bars.

To insensitive captains, it made little difference what the background of their crew was—Irish paddy, black, wasp—they were aboard to be worked hard for the season and then perhaps paid off at the end with the boom. The captain would call the crew on deck, stand them on the cabin top, and tell them that he was going to give them their wages. Then he would jibe the boat and the boom would sweep them overboard into the Bay. Some never made it to shore alive, as an account by Otis Evans of Crisfield reveals.

One time I went dredging with Wes Sneede when I was about thirteen years old. He had a little two masted flattie and Cliff and Perry were aboard. So we was becalmed there one time on Oyster Creek shore and Captain Wes says, 'Boys, about five years ago, I buried a nigger right over there on that sand spit.' Well, we were all ears. 'Yes,' he said, 'he got drownded and washed up there on the shore there, and I buried him.'

Well, we laid there about another hour. No wind at all. So Captain Wes says, 'Boys, it looks like we're going to be here a while, you might as well go ashore and pick up some driftwood for the cabin.'

So that was all we needed. We jumped into the skiff and headed straight for the sand spit. When we got there we saw something in the sand and it looked like a big gum boot with the toe sticking out. I went straight to that and grabbed it and I give it a big shake, and out dropped a human foot. Now the leg part of that boot was rotten, but that foot part looked brand new, and the foot dropped right out of that. And there was a kind of sock that we used to call 'knitting tight,' that's exactly what that foot had on so help me.

Now before that Wes Sneede had told me some tales I didn't know whether to believe or not, but after that I'd believe anything. My blessed, he had me sold. Probably every point in this Bay had a man buried on it. Bodies washed ashore; no one asks any questions, just dug a hole and put them in. That's the way they did things then. (4)

Other hands, paid off with the boom or lost overboard, survived only by the grace of God and tremendous perseverance. Captain Connell of Cambridge was bound up the Bay one evening with only the cook aboard with him. Suddenly, just off Thomas' Point, out of the darkness, walking aft, came a third man. "How did you get aboard?" the captain asked him.

"Well, I'll tell you. It's a long story, but I've been in the water for six hours. When I saw your light you were coming right for me, and when you come to me, I grabbed your bob chain and pulled myself up."

Still other watermen who jumped ship to avoid the harsh treatment, though they made it to safety, lost their minds from

the exposure. On Deal Island, Albert Brown recounted an unnerving thing that happened to his grandfather. The old man lived
near the water. One winter night a huge waterman who had
jumped ship in the Bay and swum ashore came to the house and
beat on the door. Brown, aware of the crazed condition of the
intruder, refused him entrance. The man tore down the door only
to have Brown confront him with a loaded shotgun. Brown put
the gun against the giant's chest and pulled the trigger. The gun
misfired. The waterman swept the old man aside like a cobweb
and dashed into the back of the house where he jumped into bed
with another member of the family to get warm. Brown gathered
himself together and ran down the road for help which soon
came and carted the waterman off to an institution. The following day Brown took his shotgun out in the backyard to see what
the trouble was. He cocked it, shouldered it, pulled the trigger,
and this time the gun fired.

If men could be driven to such lengths to avoid life aboard
an oyster boat, there had to be something behind it. More often
than not it was the captain's manhandling of the crew that led to
trouble, and the episodes which picture a kind of bizarre violence
live best in the memories of Eastern Shore storytellers. Al
Wheatley spoke of a captain named Pace who hung a sick man in
the rigging for refusing to work.

> Over in Virginia there was this fellow named Pace and
> he was dredging a brand new pungy boat over on Hog Is-
> land and he had this man tied half way up in the rigging with
> his arms spread out and he was hollering and squealing and
> swinging back and forth. And a man from Tangier pulled up
> along side of him and I reckon that weren't no son-of-her
> he called that Pace.
>
> And two or three days after that they brought that man
> ashore dead, with his head all tied up in bandages and held
> an inquest over him. They killed him, that's what they done.
> That fellow was sick and couldn't work and that's what they
> done to him. And he was ageable too. And at the inquest,
> one of our young fellows looked at Pace and said, 'You
> killed him, that's what you done.' Which he did. (3)

Equally calloused captains from Hooper Island treated their crews brutally. Captain Jack Lance took his men from Baltimore and when it came time to pay them off, he rowed them ashore to Hooper Island, beat them to within an inch of their lives, and left them to wander all the way back to Baltimore with nothing on but their oilskins. Wild Bill Lenmore, on the other hand, drowned men right off his boat rather than pay them their fee. And once when the police came aboard to look for him, he climbed up the mast and hid in the rigging while his son handled the law. Later, when his own son refused to obey an order, the old man hurled an oyster at him with such force that it struck him in the forehead and came completely out of the shell.

Often these men died as violently as they lived. Wild Bill fell off a bunk in his boat and died of a broken neck. Jack Lance perished when the stove on his boat exploded. Others died by the hand of their crew, as did Al Horsey.

Now this happened over here to Broad Creed. There was this man Al Horsey, and he sailed one of these skipjacks, they called them. He shipped a man down the Bay from Baltimore. (They used to shanghai them there; give them a drink of a special bottle of stuff, and then they'd ship them down the Bay.) Well, this one fellow that Horsey got was a Mason, and when they got down here to Broad Creek this man wanted to go ashore, but Horsey wouldn't let him. He told Horsey that he would repay him every cent that he'd spent to ship him. He was respectable, you know. But Horsey wouldn't do it. So he jumped overboard and he tried to swim ashore in his silk underwear and he drowned, in only three feet of water.

So I guess word got back to Baltimore, because the next time that Al Horsey went up there to ship crew, they had it set for him. He shipped a man down the Bay, and in the Potomac that fellow walked back aft and he pointed to the shore over the stern. When old Man Horsey turned around, he busted his head wide open with a handspike.

And they figured that man was planted there to do that, 'cause he wouldn't ship aboard any boat but Al Horsey's. (9)

76

Perhaps one of the figures most notorious for his fearless life-style was Captain Wynn Dunn of Smith Island. Unlike Lickin' Bill, Dunn was a small, spindly man, but he was afraid of no mortal living. He had the reputation of treating his crews extremely hard, and he was utterly intolerant of anyone aboard his boat who failed to obey orders. One time, a Negro came aboard and Dunn put him to work winding the cranks on the dredges. But every time the captain gave the order, "Wind," the man sat down. So Dunn told the first mate to hold him, and while they tussled about on the deck, Dunn took a three-foot monkey wrench and struck the Negro right across the forehead. Then he starved him for three days until he promised to work, but when he finally agreed to do his share, he turned out to be one of the best men Dunn ever shipped aboard his boat.

Captain Dunn's heartless reputation and the punishing pace at which he drove his crew forced one man aboard his boat to commit suicide.

The first time he was dredging on Middle Ground—now I heard him tell me this himself—he called the crew up on deck to go to work, and this one fellow come up and he looked out. Then he took off his hat and he threw it overboard and he div [sic] right in after it, and he didn't come up. And the rest of the crew just stood there and watched. And after a while Captain Dunn left the wheel and he walked over there to the middle of the deck where all those men were standing, scared to death, and he swore up and down, and then he said, 'All right, if there's anybody else wants to go, now's the time to do it. Otherwise, we got to go to work.'

So they went back to work. That's how cheap human life was then. (4)

Those who depicted Dunn as a ruthless man also respected him for his fearless nature. Captain Wynn, in fact, was not even afraid of his own wife. One time in court he wanted to have his wife bound over to peace.

77

The judge said, 'All right, Wynn, you mind coming and putting your left hand on the Bible and holding your right hand to God?'

He said, 'What do I have to do that for?'

Henry Dize, the judge, said, 'Well, Wynn, in order to have her bound over to peace you've got to swear to Almighty God that you're scared of her.'

'Ayeee,' he said, 'I'm damned if I will.'

Judge said, 'Wynn, I'm afraid I can't have her bound over to peace unless you'll swear you're scared of her.'

He said, 'I don't want her bound over then, if I have to swear that.' He weren't afraid of no damn woman living. (1)

Apparently, Captain Dunn's daughter possessed some of the same qualities as her father.

Now that Wynn Dunn, he was a bird. He was a little slim fellow, but the dicken couldn't scare him. He had a bugeye that he used to sail to Baltimore and he'd take his oldest daughter Betsy along for his mate. And going up there she'd put her britches and stuff on and go out there to the wheel while her father went below and went to sleep. And they said God Almighty couldn't roll up enough clouds in the northwest to scare her. No sir. (3)

Things evidently caught up with Dunn towards the end of his life. Twelve years before he died, he took two young boys and a Negro on his boat over into the Potomac River. They anchored about the edge of dark, went below, ate, and went to bed. About midnight, the Negro located an axe, crept aft into the main cabin, and laid open the skulls of Dunn and the two boys. He then scoured the cabin for money and jumped in the dingy and rowed ashore, leaving his victims for dead. But all three survived and got to shore to notify the authorities. The police caught the man and had him apprehended, but after that Captain Dunn was never the same man. The episode broke him.

Tall Tales and Windies

On the Eastern Shore the word "yarn" connotes a great many things to different people. The word is casually flipped around by storytellers to refer to almost any kind of story. A ghost story could be a yarn; so could a tale about a local character, an anecdote about a humorous event on the Bay, an international folktale, or even a joke. A conversation I had with an informant started like this:

> You know Thomas Crockett I was telling you about?
> Yes.
> Well, I'll tell you a crab yarn on him.

And out of this brief introduction would spring a story:

> Well he used to crab when crabbing increased, and he used to keep these crabs in his float. And we couldn't catch nothing but thin pealers then. Well, you sell all you catch now, pretty well. And he said he had a crab in his float which he put in there when he first started crabbing in the spring. And in September, every time he went to his float to sort the hard crabs out from the pealers, this same crab would be there whacking at him with his claws like that.
> Well one day he was out there and this crab was a-whacking at him, and he had one of these little canoes that had afterlockers in them to keep the ballast stone in the middle seat for a middle sail. And he took his crab net and he eased this crab right over into the canoe. He said, 'Never mind you son-of-her, when I get done fishing this float I'll fish you.'
> Well when he got done he went after this crab. He had

79

on a pair of hog hide boots, and he got up on the locker—that crab down there a-whacking at him,—Well, when he jumped down there for that crab, both feet went out from underneath him—and he weighed 200 pounds or more—and his shins went up against that middle seat, skinned them both the whole way up. He just lay there and grunted and groaned, and after a while he turned and raised up, and there was that crab at the end of the well a-whacking at him. He put him in his crab net and eased him overboard and he got in his skiff to go ashore. That crab followed him ashore still a-whacking at him, and when he pulled his skiff up on the bank, that crab come right up on the edge of the bank after him. (3)

Eastern Shore storytellers also term this kind of tale "a lie" as well as a yarn, and thus they have two names for what folklorists call the tall tale. In effect, the storyteller is striking out in straight-faced jest at the quixotic creature from whom the Eastern Shore waterman must make his living. The waterman sees the crab as vicious and unaccommodating, and yet he knows full well that without its appearance each spring and summer, times would be hard indeed. Yet he can laugh at this possible plight in a tale such as this, where the perennial confrontation between man and crab is amusingly depicted.

Stories similar to this crab yarn exist in great abundance on the Eastern Shore. Many surface in what are known as lying contests. Though I have never witnessed one of these personally, Link Ward, in recounting his own tall stories, reconstructed the scene verbally.

Dewey Landon began the session:

Now around Easton, Pennsylvania where I was one time, there was a place where you could holler and then take a cigarette out and light it before the echo got back. (12)

Link Ward retaliated:

That's one hell of an echo, but it ain't nothing really. We

were up to Alberta Canada, north of Montana, and me and my partner parked our truck beside the edge of the canyon to go to sleep. And we wanted to be sure to wake up in the morning, so we went over there and yelled in the canyon as loud as we could and then went back in the trunk and went to sleep. Damn if seven and one half hours later that echo didn't come back and wake us up. (13)

Then the conversation turned to ships, and Harold Hinman spoke up:

You boys ain't never seen a ship. I was down in Norfolk and one of these foreign boats came in for coal. And this one boat loaded ninety-five tons, every five minutes twenty-four hours a day for three weeks, and never even got her waterline under water. (14)

Link Ward rejoined:

Oh, that's nothing. I saw a ship once that it took one hundred and twenty-eight gallons of paint to paint a quarter of an inch bead line around her hull. (13)

And so it might go, on into the afternoon or evening at the local store, or wherever the local wags might choose to gather. And finally someone like Dewey Landon would utter a true whopper:

I was a small kid about ten years old and I have proof of this. We had a little shed out there where we used to have a cow and we closed it in and put chickens in there. There was one white hen with some black feathers into her and my mother told me to go out there and see what she had laid. So I went out and I crawled in there and I brought in this egg that was just as big as a goose egg and I gave it to her. The next morning my mother cooked that for breakfast and when she broke that on the frying pan it had six yolks in it. And that day I went out and got another egg and that had five

81

yolks in and the next day four and then three and then two and one, and the next day when she broke that egg into the pan, it didn't have any yolk in it at all. And that's not all; listen to this: I know somebody who had a chicken that laid an egg with a perfect six double domino. Now if that weren't something! (12)

Perhaps with this everyone concedes and the gathering breaks up and heads for home.

Fair Catches and Fertile Fields

In the area below Cambridge, Maryland, where the livelihood comes either out of the sea or from the ground, tall stories of fish and fertile soil flourish. At Head-of-the-Creek, Peggy Wainwright's grandfather encountered an odd situation:

One day he was coming from the Coopers boys' house walking along and he happened to look up and he saw this tremendous eagle flying along low with something hanging down. He started screaming and hollering as loud as he could, and the eagle dropped this thing from its mouth. He went over there and he looked and it was the biggest catfish you can imagine. It was so large that he put its head on his shoulder and its tail was dragging the ground. It took him nearly six hours to get it home, and when he did he hung it up just like a hog and cleaned it. He gave one half to his brother who had ten children and he kept the rest for his family of eight, and you know, they ate off of that one half a fish for a whole week. (15)

It was not always the size of the fish as the amount that was staggering. Over near St. George's Island the hard head take tested human credibility.

There was this fella, a good waterman, from over there to St. George's Island and one time in the store they got to talking about how many hard heads there used to be in the old days. And this fella spoke up, "What you people round here in Mount Vernon catch is nothing to what we catch. Why one time I set a gill net over there and I had a hard head in every hole. When it come time for me to get them out of the net I didn't have time cause the steamboat was about to leave for Baltimore, so I shipped the net and all."

Later I asked him if he ever got the net back.

He said, "No, but they sent me back the corks." (16)

Other men had lucky days. A Tangierman learned of a special place which had been marked out by stakes, but when he sailed to where it was supposed to be he couldn't find any marker. He told his partner to sound for the bottom with his fishing line. He did, and without bait, drew up three trout. "This is good enough for me," said the Captain, and when they quit the spot that evening they took home 1600 fish.

Oysters, too, might come in amazing abundance. Harry Dize set out from Tangier one Saturday morning with his two brothers. He tonged with the rest of the fleet all morning with little luck, and after the other boats gave up he decided to try one more spot. One lick and he knew he had come to the right spot. In two hours he pushed more than seventy-five bushels of oysters from the culling board into the hold of his boat.

Know-how counted as much as luck in securing a catch. Alex Kellam, known around Crisfield as a remarkable fisherman as well as raconteur acquired his reputation as a young man on Smith Island:

Well one time Captain John Whitney and I were going fishing and the night before as we were leaving the store Captain Lloyd, the store keeper, said, "John, watch out for Kellam, he's a good fisherman."

He said, "Lloyd, I intend to do just that. I'm going to show him what it's all about."

The next morning at sunrise we got up and got over to this place where we were going. And it was nice smooth water and we tied the boat so the anchor was right in the middle and let her swing crossways to the tide. Well, to make a long story short, when we finished I had 145 trout and Captain John had 37. And when we went back to the store that night Captain Lloyd said, "John, how did you make out?"

He said, "Lloyd, I learned one thing today."

"What was that?"

"I never did know how to fish." (1)

Kellam claims to have filled his eighteen foot runabout with rockfish in less than two hours. Once, a nearby fisherman sat in his boat and watched Kellam and his partner haul in the fish while he failed to get even a nibble. Finally he could stand it no longer, so he bellowed across the water, "Say what are you using?" "Skill," Kellam shot back.

Eastern Shore land is as prolific as the Bay. Kale greens grow so large down there that Dewey Landon nurtured one stock that had a stem on it twelve inches wide, and when he came to pick it he got a full bushel of greens from one plant.

The land supported watermelons well too. Link Ward affirmed that if you didn't watch Crisfield watermelons they would bust wide open. But the fact failed to disturb him. He simply drilled a hole into each one in the patch and plugged it with a bung. When he went out each morning to pull the plugs and let the pressure off, the water spurted as high as a two story house.

As in most places where gardens are common, the outside row seldom yields as well as the other rows. One year old man Tom Tyler decided to do something about it. He told his friends that spring he was damned if he was even going to plant an outside row, and he didn't. But when his crop failed totally, he despaired: "Damn if I can stand this sort of living anymore; I'm going to paint my horse, sell my boat, and go crabbing."

Foul Weather

Lush harvests demanded fair weather; but Eastern Shore

weather is not always fair. Though not so capricious as that in New England where one is told, "If you don't like it wait five minutes," Chesapeake Bay gales furnished a good deal of anxiety. Thunderstorms, bad ones anyway, produced lightning bolts that became legendary.

There was a fella over on the island one time by the name of Saul Hargis and like most of the other watermen over there he had one of these sounding poles. They used to use them over in the Potomac River and when it was real moderate they would take this fifty or sixty foot pole and sound out to find where the good oyster rocks were. Some of those beds would be large and some would be small. And if the pole stayed in shape over the season they'd bring them home and put them under the house to keep the sun from ruining it.

Old Saul Hargis said he was standing out in his field one day and a thunderstorm come up and he saw that lightning strike the lightning rod on his house, and that rod just gathered it up ZZZZZUUUUUMMMMMMM. And it went right down into the ground. He went over there and looked, and there at the bottom was a little round hole.

He said to himself: "Damn if I don't see just how deep that is," and so he took that sounding pole, pulled it out from under the house, and he started letting it down and letting it down into that hole. He got it right down so that he was just holding that with the end of his fingers and he finally let go of it and put his ear to the ground, and the last thing he heard was that sounding pole going whum whum whum whum as it rattled down that hole. (1)

Another thunderstorm packed wind so violent that it bent a piece of iron piping on a pump handle even with the ground. A southerly blow on Smith Island brought tides so high that Captain John Lew swore he stood by his house, spat in Tangier Sound and defecated into Chesapeake Bay at the same time.

Over on the mainland near Crisfield, old Willie arrived at the local store one Monday morning in time to hear the watermen complaining about the weather. One man moaned, "My blessed, did you ever see it blow like it did last night?"

Willie said, "Blow? Why my lord, you don't know nothing. Where I was the wind was coming right through the sides of the house. Why when I got up this morning it was blowing so hard in my bedroom that it white-capped the piss pot."

Things always seemed a little bit worse at Willie's place than any other. After a dreadfully cold night Willie faced his wife at breakfast the next morning.

"Wasn't it cold last night, Willie?"

"My blessed, Es, wasn't it. It was so cold in our room that I saw those bluebirds get right off the wall paper and come huddle around the stove." (17)

Sudden storms have always been the terror of the Bay. In a particularly fierce gale over on St. George's Island, Clifton Webster averred that the wind blew 125 miles an hour for about ten minutes. When he went ashore afterwards he noticed nine trees, two feet across, twisted off as if they had been "teeny little black gum."

Some captains on the Bay really liked to drive a boat, no matter how bad the storm nor how loudly the crew protested:

Willie Evans had a bugeye named the *E. C. Tyler*. She only saw one owner and when he was finished with her he wouldn't sell her, just let her die. And she was a narrow, high-sided thing and wally, she would lay right down on her side, and this one time they were going up the Potomac River and it was really blowing in a storm. And Willie's son, Ed, come out of the cabin with a caulking mallet, caulking iron, and some caulking cotton.

Willie said, "Ed, what are you gonna do with that?"

He said, "Caulk her garboard strake going up here." (1)

On board another dredge boat the weather got so miserable and the temperature dropped so low that a man could hardly draw water out of the on-deck barrel before it froze in his cup,

86

but, for some reason, the water in the barrel flowed freely. Out on the fishing banks off Smith Island, Dewey Landon sensed a blow coming on, slipped his anchor and fled back to Crisfield. No sooner had he and his party stepped ashore than the wind began to blow 100 miles an hour, but by the time he walked from his boat to his store (about 400 yards) it was so still you could hardly catch your own breath. Ramsey Laird, while fishing in Delaware Bay, saw a wave sweep the yaw boat right out of the davits of a skipjack and he witnessed the same vessel stand up so straight that he could look right up her centerboard trunk. Al Wheatley sailed into Rock Creek one time. The wind came up without warning, blew the sails to tatters, and carried away the water barrel that was lashed down to the mast, stops and all. Wheatley also experienced a gale in Cloverdale which turned the harbor into a seething tide rip.

It was along about suppertime and it was flat calm. I went down below and I remember, I was cooking up hot dogs on the stove for supper and I had just put one of them in my mouth and this storm just fell from the heavens. My boat was forty-two feet and I had her hold loaded with lumber and the water was right up to her washboards, and I thought sure she was going to turn over. The wind blew so hard that it drew ten penny nails out of those oak beams and it blew away one of them firkins that was on deck half full of water. It pulled the stake I was moored on and I went stern first right ashore and in fifteen minutes the rudder arm was completely out of water. So I jumped over and tried to get her off, but nothing doing. And all of a sudden the tide commenced to come in there, and I wish you could have seen it. It was a solid roar and in fifteen minutes more I shoved her off of there and went out and moored her on another stake in a flat calm. That tide was coming in there so fast you couldn't year your years [hear your ears] in there. (3)

Fog on the Bay comes in predominantly in the spring and the fall of the year, not in the summer. But when it comes it brings, as always, hazardous navigating conditions. Yet for the tall tale tellers, there is an easy way out of everything:

> This fella come out of the Great Wicomico River and he had just got out into the Bay, and, man, it really set in thick. But he decided to keep on going and he went and he went and he got out into the Bay channel and bye and bye he decided it was just too thick to go on to Tangier without a compass, so he turned around and come back into the Great Wicomico using the same track he'd make going out. (1)

Jim Hen Nelson did not even need to have a track to follow; he just had a sense of where he was. When he and his son had been out in a dungenous fog for three days and two nights, the old man told the boy to roust out the fog horn and give it a long blow. When the boy wanted to know why, after so long, his father wanted him to blow the horn now, Captain Jim replied, "To let old man Dicky open the drawbridge for us so we can get into Crisfield Harbor." Another thick fog bred this story:

> There was this Menhaden fisherman out of Reedsville, and he'd always go out into the Atlantic catching Menhaden. This one time he went out and he loaded his boat and he said, "All right boys, get in your nets, we're going in to unload." And they went in the Bay and when they did, it really shut in fast. They come along up the Bay for quite a while, and bye and bye the Captain slowed her down and says, "O.K. Mate, jump, that's the land."
> He said "Captain, I don't see anything."
> Captain said, "Jump, man, jump. It's got to be there." (18)

Remarkable Wildlife

Creatures in the tall tale are simply extensions in size and feats of those we know in real life. A Deal Island woman affirmed that a bite by a local mosquito required an immediate blood transfusion. In southern Dorchester County farmers had to put bells on their cows so they could find them after the mosquitoes carried them off. On Smith Island, the mosquitoes began to fornicate with the ducks which upset the hunters and the ecology not a little. When a friend told Howard Hinman a mosquito lived for only three years, be begged to differ:

Son, I think you're wrong, there. I heard something buzzing up in attic for twenty years and for all that time I thought it was a meter or something, just humming up there. After a while it got on my nerves so I went up to see what it was, and damn, there he was, a skeeta. I killed him and he dressed out at three-quarters of a pound. (14)

Around Dames Quarter the mosquitoes displayed craft as well as size:

There were some men fishing down here one time and their boat broke down and they had to come in and fish along the shore. And they decided that the mosquitoes were so bad they had to find something to protect themselves and they found some of these iron pots and they put them over their heads where the mosquitoes were really getting to them. Pretty soon the mosquitoes started sticking their bills down through the iron pots, so they took hammers and started nailing their bills down to the pot. Bye and bye the pots come off their heads, and they looked and there were those mosquitoes half way across Tangier Sound with those pots. (16)

Snakes likewise grew to miraculous size and performed amazing stunts, at least as they thrived in the yarns of the Eastern Shore raconteurs. A man who grew up in West Virginia swore he had heard a black snake bellow just like a cow. Near Head-of-the-Creek, some women went huckleberrying in a swamp called The Promised Land. After a time they spied a particularly deep laden bush and climbed up on a mossy log for better access. When the log started to squirm, they realized they had perched on the back of a black snake and fled in horror. Wes Sneede

89

told Otis Evans that on his way out fishing one morning he saw a large, fine looking trap pole sticking up out of the water about four feet, but when he went over to fetch it, it swam away.

Besides land snakes and water snakes the hoop snake churned its way through Eastern Shore tradition. Near Salisbury a man said he knew a fellow who had been standing in the cemetery at the foot of a hill and he saw a snake take its tail in mouth and roll down that hill. When it came to a certain tree it struck out and bit the bark, and the next day that tree died. Another yarn spinner was telling Link Ward just how poisonous the King Cobra and Coral snake were, but Ward cut him short:

> Hell, them ain't no snakes at all. One time I was down in Texas and we were going hunting and there was a man with a double team of horses coming along the road and one of these horses had his tongue hanging out, a walnut colored tongue. Well, I seen this hoop worm take its tail in its mouth and come rolling down the road toward them, and when he got to them, that damned snake throwed his poison tail into that horse's tongue and, man, it began to swell. We got axes and adzes and tried to keep that swelling down, by chipping, cutting it down little by little. We cut that tongue down till we got seven piles of chips as big as haystacks. Now you just tell me that Coral snake is poisonous! That ain't no snake at all. (13)

Progging and Proggers

Any man who has followed the water for a length of time or lived in one of the small bay settlements has indulged in, or at least heard of, "progging." The term is old. Dictionaries do not list it. Gilbert Byron once speculated to me in conversation that he thought the word derived from "piroque," a boat type used by older watermen. Essentially, the progger is a trapper. In the 1920's, when the diamondback terrapin was considered such a delicacy, the progger made a reasonable living flushing out these turtles from their hiding places along the Bay shore. At present,

90

the search for muskrat has eclipsed the search for terrapin. Still, with a few exceptions, progging remains a part-time affair for most watermen, something they undertake in their spare time, or when oystering and crabbing fall off. "Each winter, . . . " writes college graduate John Creighton,

> I have caught two or three dozen muskrats—not so much for the money as to keep in contact with the habits, conscience and consciousness of my grandfathers and early forbears. . . . I have always felt a special tingling on those New Year's Eves (January first is the first day of the season in Dorchester) when you set your traps before a predicted snow, and the next day crunch through ice and snowdrifts to see what passed with the tide during the night. With a hatchet to cut through the ice, a trapper can tell as soon as his blade hits whether a 'rat's been by that night. If the tide has fallen and left a fairly warm pocket of air, the pungent smell of musk comes pouring through the crust ice. *

But to the Eastern Shoreman a "progger" is not just a trapper; he is any man who sustains himself in part or in full from the things that live along the shore or in the shallow water. Dewey Landon of Crisfield provides a good example. Captain Dewey used to run a small shop down by the wharfside in town. His store catered primarily to tourists who wander in before taking the ferry boats out to Smith and Tangier Islands. Inside, strewn around on the cement floor and various tables were every conceivable kind of artifact. Landon's shop seldom opens before noon, and that frees the forenoon up for him to do his progging.

I went out with him one warm April day and as we eased out of the Little Annemessex River and around Great Point, I noticed the stakes of the gill netters who had set their rigs athwart the river to catch the fish that came in with the tide. Below the point we tied the skiff to an oar we stuck in a "tump" of marsh mud and struck out across the sand towards a shallow creek which cut into the marsh from Tangier Sound.

On a sand spit in the creek about a five minute walk from

*Swarthmore College Bulletin LXVI:5 May, 1969, p. 24.

the Sound, Landon pulled rubber protectors over the index and middle fingers of each hand and began burrowing into the sand where he saw the air holes of manoes (soft shell clams). He had to work fast as the soft sand quickly collapsed the hole leaving the clam once again to its damp solitude. To the uninitiated it was hard, hot work in the April sun, and more often than not, a great deal of pawing in the sand and mud produced a sliced finger, a broken clam shell, or nothing at all. But for Landon, who understands shoreside wildlife, it was easy work done rhythmically and effortlessly. In less than a half an hour he secured all the clams he needed for the evening stew.

On the way back, Landon turned his skiff down into Broad Creek and we skimmed along the top of that calm sluice of water until he cut the engine and we came to rest beside a channel marker. Inside the marker, towards the shore, the water shoaled to less than two feet, and the eel grass cut any view of the bottom to nothing. Landon took his eel gig, a ten foot pole which looked something like Neptune's trident, with V-shaped barbs at one end, and he began cautiously to probe the bottom. He worked intently for a time, the boat simply drifting with the tide.

He prodded away until he felt the rubbery touch, then he jammed the gig down hard and pulled it back quickly so as to impail the eel on the barb, and finally he swung the slithery, slashing thing into the boat and shook it loose in a pail.

Many men prog using the same traditional methods as Dewey Landon. It is a way of folklife, passed down generation to generation. There are probably few who today are as adept or as successful at progging as Landon. But back in the early part of the century, there was a man on Smith Island named Wes Sneede whose uncanny sense for tracking terrapin astonished his admirers. "I remember," allowed Winfred Evans of Rhodes Point,

I went out with Wes one time, and this may sound funny to you, but Wes Sneede kept seeing these markings and I couldn't see nothing. He could see where that terrapin had drug his tail on that mudflat and then burrowed. He had this progging stick and he walked along and shoved that stick down and he'd say, 'There he is, there's your terrapin,' and

92

he'd reach in there and grab him. And I couldn't see nothing. Another time we were walking along and he said, 'There a muskrat in that hole there. I know 'cause I've seen him and I'll get him someday.' And I was over to his place later on and he came up to me and said, 'Winfred, I got that rat.' (19)

Yet as uncanny as Wes Sneede and other proggers were, their way of life was not without danger. Captain Wes, who told his share of tall tales, spun Alex Kellam an incredible yarn:

One day I was up in the marsh looking for terrapin and I come across a patch of them and we were getting about $4.50 a piece for 7-inch terrapin then, and I wasn't about to let any of them go. Anyway, there was this fella up there who had a small ranch on Smith Island then called The Barn Marsh and they had some animals, and I wasn't noticing and this old ram come up behind me and hit me in the butt end and damn near killed me. I didn't know what to do so I laid as flat as I could get on my back and this ram come and stood right over me. And everytime I started to move, that old goat would rear up on his hind legs. I had this big pocket knife with me, so bye and bye I got that out and I opened it and put it in my mouth and I began to draw up and draw up. And I was quick then. And I moved little by little till I could get up and then that son-of-a-bitch come into me. Well, I caught him right by the goddamn horns and I walloped him down. I took my knife and I sawed his head off and I threw it out into the pond, and I looked out and there were those two eyes just staring right at me. (1)

Sneede had other tales to tell. He recalled once while out progging he came upon a snake and an eel having a terrible fight. The snake grabbed hold of the eel's tail and the eel took the snake's tail and they began to swallow one another, and pretty soon they completely disappeared. Captain Wes also claimed he saw a flock of ducks fly through the mainsail of a bateau he was on and come out the other side wearing canvas britches.

93

Hunting, of course, is another part of Eastern Shore life that occupies a good deal of the native's time. Watermen detest federal game wardens with an abiding passion. They picture the agents as the people who have encroached upon a share of their rightful livelihood with their restrictions and their underhanded ways of seeing these restrictions enforced. To many an Eastern Shore waterman, the shooting of game, particularly ducks, simply eased the press of hard times when food was scarce during the winter months. Dinner came very easily when a man could gun at will, his wife directing:

> There was a man over on the island and he came home one night and asked his wife what they were going to have for dinner the next night. She said, 'Black duck.'
>
> 'Highyi,' he said, 'where are we going to get it?'
>
> She said, 'There's two of them that come in every night about sundown and I know right where they are. All we have to do is go over there and get them.'
>
> So bye and bye she says, 'Get your gun.'
>
> They just had those single barrel guns. So they got over there and squatted down, and pretty soon, in these ducks came and they pushed right up in there where they were. And she said, 'Shuuuush, here they come.'
>
> And they both let go: BOOM BOOM. They weren't gone no more than half an hour and they had their Sunday dinner. (1)

However, the law all but ended gunning out of season as wardens slapped limits on everything and the Bay became strictly patrolled. Well-to-do people from out of state established gun clubs and raised the hackles of many watermen who looked upon the waterfowl as part of their livelihood. Furthermore, the watermen frequently felt that these wealthy outsiders were somehow in collusion with the game wardens. One waterman reacted hotly when I asked him if he still did any duck gunning: "Oh yes, I used to gun a lot, but I threw my gun overboard one day, 'cause

I knew if I didn't I'd shoot a game warden instead of a duck."

No matter how bitter the native hunters may be, the hunt still gives rise to some extraordinary stories on the Shore. Up near Head-of-the-Creek, a man went out gunning one time, but neglected to take more than one shell for his gun. When he came upon a quail and a rabbit at the same time, he loaded his one shell and fired. The bullet split in two and killed both the rabbit and the quail instantly, and the recoil from the gun knocked the hunter over backwards into a stream. When he came up his pockets were full to the brim with fish.

A Negro man learned from a white neighbor the best way to hunt possum: take the carcass of a horse or mule and lay it out in a field for the night. The possum will come around and burrow into the dead animal. Then go out in the morning and put a bag over the anus of the carcass. Take a couple of sticks and starting at the head beat down the body until you drive the possum out the anus and into the bag.

Other methods for taking game were less complicated. Saul Hargis loaded his gun with flour, fired at a flock of ducks, and turned them all into doughboys. Another Smith Islander winged two nice sized ducks, using nothing but a broom for his weapon. Yet, all things considered, the most successful hunters had good dogs:

> Oz Mears had a bird dog that was said to be about the best around. He carried it down to the beach one day where some men were fishing. That dog just stood there looking out into the surf, until one of the fishermen said, 'What's wrong with that dog?'
>
> Oz said, 'I don't know, but when he goes on point like that, there's usually a bird around.' Just about that time one of those fellas hooked a big red drum. When they got it ashore, Oz said, 'Cut him open.' When they did they looked and there was this quail inside of that fish. (15)

Some dogs' effectiveness lingered on posthumously:

> There was this fella down here one time and he had a

95

wonderful rabbit dog. Well, this dog died and he decided that he had to do something to remember him by so he had him skinned and made himself a pair of gloves out of that dog's hide. One time he was out in the forest working, and he pulled his gloves off and laid them on this stump and set down to eat his lunch. All of a sudden this rabbit run out of the underbrush and those two gloves jumped off of that stump and grabbed the rabbit and choked him to death. (1)

Coon hunting, long a popular amusement on the Eastern Shore, evoked a variety of tales. One afternoon Venton pranksters dragged an old coon so the scent led to a large tree in the woods. In the topmost branches they left one man. That evening their dogs led some Negro hunters to the same tree. One man climbed up. All of a sudden, he sang out in terror, slid down the tree, and headed for the clearing. When his friends finally caught him, the dazed hunter blurted out, "Man, that coon talked back to me.'

Sometimes fear made adrenalin run even in the glands of rheumatic coon hunters:

Old man Hunt Munford had the rheumatism so bad that he hadn't walked around for ten years. But he had a bunch of dogs and so his son come to him one night and said, 'Paw, we're going hunting tonight.'

The ole man said, 'Boy, I'd sure like to hear those dogs go again one more time; I ain't heard them in a good year or more.'

His boy said, 'Paw, we got a big nigger and he'll take you down in the woods with us on his back.'

So they went on down there and the dogs got after a coon and they run him for a while and the ole man sat there on a stump and he said, 'That's the sweetest sound I've heard in years.'

So the dogs got this coon up a tree pretty close to where the old man had settled and one of the boys said to the dog, 'Shay, go shake him out.'

Well, when they started to get that coon out of there,

they found it wasn't any coon but a bear. And the fella that went up the tree come down shouting, 'That's no coon, that's a bear,' and headed for the clearing. Well, they all took off out of there as fast as they could go, and when they got home there sat the ole man in his rocking chair on the porch chewing his tobacco. That ole crippled man, who hadn't walked for twenty years, got home before any of them. Now that's got to be some sort of a record. (20)

On another occasion, a Mount Vernon man discovered the devil instead of a coon. Jim Martin got liquored up Saturday night and after midnight he went by and picked up his black friend Andy. They got their dogs, and they hadn't been out long before they treed a coon. Andy went up the tree, looked through the branches and spied a creature with mouth agape and eyes that spit fire. He dropped out of the tree and bolted for home. When he encountered Jim on Monday he said, "Jim, I told you it was bad luck to hunt coons on Sunday; that was the devil we treed the other night and I ain't going in the woods again as long as I live. If it hadn't been for that whiskey you fed me, I'd have never gone on Sunday."

Fantastic Events

Like hunting yarns, simple events become magnified in the tall tale. Jack Beall used to tell his friends about the old days when they used rawhide to hook horses to equipment.

One time Jack said he went out in the thicket near his home to cut some wood, and after he had cut it up and was just getting it loaded on his wagon, it started to rain. So he ran up right quick and took the horse by the bridle and led him up to the house and tied him to a post near the barn and ran into the house. When he got into the house he looked around: the wagon was still down there by the woods. That rawhide had stretched that far. He said to himself, 'Damn if I'm gonna go down there and get that tonight. I'll wait till tomorrow when the weather is better.' But he slept late the next morning, and when he woke up, the sun had been out a while, and when he got to the barn there was that wagon hooked right up to the horses. The sun had dried out that rawhide and drawn that wagon right up there to the barn. (21)

Equally astounding, Dewey Landon admitted that his family found a snapping turtle once that lived for six years after losing its head. Moreover, one evening as a thunderstorm was dying out in the west, Landon and some friends witnessed a spectacle to make even an atheist a believer. The clouds unfolded replicas of beautiful lakes and beaches, a submarine and battleship, and palm trees bending over in the wind. When Landon went home that night he discovered that his wife's mother had seen the same thing in her bedroom mirror. As it turned out later, that was the same night that her son arrived in the Hawaiian Islands. Landon also maintained that his father, against the advice of his crew, picked up thirteen corpses after the *Slocum* sank in the Potomac River. The thirteenth corpse turned out to be a lovely woman with black hair. They brought her back to the Eastern Shore and buried her, and not long after that her brother appeared from Baltimore with a chart of her teeth. When they dug her up and identified her, Landon's father received $500.00 in cash.

If Baltimore had philanthropists who came seeking their drowned siblings, the town also had a plethora of dogs.

There was an old captain around here one time called George Jones and he was a great storyteller and he used to hang around my father's store quite frequently and if strangers would come around he would delight in telling yarns. And one story that he used to tell was about an old Bay Captain, who used to go up to Baltimore a lot. And every time he would go in the harbor there—you see, in those days they didn't have any refrigeration on boat or anything like that and they kept their stores and meat stuffs covered outside on the deck where the cold air could get at them. Well, every time he would go into Baltimore, there were these dogs that used to come aboard his boat and steal his meat out from under the covers. So he said he'd fix that. So this one time they came in he set up a dead fall over the hold of the boat. He went to bed real early that night and it wasn't long after dark before he heard a dog come aboard and walk up the deck, strike this board and go down in the hold. A little while later, another dog came aboard and he struck the dead fall and down he went into the hold.

He said he caught dogs all that night and when he got up the next morning and looked down in the hold, there were big dogs, little dogs, police dogs, poodle dogs, fox terriers—every kind of dog you can imagine. He had his hold full of dogs. And it scared him. He didn't know what to do. He said, 'Oh my blessed, if these people find out I've got their dogs aboard this boat I'll be arrested and I'll never get out of here.'

So he thought the best thing to do was to get underway.

As he was sailing down the Bay he was wondering what to do with all these dogs. He said to himself, 'I've got to get rid of them somehow.' So he begun to fix himself up a big strong dip net to see if he could get rid of some of these dogs. And when he got off of Holland's Island he hove to. He begun to dip these dogs out, and he dipped out dogs for three or four hours and there were five acres of dogs swimming ashore, and when they hit Hollands Island the women begun to shriek. He said that was some time, and he got underway again and got as far from that island as he could. (16)

Five acres of dogs in the water was an undesired commodity to Holland Islanders, but so was a tadpole in a glass of whiskey to a man who had purchased a drink:

At one time there was an old gentleman who ran a country store down here on the Wicomico River and he used to sell drinks to tipplers, and those who frequented the store a lot were of the opinion that the store keeper watered the drinks. Yet no one could ever make sure. And in those days the whiskey came down from Baltimore in barrels, and this one year the owner had sold down this barrel of whiskey quite low, and he was worried when he would be able to get another shipment in. So he began adding water to the barrel from the ditch just outside the door, and all the customers were quite sure what was happening but they couldn't ever prove it until one day this drinker came in and he ordered a drink. When they brought it to him, he picked it up and there swimming around in the shot glass was a tadpole. (16)

Remarkable Personal Traits

All men have certain characteristics that set them apart from their fellows. They may be brave or timid, prodigal or niggardly, lazy or foolish. In a folk community the tall tale-teller latches onto individual characteristics and tailors them to fit his audience. Some yarns, for instance, play up the timidness of Tangier Islanders towards such modern conveniences as eyeglasses and dentistry. Standing around the Kozy Korner in Crisfield watching John Glenn go into orbit, Alex Kellam turned to Lester Crokett and commented, "Boy, it really takes nerve to do that." "Yeah," shot back Crockett, "as much nerve as Mom: she had to have gas to be fitted for eyeglasses."

One night another Tangierman awoke with a terrible toothache, and the next morning he took the boat ashore to have the tooth pulled. When he returned a sizeable group had gathered to find out what it was like.

"Did it hurt much?"

"No, not much, about like a greenhead fly."

"A greenhead fly?! My blessed father, man, you were killed!"

Sugar diabetes also got out of hand at times. When a Mount Vernon man took a specimen of his wife's urine to have it tested at the doctor's, the physician took it back to his office and emerged shortly with a bucket full of stick candy.

Sick men in Byrdtown often live on borrowed time. Making

his rounds one morning, the local preacher approached one of the older watermen in front of the store:

> 'My lord, Captain, I thought you'd been sick.'
> 'Sick? Why my good lord, I've been dead for four days and I don't know what it is that keeps me up and around.'

Indolence and miserliness qualified along with bad health as part of the human condition worthy of tall stories. Old Joe Morse from Georgia was a terribly lazy man. He found it too exerting to say his prayers at night, so he made himself a plaque with a prayer stencilled on it and hung it over his bed. When he crawled into bed at night he'd point to the plaque and say simply, "Lord, them's my sentiments."

Attention always focused on the skinflints as well as the slothful. Captain Ander over on the Wicomico River held the distinction of being a very penurious man:

> Captain Ander was a very industrious person but he was also a most scrupulous and economical man. He watched every penny, and one year on this small farm he had, he got a nice corn crop. Well, he got this colored man by the name of Spence to help him strip that corn off in the fall. When lunchtime came along, Captain Ander asked Spence to come in and have lunch with him. When they finished up the work in the afternoon Captain Ander paid Spence off, but he told him, 'Spence, I hate to do this but I'm afraid I've got to take off for your dinner. If it was me, I wouldn't do it, but you know we had a duck dinner, and that was my wife Betty's duck, and you know, my God, I've got to pay Betty for that duck.' (16)

Some men even carried their miserly habits to the grave.

> Now old man Barker Trull was one of the most money hungry men around Marion. They claim that at the end of his life, money drove him mad and he went around here just looking for something he could sell or make money on.

Now there's a graveyard around here where almost everybody's buried. There's a road that runs through the graveyard and on one side they put the Episcopalians and on the other the Methodists. Well, old man Trull was an Episcopalian, and when he died they stuck him on that side of the road. And a couple of days later a Methodist fella died and they put him on the other side of the road. Well, that night somebody was driving down that road and they swore they had to throw on the brakes to stop the car, 'cause there came old man Trull's ghost back to his own grave with a bunch of flowers from that other man's plot. (21)

Other Eastern Shore windies centered on people with remarkable physical attributes or talents. Two Negroes recently discharged from the service were arguing about the buglars in their company. "Boy," said one, "we had a fellow who was so good that when he blew taps it sounded like a whole orchestra playing the Rosary."

"Oh Sam," said the other, "you didn't have no buglar; when that man in our company wrapped his lips around his bugle and blowed mess call, I looked down on them beans and said, 'Strawberries, quit kicking the whipped cream out of my mess kit.' "

On a summer's day, two retired watermen sat on the Liar's Bench in Crisfield. One turned to the other and remarked, "Captain, I'll bet you can't see those two flies crawling up that roof on the other side of the harbor, can you?" "No," quipped the other, "but I know they're there, 'cause I can hear them crawling." The voice of Uncle Rubin on Tangier Island marked him as a man worthy of note: when he hollered "Whoa" to his team, a man's horses on the western side of the island two miles away came to a halt.

If storytellers could yarn about the strength of a man's voice, they could also yarn about the size of women. Captain George ended a lying contest in the Mount Vernon local store when he observed: "Boys, I can tell you this: you have never seen a large woman. I went to Baltimore and there was a woman there that gave birth to a 500 pound baby." Conversely, there was the tale about the small woman who entered Scorchy Tawes' restaurant in Crisfield. Someone commented on her size, but he

102

was immediately eclipsed by a Tangierman: "My God, man, you think she's short; why I know a woman down on the Eastern Shore of Virginia who is so short she has to stand up to pick strawberries."

Perhaps most common was the liar who lacked the time to lie:

> Casey Jones was a big liar. One day these three men were going to work and they met Casey and they said, 'Come on, Casey, tell us a lie.'
>
> He said, 'Man, I ain't got no time to tell you a lie today, I've got to go to Tony Tank to pull two horses out of the river.'
>
> So these fellas took off to go down there to Tony Tank to see what was going on, but when they got down there they didn't see any horses anywhere. Next week when they saw Casey again they asked him why he'd lied to them the other day.
>
> He said, 'Man, you asked me for a big lie and I told you one.' (22)

Fools and Simpletons

Tales about foolish people capture the imagination of raconteurs. Often the uninitiated outsider became the butt of humor. Down near Pocomoke, a man stopped to chat with a farmer across the fence:

> 'I see that's the yellow corn you got there.'
> 'Yeah, that's the kind I planted.'
> 'It don't look like you'll get more than half a crop.'
> 'Yeah, that's the way I raise it, half a crop.'
> 'Good Lord, there's not much difference between you and a damn fool.'
> 'No, just a fence.'

And then, of course, there were those tourists who got lost in the same area.

103

'Do you know if this road will take me to Pocomoke City?'

'I don't know.'

'Well, where will I end up if I take this road?'

'I don't know.'

'Boy, you sure don't know much, do you?'

'No, I don't know nothing, but I ain't lost.'

Some visitors never quite understood the oyster. When Captain Parker of Cambridge threw some of his catch over the side of the boat they landed on the bottom, still plainly visible from the wharf. A young innocent strolled by and looked down at them a long time. Finally he turned to Parker and said, "Captain, how long does it take before they crawl away?"

Horse stories inevitably revealed a fool and a clever man, and it appears that the old Yankee horse trader moved south to the Eastern Shore.

There was this Yankee farmer and he advertized a horse for sale. Well, the people in the immediate vicinity, they knew all about the horse and they didn't want anything to do with it. So this stranger came by and was interested in him and he told the Yankee, 'That's a beautiful horse, what do you want for him?'

He said, '$150.'

'Well, what's wrong with him?'

'Oh, there's nothing wrong with him.'

'Look,' said the stranger, 'you wouldn't ask less than $350 unless there was something wrong with this horse.'

The Yankee said, 'No, I've just got no use for him and I want to get rid him, and I'm willing to sacrifice him.'

So the stranger felt his legs and he looked at his hooves and he thumped his belly, and looked at his teeth. Finally he said, 'Come on now, what's wrong with this horse?' Then he went over and looked the horse in the eye. 'My God,' he said, 'I believe he's blind.'

'No,' said the Yankee, 'he's not blind.'

'Well, open the gate,' said the stranger. So the farmer

opened the gate and that horse ran out and he ran down and ran right into a tree. The stranger said, 'That's what I thought, he's blind.'

"No, dammit, he's not blind.'

'Well, what made him run into that tree?'

'Oh,' said the Yankee, 'he just don't give a damn.' (23)

Some horses were just stubborn.

At one time Captain Tom Bradshaw had a big horse that he worked in the fields practically every day. And every day Captain Tom would bring the horse in and water him when he came back to get his dinner. Between the water well and the field was a big ditch and if you didn't go across it you had to go about two hundred yards around. Captain Tom would bring that horse to the ditch and try to coax him across it, talk to it, pull on the reins and even whip the animal sometimes. One real hot summer day Captain Tom was trying to get the horse across and when the horse wouldn't go, he went back and got his bull whip and started to beat on the horse but nothing happened. Then Captain Tom got mad. He said, 'Yancer, you'll come across this ditch or a piece of you will.' And he walked right over there and bit that horse on the end of the nose. They say the blood flew and the horse reared back, and Captain Tom bit him again. But they say he never did get that horse to come over the ditch. (24)

Similarly, a horse in Crisfield got Charlie Crockett terribly riled up. He was walking down to his boat and he walked right under the head of this animal and the horse bit him on the shoulder. He thought little about it until he got in his boat and sailed out around Great Point, when all of a sudden it came to him what had happened. He turned his boat around, came back to Crisfield, walked back up the street and hit that horse right in the nose with his fist.

A witless fellow on another occasion asked his neighbor what it was he gave his horse when it was sick. "Turpentine." When he saw his neighbor several days later:

'What was it you gave your horse when he got sick?'
'I told you, turpentine.'
'Well, I gave mine turpentine, and he died.'
'Mine did too.' (1)

Fools came in many guises. A simpleton approached a waterman one morning:

'Captain, if you can tell me how many pigs I've got in this bag, I'll give you both of them.'
'I'd say you had two.'
'My God, you must be a witch.' (18)

And from Tangier Island came another yarn about a pig in a poke:

Well, there was a priest one time and he come to a place where these two old bachelor brothers were living together. And these brothers raised a lot of pigs, and they told this priest they were going to give him a pig. They told him to get his pen ready and one of them would bring it up. So when the priest let them know his pen was ready, one of these bachelors got a nice pig and put him in a bag.

Well, on the way to the priest's place, there was a barroom and this fella went in there to get a drink and he left that bag outdoors. Some mischevious boys came along and they took the pig out of there and they put a dog in. Well, when this fella got to the priest's home he told him he had his pig and he carried him out to the pen and dumped him out and there was this dog.

He said, 'When I put him in there, he was a pig. I'll carry him back and the next time I'll bring you a pig.'

Well, on the way back he stopped and got himself another drink and he left that bag outside the barroom. And those boys got the dog out and put the pig back in. So when that old bachelor got home he went to his pen and he dumped out that bag and there was a pig.

'Now,' he said, 'Look here, if you're going to be a pig,

be a pig; if you're going to be a dog, be a dog.' (3)

Old man Tommy Dyke also enjoyed his liquor, and as with most men it confused him at times. Once he took his ox cart to Princess Anne and while he was there he consumed his fill. On the way home he stopped to take a snooze under a tree and when he woke up his two oxen were gone, and his cart was out in the middle of the road. So he said to himself: "If I'm Tommy Dyke, I've lost two oxen; if I'm not Tommy Dyke, I've found myself a good ox cart."

Some men's simplemindedness caused difficulties for islanders. Smith Island dwellers had to depend on an illiterate delivery man:

There used to be this fella who delivered stuff to the island, and if somebody wanted ten pounds of scrap iron, he'd draw a picture of it on the side of his cabin 'cause he couldn't write. His cabin was almost totally covered with markings. Well, one time Captain Otis' father wanted one of these small size grindstones to sharpen his axe on, and this stone had a square hole in the center of it to keep it revolving. So Captain Shore, the delivery fellow, drew this on the side of his boat and he went over to Crisfield and made the purchase and when he came back he handed Otis' father this great big cheese. When Otis' father said he didn't want a cheese, he wanted a grindstone, Captain Shore said, 'Oh no, Job, you're wrong; I know because I remember the picture I put on there—Oh my God, you're right. I forgot to put a hole in that thing.' (25)

Several stories turned their humor on naivete. Uncle Ben had never seen a car. When a Model T Ford turned down his dirt road one morning, he grabbed his shotgun and unloaded both barrels at it. His wife called out:

'Did you get it, Ben?'
'No, dammit, but I made him turn that man loose.'

107

Jake Bradshaw collected junk. He learned of some excellent places for gathering it down in North Carolina, but he knew nothing about navigation. So he went to Captain John Sterling: "Captain John, I can't read these government charts and I certainly appreciate it if you'd make up a simple scale readable chart so I can find my way."

Captain John agreed. He outlined and charted him a course all the way down to North Carolina, and gave it to him.

"Oh, Johnny, that's fine for going down; now will you make me something so I can get back here to Crisfield?"

At times what seemed the simplest problems caused the most difficulties. Two Lawsonia men fell to arguing about the light of the moon and the sun:

'You're a damn fool, the sun doesn't give no light at all compared to the moon!'

'What do you mean?'

'I mean the moon gives twice as much light as the sun and I'll prove it. Look, when the sun comes up it's already light, and the moon comes up in the night when you really need light. Now if the moon came up when the sun was out in the day, damn if you wouldn't see some light.'

'My God, you're right, I never thought of that.' (26)

For others, it was not celestial bodies that caused dilemma, but the face of a watch:

There was this fella over on one of the islands there, and he always wore a watch, but he didn't have any idea how to tell time. And this fella he was working with couldn't tell time either, and he came up to him and he said, 'What time you got?'

The fella showed him his watch. 'There it is,' he says.

'Damned if it ain't,' says the other. (1)

108

Anecdotes, jests, and local history fuse easily in the folk mind. One of the best examples of this coupling of local history and floating jest came to me from the lips of Captain Otis Evans. It was a story told to him by his uncle as true, and Captain Evans was not about to dispute it.

My uncle told me this happened to my great, great grandfather, and I suppose it's true. His name was William Evans and he was living on the Bay side of Smith Island, and at that time Smith Island was sparsely settled. They were scattered from Kedges Straits half way to Tangiers. The old man had a farm and a herd of cattle and he thought enough of them as if they'd of been Aberdeen Angus. But they were hide and horn mostly.

When the British left Baltimore after they got whipped [in 1814] they were becalmed off Smith Island and their provisions were about gone. They looked over through their binoculars and they could tell that there were cattle roaming around on the beach. So when the old man got up this morning, he looked down there and there was a long boat on the Bay shore and a bunch of bluecoats there around his cattle. Well, he saw the fire right away, so he grabbed his old walking stick and he got down there to the beach and he started waving that thing around, you know, so those men gathered him up, tied him and put him in the long boat, and took him aboard the boat.

Now this all happened when tobacco chewing come in. The old man was a great chewer—grew his own tobacco.

So he sat out there in the main cabin of the ship chewing his tobacco. But he didn't know where to spit. Oh, they had a plush carpet you would sink down into. So by and by he found himself a corner and he spit into it. Here comes a little fella dress up in white and he put down a big silver looking thing, all bright and shiny. So after a little while the old man felt he had to spit again. He looked around—couldn't spit in that beautiful thing—so he found himself another corner and he let loose. And that fella run and grabbed that silver thing and put it in this corner. So this finally got on the old man's nerves and he said, 'If you don't take that *dahmn* thing out of my way, I'll spit right into it.'

'Oh, Captain Evans, that's just what we want you to do.'

'Well,' he says, 'good enough.' So he sat there. Said he had the greatest evening of his life. But later on it breezed up, so they went on down to Tangiers, 'cause they had a deep water harbor there. They went there for repairs before they went back to England. And they told Captain Evans —he had been as contrary as he could be—

'Mr. Evans, we're going to take you to England.'

He said, 'That's just what I want you to do, take me to England. I want to tell the *dahmn* queen just what kind of a bunch of cut throats she sent over here, anyhow. You're no good.'

(And according to my uncle, my grandparents did hate the British. Oh yes, they called them *dahmn* Britishers, and they weren't cussing men as a rule. They were church abiding men, but they'd use that word: *dahmn* Britishers.)

But anyhow, the day came that the British were all ready to sail back to England, and they changed their mind on grandpap. They said, 'Mr. Evans, you're too brave a man to keep in custody. We're going to send you back home.'

And so the man in charge put an officer over him and said, 'You take Mr. Evans back to Smith Island and you be sure to put him on dry land.' So when they got up there to Horse Hammock, the tide was down low and there was this sand bar going out there for one hundred yards or more from the shore. They said, 'Mr. Evans, you'll have to walk from here. This is as close as we can get.'

He said, 'I heard your commanding officer tell you: Put me on dry land! And you'd better do it or there's going to be trouble. I'll report you certain.' So the four of them picked him up, one a-hold of each arm and they carried him ashore and set him down on the grass. 'Now,' he said, 'you can go.' (4)

Somewhere in the transmission of this family story, as it has been passed down for three generations, someone has injected the traditional account of the cuspidor. The yarn of the man who swears he will spit right into the cuspidor unless it is moved has been attributed to such folk heroes as Davy Crockett who faced the same situation while on a trip to New York.

Older and still more widespread is a story told about a man and an oar. Recorded by Homer in *The Odyssey,* the tale still lives in oral tradition today along the Maine coast and on the Eastern Shore.

> When I was to the store the other day, there was an old fella sitting out in front smoking his pipe. He'd followed the water all his life and made his living oystering, crabbing and fishing. Just as I came in I heard him say:
> "I've lived here all my life and I've worked on the water and I'm getting kind of sick of it all. When I retire I'm gonna get me a rowboat and oar down the river. I'm gonna go and go until somebody asks me what that is I've got in my hand. Then I'll say, 'You don't know what an oar is?' And if he says 'No,' I'm gonna throw my oars away and let that rowboat go with the tide, and then I'm gonna spend the rest of my life right there." (27)

In another widely told tale one begins to see cultural adaptation as the story-teller fits his anecdote to an Eastern Shore occupation.

> There was this colored man who had been drowned at least for three or four days. These two Tangiermen were

111

poling up a gut soft crabbing when they come across the body of this drowned fella. They tied his body to a stake and went off crabbing. Bye and bye when they came back, there were crabs all over that corpse eating away. They fished them off and put them in their boat, and then went on to crab some more. When they came back again, there were more crabs all over that colored man. So they fished them off and filled their baskets, and one of them said to the other, 'Ready to go to town?'

The other fella said, 'No, let's fish him one more time.' (28)

A similar version of this story occurs in Maine where it is told on a lobsterman and his nagging wife who drowns and acts as lobster bait for him in the same way. In the lumbering woods the victim is caught beneath a log jam. After two days they finally rescue the body and find it filled with eels. The lumbermen sell the eels for ten dollars to give the widow as a condolence gift. Finally after everything is explained, they ask the woman what she wants done with the body. She says, "Throw it back in; that's the first ten dollars I ever had in my life."

The Preacher and the Church

Invariably, traditional jests depict the shortcomings of a particular group: lawyers, schoolteachers, preachers, or just dern fools. Amid the Methodist stronghold of the lower Eastern Shore, it is hardly surprising to find that one of the chief subjects for amusement is the preacher and his sanctuary, the church. Nor is it surprising to find, in a strictly maritime culture, that the water and spiritual life are never far apart. On every dredge boat that I have ever been aboard, grace is always said before meals, as the crew bow their heads while the captain utters the simple words of thanks in what is obviously a very traditional ceremony. On certain gravestones in cemeteries on Deal Island engraved pungies or skipjacks replace the more traditional motifs of weeping willows or doves on the headstones, and the inscriptions indicate that the dead have anchored at last in a snug harbor. In a more amusing vein, one Deal Islander, convinced that her husband loved his "damned old boat" more than anything in the world, swore that when he died she was going to construct him a casket in the shape of a boat and have done with it.

On Smith Island they tell another story of a young lad who, when asked in prayer meeting what the most important commandment was, replied without batting an eye: "Never rub a buckram." The story is well-founded. It united both sea and sacrament. A buckram is a crab which has just shed and begun to form its new shell, but if it is rubbed enough it can be illegally passed off as a soft shell crab for more money. To the young boy who made the reply, if indeed he did, there was unquestionably an extra commandment that Moses left off the tablet. But Moses never fished for crabs in Tangier Sound.

The humor derived from the church and from the ubiquitous preacher. It would be shameful to make fun of the minister to his face or to recall his sometimes foolish antics in front of him. But behind his back, this covert humor seems acceptable to the folk, and they indulge in it as a sort of release. The situation comedy that surfaces with stories of witty retorts inside the church proper—and some are quite obscene—would, if experienced personally by the tale-teller or listener, be exceedingly embarrassing and uncomfortable. Yet, outside the walls of the sanctuary, a different perspective allows the storyteller to indulge in a taboo, namely mocking, that which is ordinarily a serious matter. Certainly the stories and jokes on preachers which are common on the Eastern Shore provide ample evidence of a kind of covert protest tale which in a very round about way gets back at that figure of righteousness and authority whom everyone knows is not always that righteous or that authoritative. In these tales the preacher appears in every conceivable role: a hypocrite, a drunk, a fool, a poor speaker, a coward, a wit, a fraud, and a pauper.

For every young man, there is always the question of what profession to pursue. For potential men of the cloth, the decision sometimes came after a sign:

Now there was this preacher we used to have out on Smith Island. I'll say his name was Ralph. He used to be a

113

farmer up in Delaware, and he was out in his field plowing
one day and he looked up and there was this cloud forma-
tion and it said, 'P. C.'

He said to himself, 'Of course, that's "Preach Christ" and
that's exactly what I'm going to do.'

So he put down his plow and he went to preaching and
pretty soon fate brought him over to the island. He stayed
there a while, but the more he preached, the worse he got,
and the congregation got more and more dissatisfied. So he
got to thinking over that perhaps 'P. C.' really meant, 'Plow
Corn' so he went back to that farm in Delaware and that is
where he stayed.

Now I don't know if that's really true or not, but the
story fits this preacher we used to have so well that I've
always told it on him. (4)

Once a man elected to follow the ministry, his troubles
often began when he moved into a new community and tried to
establish communication with his parishioners:

Now this really happened down here in Lawsonia. There
had been a change of preachers here, and this new man he
come into that institution of learning, the country store. What
you couldn't learn in there wasn't worth learning. Well, there
was this old fella laying round there after a day's work and
this preacher was trying to get acquainted with the future
flock and he walked into the store and he greeted the old
man who was laying on the bench chewing tobacco.

'Good evening.' The old fella spoke to him and spit. 'I'm
your new preacher around here and I'm trying to get acquainted with the members of the church.' The old guy
never noticed him. 'I noticed the soil seems to be fertile
around here. Looks like you could raise almost anything
on it. What crop do you raise the most of?'

The old fella looked at him and spit again. 'Well, all I
ever knowed them to raise around here was a lot of hell,
and they get about 500 good crops of that every year.' (26)

Trouble plagued the preacher even further when it came

114

to the matter of pay. Preachers, like schoolteachers, receive less than their fair share no matter where they go, and the Eastern Shore is no exception. At Mariners, outside of Crisfield, Reverend Moffert sat in on a meeting where they got to talking about raising his salary. Before too long he interrupted the discussion: "Gentlemen, I appreciate your wishing to raise my salary, but I'd appreciate it even more if you'd pay me last year's first."

Over on Smith Island, a minister's wages fluctuated with the price of crabs.

They told this on this fella James Bradshaw. No, it was his brother John, that's right. They said the preacher over there asked for an increase in salary. Now, over on the Island, each part pays according to their population. Ewell and Tylerton and Rhodes Point. Them that has the most population pays the most money.

So this preacher asked for an increase in salary and they called the official board together to see what they were going to do, to see if they were going to meet his demands. So they all gathered in the basement of the church, and Captain Arch called the meeting together and said, 'Gentlemen, we're here tonight to see if we're gonna give the preacher an increase in salary he was asking.' And of course in a matter of minutes they got completely off the subject.

Well, you know each crabber gets paid by the peck with the pealer soft crabs, and at that time they were paying two cents for the crabs. So Captain Arch rattled his gavel and he said, 'Boys, we got off the subject. We've gathered here to see what we're going to pay the preacher.'

John Lewis Bradshaw said, 'Pay him the market.' (1)

Further south, times for preacher were equally hard, but there were better reasons.

Well, several years ago my father and two other men were on a boat and they went down to North Carolina to buy oysters. They were in this small village on Sunday and they went into this colored church where they had this colored preacher. When the collection plate went around they

115

noticed that it just had some pennies, a few nickels, and some buttons in it. So each of them put a dollar in and after the sermon was over the preacher came up to them and thanked them. One of the fellas with my father asked him how much salary he got.

He said, 'They only pay me one hundred dollars a year, but when they kill the hogs they bring me some meat and when they harvest their crops I get some of that.'

This fella said to the preacher, 'Boy, that's damn poor pay for a preacher.'

The preacher looked at him and laughed and said, 'Yeah, it's damn poor preaching too.'

Now that really happened. (24)

Ministers might suffer ignominy and abuse right within the walls of their own sanctuary. The jest which turns on the clever retort uttered in church, or which places the preacher humorously in an embarrassing position finds great acceptance among Eastern Shore raconteurs. When a long-winded Tangier preacher put a member of the congregation to sleep, he asked for help.

'Captain, would you wake up that man sitting next to you?'

'Why should I, Reverend? You wake him up, you put him to sleep.'

An especially tedious sermon in Lawsonia put every parishioner to sleep except one elder. After the service the preacher met the elder at the door:

'Well, what did you think of my text today?'

'My God, five more minutes of that and it would have killed the devil.'

Out on Smith Island during a camp meeting the preacher worked the congregation into high frenzy with his hell and damnation sermon. As he reached a crescendo he cried out: "Everybody who wants to go to heaven, stand up." The whole congre-

116

gation rose but one man way in the back of the church. When things quieted down the preacher inquired:

'Captain, I noticed that when I asked the question about going to heaven, you didn't stand up.'
'No sir, I didn't.'
'Well, don't you want to go to heaven?'
'Yes sir, I do when I die, but I thought you were getting up a load right now.' (1)

Similar church meetings elsewhere drew inauspicious remarks from the congregation and doubtless caused the preacher no little embarrassment. In Sharptown, a village once known for its boat building, a preacher exhorted the flock to a high emotional pitch. Suddenly a young woman jumped up and announced: "Oh, my Christian brothers, I feel so good; I feel like I just had my bottom scraped and my shafthole rebored." Outside Crisfield, "Mealbags" Lawson became enthralled one Sunday with Horace Nelson's preaching. He sat in his pew, rocked back and forth and clapped his hands and cried "Amen" as Horace spoke of the trials and tribulation of Lazarus. When the preacher told how the rich man had cast Lazarus into the street, "Mealbags" jumped up and shouted: "The goddamn son-of-a-bitch."
A similar tale again places the preacher in an unenviable position. In one particular town where no one spoke to their neighbors, the preacher tried to heal the breaches. He called, one Sunday, for anyone in the congregation without an enemy to hold up his hand. When an old man in the last pew responded, the preacher asked him to stand and explain to the congregation how it was he had not an enemy in the world. "Oh," confessed the old man, "that's easy, all the sons-of-bitches died."
In another community it was church membership that needed revision.

Now in this church I'm going to tell you about they were very high-faluting and wore stiff collars. Well, one night, this man about town came down there and he sat down in the back row and at the end of the service he came

117

down in front, and the people looked at each other and the preacher wondered how he was going to get this man out of there. So the preacher told him that before he joined the church perhaps he should go home and think it over and decide if he really wanted to.

So the next Sunday there he was again on that last seat, and the preacher thought, 'How will I ever get my salary if that man comes into this church.' So when they sang the invitation hymn, the preacher said, 'Brother, do you think you should like to join with us good people?'

He said, 'Yes, I'd like to join with you.'

The preacher said, 'Well, I tell you what to do: you go home and pray to the Lord and ask him if He thinks you should join with us or not.'

So he got rid of him again, but the following Sunday, the preacher looked back on that seat and there he was again. When the invitation hymn was over, the minister went up to him and shook his hand and said, 'Did you ask the Lord if He thought you should join with us good people?'

He said, 'Yes, I did ask Him, and He said it would be a fine thing if I could join with you. He said He had been trying for twenty years to get into this church.' (23)

Also within the church proper, there were occasions when the preacher himself did not act with all the aplomb imputed to him:

There was this hunchback who died in his 70's and the undertaker had a terrible time getting him into a casket. He'd put his upper body down and his feet would fly up in the air and when he shoved the lower part of the body down into the casket, the corpse sat up. Well, finally he strapped the dead man down in there somehow and got the casket over to the church.

Well, in the middle of the service, the straps broke and the corpse sat right up there in the casket. The congregation took one look at this and out the door they went. And

118

pretty soon the preacher looked up from his text and saw what was happening and headed for the nearest window, and the last they saw of him he was headed across a field, with a window sash around his neck shouting, 'Damn a church that's got only one door.' (16)

An Oakville preacher thought to give his cause a bit more advertisement so he told the ushers to

> Open them doors and open them wide
> So all my voice can go outside.

But when the only thing to come in from outside was a brick he hollered:

> Close them doors and close them quick
> Some son-of-a-bitch just throwed a brick.

If the preachers confronted unnerving experiences inside their churches, they became an even more liable target for humor outside, at least in Eastern Shore narrative. One story unearthed a witty, though hypocritical, minister:

Around Marion one time, there was this Baptist preacher and he preached a sermon on Sunday on all the ills of drinking and what damnation it had brought to all the people who had tried it. Well, the next day these two women in the congregation were parked right across from the dispensary eating their lunch. The Reverend come by with a little black bag that had Sunday's collection in it. He went right into the dispensary with it and when he come out one of the ladies said to him, 'Reverend, what are you doing coming out of a place like that after what you said yesterday about drinking? You ought to be ashamed of yourself.'

'Well,' he said, 'my wife has caught the fever and she is terribly constipated.'

So these ladies understood, but a short time later they saw the Reverend come by again and he was tacking up the street. They called to him and said, 'Reverend, didn't we hear you say that you were going to use that whiskey to help your wife's constipation?'

He said, 'Ladies, I'll tell you, when I get home, you can bet she's gonna shit.' (20)

And even the dialogue between laymen did little to extoll the preacher. A conversation between a white man and a Negro sparked this exchange at Mariners:

Negro: I understand you've got a new preacher up your way. How is he?

White: Well, to tell you the truth, I don't know. He just come here and I don't know how he is. But they say you've got a new man over your way. How is he?

Negro: Well, I'll tell you. He don't put out much. He can preach two Sundays on one white shirt. (10)

Though the preacher himself might not be intoxicated, he encountered difficulties with those who were. One Sunday morning up near Federalsburg, a drunk weaved along a back road in front of a preacher anxious to get to church to preach. Finally the minister tried to pass only to be driven off the road when the drunk turned into him. The offender reeled back to assess things:

'Reverend, who's in that car with you?'
'Jesus.'
'Who?'
'Jesus.'
'Well, you'd better give him to me, 'cause the way you're driving, you're going to kill him, sure.'

But on infrequent occasions the preacher did have his moment in the sun. He at times rallied with a succinct remark that left his adversary non-plussed. A Lawsonia parishioner deeply aggravated his minister with some cutting remarks. The reverend retaliated: "I'm not going to tell you what I think of you, but I will say this: I hope that when you go home your mother comes out from underneath the front porch and bites you in the leg."

Another encounter between a preacher and a drunk provided this dialogue:

'Aren't you the new preacher over there in that big church?'
'Yes, I am.'
'Do you mind if I ask you some questions?'
'No, I don't.'
'Do you believe that Jonah was swallowed by the whale?'
'Yes, I do.'
'Can you prove it?'
'Yes, when I get to heaven I'll ask Jonah about it.'
'Suppose Jonah don't get to heaven.'
'Then you can ask him.'

Other church related situations provoked mirth on the Eastern Shore, even though the preacher himself was not directly involved. On Smith Island it was often the custom to have one of the lay members of the church talk at the prayer meeting or at Sunday school, and the Socratic method was invariably employed. Captain Archie Marsh talked one Sunday and his theme was Christ's temptation on the Mount. When he asked James Bradshaw what he would have done had the devil told him to turn stone into bread, James replied: "Why Arch, I'd of showed him the prettiest pan of biscuits you ever saw." On another Sunday in the same church the lesson was on Jacob going into Egypt. It was the same weekend that Wes Marsh and Albert Evans went over to Virginia to swap their fish for corn. And when Aaron Bradshaw sprung the question: "Who went down into Egypt to buy corn," young Walter Marsh lept up and said, "Pa and Uncle Albert."

Another traditional tale told on the Eastern Shore depicts similar communication breakdowns:

A young housewife went to church one Sunday morning. Her son stayed at home. But before she left for church she put a pot of stew on to cook. By and by the stew started to boil and it came out over the sides of the pot, and her son ran down to the church to let his mother know. He stood in the door trying to get her attention and when she saw him she nodded her head and winked at him trying to tell him to go on home. But he looked at her and said, 'You can wink and you can blink, but sheep's head is pushing the stew out of the pot.' (24)

Stories about the power of prayer fostered considerable amusement. Two Smith Islanders went over to the western shore of Virginia for wood one fall. They lay there several days, and on the third day they decided that perhaps the best way to break the weather was to pray. So that night they both knelt down and prayed for a fair breeze. The next morning at dawn the captain stuck his head up through the companionway.

"How is it, Captain?"

"Just as I expected, still northeast and blowing."

Miss Taylor had better luck with prayer, or at least she thought her method effective. She lived in Crisfield and never knew much of the ways of the world; but she knew a good thing when she saw one. She lasted to a ripe old age, always on the edge, little money and not much food. Yet each night she knelt down and prayed for her sustenance. One evening two boys overheard her and planted some food on her stoop. When she collected the gift the next morning, she thanked the Lord personally. The boys tried to explain that they were the real benefactors, but Miss Taylor knew differently: "It don't matter if the devil put it there the Lord sent it."

Out on Smith Island, the Lord sent more than was asked for in one instance.

Old Haynie Bradshaw over on Smith Island used to have a pretty good sized garden. Everyone had gardens then, but Haynie had one of the biggest. He used to raise corn and beans and things like that. Well, they had a bad drought; everything dried right up. So Haynie called a meeting to pray for rain. And the first thing you know, along overhead came this big black cloud, and Haynie's wife said, 'I think our prayers are going to be answered. Here it comes.'

Well, it didn't come only rain, it come wind, and it come down in torrents and it blowed a tornader. And after it was all over the old man went out and he looked around, and he come back in with his head down. His wife said, 'Well Haynie, how was it? You got your rain.'

He said, 'Well, I'll tell you, I believe the Lord sent the rain, but he sent the wind, too. Take the Lord on the average, he does about as much harm as he does good.' (2)

On Hollands Island, Captain Todd questioned more than just the efficacy of prayer. Todd held the dubious distinction of being the only sinner on the island. He took more than an occasional nip and did his share of carousing when the opportunity presented itself. One Sunday he appeared at the church meeting which took place before the service, and he listened intently as watermen and their wives stood up and catalogued all the good things the Lord had done for them that week; helping them oyster and fish, and benefitting them in their daily routines. Just before it all ended, Captain Todd rose to testify.

Christian friends, you've been telling how good you've been to the Lord and how good the Lord's been to you during the past week. Well, as far as I'm concerned, he's been no great shakes to me. In the first place, I had three sows down there in the pen and the colery struck them and killed all three and I had to bury them out on the sand beach. Thursday, we had one of them genuine northwesters and that little bark of mine was anchored just north of Hollands Island and she sank on me. She's a total loss. Now I'll tell you how I feel about the Lord: in the past I used to take one little nip, in the future I think I'll have two. (28)

And down he sat.

Eastern Shore narrators frequently employ themes about couples and human relationships to evoke jocular reactions. Some of the material is merely personal and anecdotal, such as the story of the storekeeper in Ewell who accused Alice Middleton's father of winking at his wife. "If I did, Captain, I surely must have had something in me eye." Another story, however, exhibits all the earmarks of having been in tradition for some time. John Custis and his wife had little in common. One time, after they had gone four days without speaking, they took their horse and buggy for a drive and came to a deep stream across the road. Mrs. Custis broke the silence:

> 'Brother Custis, where are you going?'
> 'Sister, I'm going to hell.'
> 'Drive on.'

A Virginia informant hangs the same tale on a relative of Martha Washington's:

> In Northampton County on the Eastern Shore of Virginia, there lived about the time of the Revolutionary War, a wealthy land-owning family named Custis, cousin in fact to Martha Washington. For an unremembered reason, General and Mrs. Custis had stopped talking to each other. Any messages they wanted to give each other were passed through the mouths of servants, like, 'Jonas, tell Mrs. Custis we have four people for dinner this evening.'
>
> After twenty years of this, General Custis decided he would make his wife speak to him. He asked the butler to ask her if she cared to accompany him on a drive. She told the butler to tell him that she would be happy to. In their beautiful coach drawn by a matched pair of horses, they drove out into the country towards the shores of the Chesapeake Bay. When they drove onto the beach, General Custis didn't hesitate, but drove the horses into the water, saying,

'Mrs. Custis, I'm going to drive you straight to hell.'

'Drive on, General Custis,' she said, 'I have as many friends there as you do.' (29)

More divisive still, Webb White and his wife separated and agreed to split their possessions evenly. Good to his word, when it came to distributing his boat he took out a saw and cut it in two. Lennie and Clara Rebel never got on well either. When she passed away Lennie wandered past her coffin, bent down, and whispered, "You're gone, Clara old girl, and if you don't care, I don't." When a local Crisfield boy contracted a social disease, he needed an excuse to give his wife. He asked Doc. S. if such a thing could be picked up off a toilet seat. "Captain," said the doctor, "you could get it up a tree if you had a whore up there with you."

For others the problem was not disease but drink:

Now there was this fella that lived above Crisfield here and he had a terrible drinking problem. And it really upset his wife, and so she made an arrangement with a friend of hers. He said he would dress up like the devil and when her husband came through Handy's Woods the next night he would scare some sense into him.

So the next night when the old man came up through those woods, that friend hid in the bushes dressed like the devil and when the drunk went by he made an awful noise. The woman's husband said, 'Who's that?'

He said, 'I'm the devil.'

'My God, man, I'm not afraid of you, I married your sister Nancy.' (30)

On Smith Island, Harry Low lost his girl, and a friend consoled him: "Don't worry about it Harry, there's plenty of fish in the sea. Why, when I was courting my wife I thought she was so sweet, I could have commenced with her toes and eaten her right up. And now, by God, I wish I had."

Another Smith Island man learned the hard way about the dangers of infidelity:

There was this fella living up to Hog Neck Marsh and he was going out with this other woman, and he paid her off with a ham. So this woman he was going with got a little remorseful and she went and told his wife about it. She said, 'I have a date to meet him tonight down there and I can't go on with it no more so you can do what you want.'

So the wife said, 'I'd like to borrow some of your clothes and then I'll go down there and meet him.'

That night he got in his skiff and when her husband left, she run down there as hard as she could and got to the meeting place before him. And when he come in there, he began loving her and telling her how much better she was than his wife, and when he got all done, he give her this ham. And so when he got in the boat, she took the ham and she run like the devil and beat him home.

The next morning she got up real early and she sliced that ham and when he come down, there was that whole ham sliced and fried right up. He said, 'What in the hell's the idea of cooking all that ham?'

She said, 'You gave it to me last night.'

Well, that man pulled right up and left and never came back. Man who told me that said it was a fact. (1)

Courtroom Antics

Anecdotal humor from time to time depicted amusing situations in court. In several stories a black man became the butt of white humor. One Negro defendant, arraigned for shooting his neighbor with a shotgun was asked if the act was done in self defense. "Oh no, judge, I shot him in the ass and he jumped de fence." Another black man saw two of his companions get extended sentences for delivering different answers to the judge's question, "How do you feel today?" When the judge fired the same question at him, he replied, "I feel just like a bride, I know I'm going to get something but I don't know how long it's going to be."

A man by the name of Boggs was the only Negro to live on

Smith Island. He worked as a general handy man for the island residents and lived in a house off by itself. He apparently had trouble with his wife one time:

Boggs and his wife lived out there between Rhodes Point and Ewell and his wife kept a spare bedroom for white folks who got caught in the rainstorms. So one night old Boggs come home drunker than hell, and he bolted right in there, muddy shoes and all. And man, when his wife saw him in there, she took the rolling pin and clobbered the hell out of him. When he sobered up and found out what she'd done, he did likewise to her, and she had him arrested.

And so it came up in court. The judge heard each side of it and he said, 'Boggs, when you start to beating a woman, you know a woman is a weak vessel.'

He said, 'Yessir, your honor, but could I say a word? I know that a woman is a weak vessel, but being a weak vessel, your honor, don't you think they carries too much sail sometimes?' (1)

Other men likewise met the judge's question with apt replies. Irishman Bill O'Connell was hauled in up the Bay for selling liquor illegally and he faced the local magistrate:

'Are you Bill O'Connell?'
'To tell the truth, judge, I dont' know if I am or not. My mother was a poor widder woman and she got her children anywhere she could.

An illiterate by the name of George Nelson witnessed a murder on Persimmons Point. He was called to the stand:

'Mr. Nelson, where were you when this man was shot?'
'By God, Judge, I was standing right there.'
'How many shots were fired?'
'By God, Judge, two.'
'Where were you when the first shot was fired?'
'By God, Judge, I was standing right beside him; I was looking right at him when he was shot.'

'Well, where were you when the second shot was fired?'

'By God, Judge, I was in front of Mapsville Church.'

'That's two miles away.'

'By God, Judge, I know.'

'Well Mr. Nelson, how close together were the shots?'

'By God, Judge, they were just like that, SHE-BANG, SHE-BANG. (31)

On occasions, it was the judge himself who carried the day. Near Snow Hill knowledge of the scripture stood a judge in good stead.

One time just before Christmas, a fella that lived outside of Cedartown stole fourteen turkeys and carried them to a poultry buyer. The buyer noticed that something was wrong so he wrote down the license number on the Model T. Well, this fella, Em, was arrested and he come before me —I was judge then.

'Em,' I said, 'how come you stole those turkeys?'

'I took them according to the scriptures,' he said.

'Well,' I said, 'O.K., but I've done a little studying of the scriptures and I've never come across anything like that.'

But Em says, 'It says in the scriptures that the Lord helps them that helps themselves.'

I said, 'Em, I believe that Benjamin Franklin said that, but I'll give you the benefit. Do you believe all you read in the Bible?'

'Yes I do, Judge.'

'Then read a bit further, Em, to the Sermon on the Mount where it says "The Lord loveth a cheerful giver," and very cheerfully I'm going to give you eighteen months.' (31)

Clever Retorts

A good deal of Eastern Shore humor springs from quick and pertinent responses. Stories of those who have weasled their way out of a tight situation with a smart remark or laid low an establishment figure with a well-timed witticism find ready acceptance among narrators and listeners. Whether or not the event recounted actually occurred matters little; the incident has found its way into anecdote which has been passed on orally and gained a local tradition. One such tale concerns a young Tangierman who took his crab boat outside the Virginia Capes one spring and came upon the Chesapeake Bay Light Ship for the first time. He motored alongside and called up:

'Captain, are you broke down?'
'No, I'm the Light Ship.'
'I don't care if you're light or loaded, I can tow ye.' (1)

On another occasion a Smith Islander in a rowboat encountered a battleship coming down the Bay. A crewman in the bow called down:

'Get that goddammed thing out of the way down there.'
'Are you the captain of that ship?'
'No.'
'Well, speak to your equals, 'cause I'm the captain of this one.' (1)

Bay authorities frequently caught the barbs of local watermen. When the Coast Guard came aboard to inspect Charlie McMann's crab boat he failed to have the necessary fire extinguishers on board. The Chief spoke up:

'Why in the devil don't you carry a fire extinguisher aboard this boat like you're suppose to? What would you do if this boat caught fire?'
'Why, I'd come aboard yours.'

Bay oyster inspectors likewise confronted puzzling situations:

This man, Captain Sam, they called him, lived up there to the Nanticoke River near Mount Vernon. He handled his oyster pretty rough and he knew the law was going to get him sooner or later. Well, he had this colored man working with him, you know. So this one morning, there was this inspector in a row boat trying to sneak up on him. Well, Sam saw him and he turned to the nigger and he said, 'John, shovel the oysters up on the end of this culling board.' He had maybe two or three bushels. John shoveled them right up there and got them all ready. Well, the inspector inched his way to the place where he thought he had him and he come a rowing as hard as he could, and as he come up along side Captain Sam and John upended that culling board and cccuuussshhhh, them oysters went right back overboard. That inspector looked right at him and said, 'Sam, what in the hell are you doing?'

Sam said, 'Fulfilling the scriptures.'

Inspector said, 'Fulfilling the scriptures, what do you mean?'

He said, 'Well, you know the scriptures say, "Be ye ever so ready for you know not the minute or the hour when the son-of-a-bitch cometh."' (1)

Visitors to the island communities quickly learned that it seldom paid to criticize the way of life. When a female tourist took one look at Tangier Island she was aghast. "My Lord," she said, "what in the world do you ever do in such a desolate place as this?" "Well," observed a resident, "in the summer we crab and fornicate, and in the winter we don't crab." A Singer Sewing Machine salesman learned a similar lesson on Smith Island.

My wife's uncle who was a very religious man told me this one. There was a sewing machine salesman and he was coming out to the island to do some selling, and after he was finished with what he wanted to do here, he got my wife's uncle to take him ashore. This was in the days of sailing. When they started out, the wind was ahead so they had to tack and each time they'd come about in that narrow creek he'd have to ask the salesman to duck his head. Pretty soon

130

the wind went slick calm and they just lay there and slatted back and forth. After they'd rolled around a long time, this salesman spoke up and he said, 'Well, let me tell you something Captain, I don't know how you people ever stand it out on this island. This is the most God-forsaken spot I've ever seen, and I don't think the good Lord could ever find it.'

'Well, I don't know about that,' said the captain, 'I don't think He'll have such a hard time as all that. If a Singer Sewing Machine salesman can find it, seems He can too.' (32)

Away from home, Smith Island watermen also met new experiences with well turned wit. When Caleb Jones went into a Baltimore restaurant and saw french fried potatoes for the first time, he ordered a plateful, but he was not fooled at all. "Ain't a Christ thing but hashed tater," he informed the waitress. On a trip to the Potomac River, Captain Noahy Jeems came close to becoming a Catholic:

Captain Noahy Jeems was over buying oysters in Britains Bay, one of those tributaries to the Potomac River. So one week he didn't get enough oysters so he laid over the weekend and on Sunday morning he went ashore to a place where they served whiskey and gambled. It was a combination of grocery store and everything. So while he was in there three or four of these oyster tongers who worked for him came in. They had their guns with them and they'd just come from early morning mass. So they propped their guns up in the corner, went up to the bar and ordered a couple of drinks and then they sat down and played two or three rounds of poker. Finally they said, 'Well boys, it's time to go hunting.' So they took up their guns and off they went.

Well, the next day they come along side of Noahy Jeems' boat to sell their oysters and one of them said, 'Captain Noahy, what denomination are you?'

'Well,' he said, 'I suppose you can call me a Methodist.'

131

Boy said, 'Well, it's a wonder you wouldn't join the Catholic faith.'

'Well,' he said, 'I'll tell you. If you can get up first thing on a Sunday morning and go to church and pick your guns up on your shoulders and go a-hunting and come in and drink whiskey and gamble and expect to go to heaven, it's worth considering.' (1)

Other men faced more desperate predicaments when they left home to go dredging on the Potomac River. A quick turn of wit saved a Fairmount waterman a sound thrashing:

Now Cecil Ford's grandfather, he was a big strapping, rawboned fellow and he had a pal, Frank Hale, who was a little fellow, no bigger than me. And they were over there on the Potomac in one of them joints there. And they got pretty liquored up, and this big Eastern Shore Virginian knocked Frank Hale down. So someone went in there and told Cecil Ford's grandfather that some fellow outside had knocked Frank Hale down. Well, he went out there, and he was kind of a bully anyhow, and he walked right up and said, 'Where's the man that struck Frank Hale?'

And this great big Eastern Shoreman from Virginia, rawboned and tall, walked up and said, 'I'm the man.'

Well, Cecil's grandfather looked at him all over and said, 'Well, I'm obligated to say, you sure struck him one hell of a crack.' (33)

Still others left home to go prospecting for junk. A Crisfield man named Mason took his vessel and went all the way to North Carolina. Up one of the rivers there he came across a huge pile of debris, but when he went ashore to explore it, he confronted a laconic attendant who wasn't anxious to sell him a thing. Finally he got the man to agree to release an old cookstove for a quarter. As he departed Mason thought he would have the last word.

'I must say, this is the first time I've ever been up this

river, but this is the goddam poorest place that I have ever seen.'

'Where are you from?'

'I'm from Crisfield.'

'Where the hell is that?'

'Well, that's about 75 miles up the Bay from Cape Henry.'

'Well, it must not be too damn great up there.'

'Why is that?'

'It's got to be a pretty poor place if you have to come all the way down here to buy a cookstove for a quarter.' (23)

As with any other profession, working on the water produced good days and bad. Sometimes nothing went right. When Winfred Evans was running the ferry boat to Smith Island he wound a crab pot line around his propeller and had to dive over the stern and pull the line off with a pair of pliers. After he struggled for a long while he surfaced and a greenhead fly bit him on the forehead. "John Smith, you grey-headed old son-of-a-bitch," he cried, "I wish you'd been in hell the day you ever discovered this place."

Another Smith Islander, Captain Oscar Smith, also had his set of problems. He left the dock one morning and no sooner had he set out his trot lines than his engine broke down. He failed to get it running until late in the afternoon, and when he finally fished his lines, he didn't catch one crab. When he got back to the wharf, Captain John Lewis Bradshaw sat there smoking his pipe.

'Well, sir, Captain John, the Devil's been aboard of this boat all day long, and the hard part of it is he's still aboard.'

'Captain Oscar, birds of a feather stick together.'

Everyone in Tylerton knew that Will Marsh had never learned how to bring his sailboat into the dock. He always shot it up into the wind too soon and rammed the dock. One afternoon a group of men from the Fulton Fish Market sat in the

133

crab shanty on the dock smoking big cigars and talking with the watermen. Suddenly the wharf reverberated. "That's Will," said one of the men.

"You're damn right it's Will; you can't see the dock for all the cigar smoke."

Both Seward and John Crockett turned their wit to good advantage. Seward returned home at Christmas after dredging all fall, and his first night back some neighbors came over and stayed on and on. About eleven o'clock Seward stood up and said to his wife, "Sally, we might just as well go to bed; these folks want to go home." John Crockett, on the other hand, had the reputation for having the slowest freight boat on the Bay, the *John T. Hardy*. One day in the store, the local wags got to ribbing him about it. "Boys," he said, "the way I figure it, Saturday comes as fast on a slow boat as it does on a fast one."

Once in a while, clever remarks combined rhyme with humor. Two vessels crossed paths on the Bay and a very courteous young man aboard one called across the water:

'Where are you from, Captain?'
'Piankitank.'
'What are you hauling?'
'Pine plank.'
'Where are you bound?'
'Choptank.'

A spate of six other anecdotes, all actively told on the Bay, reflect typical aspects of Eastern Shore wit.

A Star to Steer Her By

One time Captain Ben 'Fudd' Evans was sailing up the Bay and he was short-handed on the trip so he had to use a greenhorn to help him out. It got pretty late one night and Captain Evans got sleepy at the wheel so in order to get a little sleep, he called this young boy to see if he could steer the boat. He didn't have no lights to see the compass, so Captain Evans picked out a bright star, and told the boy to steer for that.

A couple of hours later he called up, 'Boy, you still got that star I gave you to go by?'

Boy said, 'No, Captain, but that's all right, I lost that one but I've found another one just as good.' (1)

A Stuttering Crew Member

One time there was this boat and they had a crew of thirty-two, and one of them had a terrible time talking, stuttered everything he said. So one day he runs up to the captain and starts to speak, but all that came out was 'Ahahahahahah.' And the Captain says, 'Oh, come on now, I haven't got time to hear you out, go ask the mate.'

So he goes to the mate and the mate says, 'Damn, man, don't bother me, tell it to Sweeney.' And it goes on like that through the whole crew and nobody would listen to him. Well, during this time they were beginning to wonder why dinner was so late on board, and by and by this fella comes running back to the captain. And just then the captain remembered that when this man sang he didn't stutter. In fact, he was a good singer. So the captain says, 'If you can't talk, sing.' And so he did:

Should old acquaintance be forgot and
    never brought to mind,
The colored cook fell overboard, about
    twenty miles behind. (16)

My End of the Boat

Well, one time there was this lumberjack schooner loaded with lumber and she left Baltimore and was on her way down the Bay, and they had this good stiff breeze right about north. About two o'clock in the morning, this Irishman who was crew got sleepy and he climbed back aft over the lumber pile and he went to the captain and said, 'Captain, what do you say we go to bed?'

'No,' he said, 'Pat, we can't go to bed. We've got to use this fair wind to get where we can unload this lumber. You go forward and tend to that end of the boat and I'll tend to this end back here.'

Well, about an hour later, the Irishman was back again, and he did this several times and it sort of peeved the captain. So the last time he come back, the captain got a little mad. He said, 'Now Pat, you get the hell up there forward and take care of your end of the boat like I told you, and I'll take care of mine.'

So the Irishman climbed back over the lumber and he went about twenty minutes and the anchor went overboard, BRRRRUUUUMMMM, and the chain went out through that hawse hole, RRRRRRRRRRRR. The first thing you know she took up, one half the load of lumber went overboard, and she almost capsized and finally she come head to and her sails were shaking. The captain went up there and said, 'Pat, what in the hell have you done?'

He said, 'I've anchored my end of the boat, you can do what you damn please with yours.' (1)

Framing Up the New Herd

One time a couple of watermen brought their boat into a creek near where old man Sanford had his place. The old man had a lot of land there and he owned a good many cattle, but they were a rundown stock and this was in the last of February and they were nothing but skin and bones. So one of those fellas looked over there and he saw them cattle standing pretty close by and he busted out laughing. 'Oh,' he said, 'I see where old man Sanford's going to build himself a new herd of cattle.'

'Build himself a new herd of cattle?'

'Yeah, he's got the frames up.' (4)

Hard-A-Lee

Over there on Smith Island the people used to keep cattle in the old days. That was before they had refrigeration and they needed them for their milk purposes. They used to let them run up and down the roads just as they wanted. Well, this one had just let a big five lair one go right in the middle of the highway. The road was narrow with houses up on one side and water on the other, and these men were sitting around on the fence in the spring of the year 'cause there wasn't much doing then. Well, this girl come along and she seed them, and in them days they was awful sensitive anyway, and she headed right for this cow pie in the middle of the road. She had her head high in the air, 'cause she knew they were going to give her the once over. But just before she got to it this old sea captain hollers, 'Hard-a-lee.' (They always said that when they were changing tacks, you know.) (1)

Delivering the Manure

There was this fella Brown, and he lived up here on the Nanticoke River and he had the Midas touch. Everything he touched turned to money and he accumulated six or eight pungy boats and five or six farms and he built him this big home on the knoll and he and his wife got real stuck up. So he had one fella who was running these pungy boats and he sent him up the Nanticoke River after a load of manure for one of his farms. Well, the fella left that morning with a strong southwester and he got up the river where he was going and he got his load of manure aboard and later that evening the wind shifted into the northeast and he upped sail and at twelve o'clock that night he was anchored right off the house.

He'd made such a flying trip he wanted Mr. Brown to know he was back. So he went ashore and he walked up to the house and he rang the door bell. Finally Mrs. Brown came down and she opened the door and she said in a very affected way, 'Yeass?'

He said, 'Is Mr. Brown home?'

'Mr. Brown don't live here, however, there is a Mr. Breerrown.'

'Oh,' he said, 'I beg your humble pardon lady, would you mind telling Mr. Breerown that his beehoat is out heaah leehoded with sheehit.' (1)

If local store gatherings acted as catalysts for some of the best storytelling to issue from the Eastern Shore, it is hardly sur-

137

prising that some of the stories dwelt on incidents that actually occurred in the stores themselves. One Crisfield raconteur told this as happening on Deal Island where apparently there was also a snob named Brown.

There were two families over there one time, one named White and the other named Brown. And the heads of those families would get around the local stores from time to time and they would argue and brag about whose family was the best. This particular evening Brown said, 'My people have always been the most outstanding people in the community; my father was a Brown, and all my generations have been Brown. And he thought this was a pretty good line so he kept it up for a long time, night after night. And finally White countered with him.

He said, 'My father was a White and my grandfather was a White and my great grandfather, and all my generations have been White, and we're mighty proud of the fact that our name is White, but there's one little thing that we sort of regret: around our ass there's a little rim, and that's Brown. (1)

The store in Tylerton on Smith Island likewise afforded several anecdotes. A young island boy approached his grandfather in the store one day.

'Here I am, Grandpap, seven years old and only one copper.'
'Well, Son, here I am, seventy-six, and only another.'

Captain James Bradley came into that same store on another occasion while Ed Smith was there. He walked over, sat right down next to him and immediately passed wind. Ed sprang up.

'Good God Almighty, whoooooooo.'
'What's the matter, Ed?'
'My Lord, you could put that under a fresh hill of planted beans and dig them a-Thursday.'

138

There was other amusement that emanated from gatherings at the local store. In the old days on Smith Island residents enjoyed testing their friends and neighbors with esoteric questions about the scriptures. A waterman might stay up late at night trying to think up an obscure question on biblical lore which he could present at the store the next evening as a problem to be solved. The purpose was to gain respect by stumping the others in the store. But at times the process provided ludicrous sidelights as it did one night when Will Torg came into the store and said:

'I guess I got one that will stump you. Does anyone know how long King Solomon's been dead?'

Well, nobody didn't know and just about this time this character walked in there. His name was Harry Low. So someone said, 'Will Torg, ask him, ask Harry Low.'

And Will Torg stood up there and said, 'Harry, do you know?'

'Know what, Will Torg?'

'Do you know how long King Solomon's been dead?'

Harry said, 'Well, hell, man, I didn't even know he'd been sick.' (1)

At a different time in the same place Will Torg was the questioner, but his problem inclined more towards science than it did religion. He confronted Charlie Marsh:

'Charlie, how far can you see with the naked eye?'

'Well, Torg, I have seen the Patuxent Cliffs and they say that's about thirty-five or forty miles, but I'm sure you can beat that.'

'Yes, I sure can, I can beat that all to hell.'

'Torg, how far can you see?'

'Ninety-three million miles.'

'You damn, no sense fool, you. How's that?'

'I can see the sun, can't I?' (1)

139

"We are," observed one informant from Mount Vernon, "one of the poorest counties in the state and I suppose the world, but there is one thing that we're very rich in and that's personalities." In his succinct way this man put his finger on a source of much of the oral humor which pervades the creek and bayside towns of the Eastern Shore: the local character. Though in some cases raconteurs do unwind anecdotes about themselves and their experiences, they seldom, if ever, depict themselves in the eccentric guise which they reserve for local characters. Like stories of legendary folk heroes, tales about colorful personalities move fluidly from one community to another, attaching themselves to the appropriate character. At times the chief local personality may be some years dead, but his memory is kept fresh by the active circulation of tales about him, some of them true, all of them fitting.

On Smith Island, one subject of considerable mirth was Charlie Marsh who went by the nickname of Pilgrim. Pilgrim was widely known for his response to Sears and Roebuck:

Now the Sears Company, they were about the first people who sold catalogues on installment contract. So Pilgrim, he got his wife a sewing machine on time. Well, they shipped it to him and they had it for a while, but his wife never could learn to use it, and he couldn't afford to make the payments on something that he couldn't use, so he sold it. And the company wrote him a bunch of letters. Finally he got tired of receiving all this mail and he sat down and he wrote them a letter. He said:
Dear Sears:
Stop writing me letters. I sold that machine and the people I sold it to have never paid me. If they ever pay me, then I'll pay thee. Don't write me any more letters.
Signed,
Charles (24)
And that was the end of it.

Pilgrim had doubtless inherited his letter writing ability from his father. When a young man, Pilgrim went on the road, ran

140

out of money, and wrote home to the old man:

> Dear Dad:
> Please send me $10.00—I'm on the hog.
>
> Pilgrim

His father replied:

> Dear Pilgrim:
> You say you're on the hog. Well, ride the son-of-a-bitch home.
>
> Dad (24)

Pilgrim's companions enjoyed playing tricks on him just to hear the remarks he would utter. As cook one time aboard a dredge boat, Pilgrim put a duck in the pot. When he went on deck, one of the crew pulled it out and hid it. Pilgrim seemed little disturbed at the turn of events, and when he was out of the cabin a second time the duck was replaced. He returned, lifted the pot lid and met the situation solemnly: "Humm. The duck goeth, the duck cometh; blessed be the name of the duck."

One Monday, aboard the same skipjack, the weather came in thick and the fleet stayed in port that day. As a joke, one of the crew planted a stink bomb below deck where Pilgrim and the captain sat talking. When the bomb began to smell both men went out on deck where the rest of the crew stood waiting for a reaction. The captain turned to them and said, "I don't know about Pilgrim; a man who would come down there in the cabin and do something like that."

Pilgrim stepped up. "Well boys, I'll tell you this: we can bury the captain tomorrow, 'cause he's dead and rotten right now."

People may have made fun of Pilgrim, laughed at his idiosyncracies and enjoyed his reputed witicisms, but there was no gainsaying his honesty. Pilgrim was a man of his word as Captain Morgan found out one day when he and Pilgrim were dredging near one another. Morgan noticed that Pilgrim had been working the same oyster rock for a long time, so he came up along side and called over.

'Captain Pilgrim, are you catching any?'

'No, Captain Morgan, I'm not catching nary a one.'

'Oh, come now Captain Pilgrim, I've been watching you and you've been here for three or four hours and you must have caught some.'

'Captain Morgan, I'm a truth telling man and a Christian, and when I say I'm not catching nary a one, I mean nary a goddamn one.' (24)

As a "truth telling man and a Christian," Pilgrim was often called to be a lay leader in the church. When asked to welcome outsiders to the annual camp meeting on Smith Island, he did it with style.

One time at that Smith Island camp meeting they were waiting for the people from Hollands Island and Deal Island to arrive. Old man Pilgrim was to open the meeting and he noticed that everybody was getting anxious so he finally started things off. Well, down in front of the altar there was a pile of straw and an old dog was laying down in there and Pilgrim hadn't noticed him. So he started; there was some singing and a bit of prayer, and then Pilgrim started to do a little preaching to kill time and he swayed back and forth there and as he did he stepped on that dog just as those people from the other islands arrived. That dog jumped up and went 'Grrrrrrrrrr.' Pilgrim shouted, 'Get out of here you son-of-a-bitch, come in my Christian friends. We're having a hell of a time in here this morning.' (24)

Local characters flourished elsewhere on the Eastern Shore. Near Modest Town, Virginia, old man Sam Doan hauled his potatoes to market at Bloxom one morning to sell them. When he got there he found a long line of other farmers who had got there before him. No sooner had he got in line to wait his turn, than foolish Bill Williams jumped in ahead of him.

'Bill, what are you doing in there ahead of me? Do you want to fight?'

'All right, Sam, I'll fight you for a nickle.'

'I'll tell you, Bill, you can buy a fight too damn cheaply around here this morning.'

Bill stayed in line.

Edgar Rayfield coached the local ball team in Modest Town and one Saturday he failed to locate a team to play. When one of the townspeople suggested that he try and get a team on the newly installed telephone, he dialed the operator: "Hello, Central, is that you? I want to talk to some of the ball boys around here."

Out on Smith Island, Al Suggs was a gullable old man. He worked for the White family and became the butt of a number of practical jokes.

One time all the men on Rhodes Point and Ewell got together and made a plot to get old Al married. Ben Evans took that part of the woman and John Wes Marsh played the preacher. When they all got down to John Wes' for the wedding, he used a Sears and Roebuck catalogue for the Bible and he started out marrying them like this:
'Dark is the night, dismal is the weather,
I now join this whore and thief together,
Run thief, catch him whore,
Live together for evermore.

Amen'
And so they went home to this place that had been got ready and finally old Ben said to him, 'Al, you damn fool.' (Everybody was there a-peeping in.) Al grabbed his clothes without dressing and went flying up the road, and always after that he said he knew the whole time what was going on. (1)

Another time Al crammed a sausage into his pocket while Spriggs, the storekeeper, waited on another customer. When he started out of the store, the whole chain came with him and Spriggs stopped him: "Damn, Al, leave me one in here, won't you?"

Al turned at the door: "I don't know how that doggone thing got hooked in my pocket."

Ware Evans also lived out on the island, and though he was a highly intelligent and well-read man, the practical side of him was missing, at least insofar as the water was concerned. He had a four cycle engine in his boat that he purchased from Sears, and it gave him a lot of trouble, sometimes because he didn't understand it and sometimes because he was just plain stubborn. Alex Kellam met him poling back to the island one day.

'Ware, what's the trouble with your engine?'
'Nothing, I put maybe a gallon or a gallon and a half in her and it's all used up.'
'Don't you have any more.'
'Yup, but I'm damned if I'm gonna humor her anymore today.' (1)

One morning Evans got up at two AM so he could get out to the fishing ground first and get the choice spot. When he got down to his boat he said, "Lord, I want this motor to go now; please let it go." Nothing happened. "Lord, I've got up now, and I want to get down there before the rest of them does, and I want her to go." Nothing. And he sat there about ten more minutes before the final demand: "Lord, I'm just gonna ask you one more time."

Crisfield also had its cast of colorful personages. Leff Webb was a butcher and he had nine children. He took them all on a boat excursion one Sunday and when they returned he counted them off, one to nine, as they stepped from the boat. Suddenly a young woman rushed up to him and insisted that he had one of her children: "Madam, I'm sorry, but it doesn't really matter; I came with nine and I'm going home, with nine."

Bob Taylor was a terribly superstitious man. He constantly looked for signs and every morning before he went to work he religiously stood on the Crisfield wharf, looked westward, and saluted Smith Island where he came from. If someone offered him a ride downtown, he always got in on a certain side of the car. Bob packed crabs for a living and did very well. But in the routine he built in certain rituals to insure his good fortune. In his crab house, no one used Bob's hatchet in the morning before he did. Nor did they call on his office phone before he

144

did. Pranksters often entered his office early in the morning and asked Bob if they might use the phone, just so they could watch while he made a foolish call so as to be on the phone first. Bob's belief in superstition and ritual carried over into other areas of his life. Every New Year's morning he paid a Negro man to come to his door seconds after midnight to avoid the bad luck of having a woman enter the house first on New Year's Day. Bob also had a fetish for horseshoes. A friend brought him a set from a Pennsylvania race horse and Bob was so elated he gave the friend two dozen soft crabs on the spot.

Unlike Taylor, Gus Ward was a local character known more for his practical jokes than his superstition. He even collected some of his pranks in a small book, though most of the people who knew Gus when he was alive admitted that the stories came across much better when the old man told them orally than when they were printed. One time, when Gus had a boarder he couldn't get rid of, he painted red pox marks all over his own face and told the man the doctor's diagnosis had been an unquestionable case of smallpox. The boarder departed and took the door with him. Gus never thought much of black-eyed peas and when asked to say grace at a meal where they were served, he blessed them accordingly: "Oh Lord, You made mountains out of molehills; You turned water into wine; oh Lord, please turn these black-eyed peas into goose turds." And he sat down.

Up near Marion it was a local eccentric named Jack Beall whose poverty allowed him to advocate socialism:

> One time Jack Beall was talking to Bob Whittington about the economical situation in the country. Mr. Bob was financially well-fixed and Jack Beall was one of the poorest men in the county. Jack said, 'Mr. Bob, it ain't fair. You got all the money and I got none. Something ought to be done about it.'
>
> Mr. Bob said, 'Well, Jack, what do you think ought to be done?'
>
> He said, 'Vide it up.'
>
> Mr. Bob said, 'Well, Jack, if we divided all the money, at the end of the year I'd have it all back again. What would we do then?'

'Well, goddamm it, 'vide it up again.' (21)

Jack had a way of gaining the last word. When Tony Green shot Tom Shelton for running with his wife, they laid Shelton in the St. Paul's cemetery and put a fancy inscription on his tombstone:

> Remember friends as you pass by,
> As you are now; so once was I.
> As I am now you soon shall be,
> Prepare for death and follow me.

Jack and Tony were good friends, so one night Jack took a black crayon and scribbled beneath the epitaph:

> Where you are now, I cannot tell,
> But I'll bet $10 you've gone to hell. (21)

Sometimes the expressions of local characters bred proverbial phrases in a particular area. Near Cambridge, Aunt Sarah had lived a rather sheltered life. She had seen plenty of bugeyes and bateaux on the Bay, but never a steamboat. One morning, when she watched one pull into the wharf, she reputedly cried: "Stand back, Beck, here she comes, big as a drugstore." Everyone knew she had never seen a drugstore and so humorously incongruous was the whole situation to the local people that they proverbialized her remark and utter it still.

Near Elliott Island lived Sammy "I" and his brother Lisha. They lived in adjacent houses for years and though they talked of making the two houses into one all they ever got around to doing was to laying a board plank between their homes. Whenever collections were taken up for any kind of charity, solicitors at Lisha's door were always met with, "Sammy 'I' pays for all." And again, the local residents, familiar with the characters involved, picked up the phrase and put it into oral tradition.

Likewise, in Mount Vernon old man Clarence Street lost his faith in paper money. He transacted everything with silver and one day he ran an advertisement in a local paper. "Fat hen, 19¢ a pound. All cash, no goat money." The expression held, though the event is virtually forgotten.

146

Legends

Legends differ from other types of folktales in that they deal with real persons, places and events. They are stories known by a number of people and for the most part they are recounted as true, though some listeners are more than a little skeptical. One Fairmount waterman who had heard a number of the "old timey yarns" held firmly to the belief that "the Lord's running the world," and felt stories like these were simply entertainment for the foolish, and he included his wife in that category.

Others were much less skeptical. After delivering a lecture on folklore before an Eastern Shore audience, I was approached by an elderly lady who looked at me with grim determination and recounted the story of an early settler, cursed by a dying Indian to suffer blindness in his family every generation thereafter. "And that," she concluded, 'is true, because I know some of the descendents living today, and THEY ARE BLIND!" Similarly, Captain Wheatley of Tangier Island placed an undying trust in what he heard from older inhabitants on the island. "When them people told you something," he explained, "it was the truth; 'cause they don't lie." Even the young find tales of older watermen quite creditable. Driving along the Deal Island-Princess Anne Road, I picked up a nineteen-year-old hitchiker from Dames Quarter who retold, without mark of suspicion, four supernatural tales heard in the local store. To those who contend that Eastern Shore legendry is dying out, I say we have a long wait before the death rattle sounds.

Treasure Legends

Dreams of unearthing hidden treasure fasten easily on the

human imagination. All one needs is the slightest suspicion that some wayward pirate or foolish millionaire deposited his fortune along the shores of Chesapeake Bay or up on inlying creeks, and the greedy are out with pick and shovel. On the New England coast the wayward pirate is Captain Kidd, and his treasure lies secluded in inlets and coves from Block Island to Portland, Maine. On the Eastern Shore the treasure belongs to Black Beard who, according to some historians, cruised in the waters around the James River in 1717 until he was finally taken and beheaded. How much treasure he deposited on the Eastern Shore remains a mystery, but we know that the night before his capture one of his crew asked Black Beard if even his own wife knew where the treasure lay buried. "Nobody," he replied, "but [myself] and the devil [knows] where it is, and the longest liver [will] take all."

Hope of uncovering the ill-gotten wealth lingered in the minds of many watermen and their families, fostered by legendary accounts such as this one, told by a Rehobeth woman who gave the infamous pirates name as "Blue Beard":

My children's grandmother used to keep them spellbound for hours telling them the story of Blue Beard, the pirate. He got that name 'cause he had a long blue beard, but anyhow, the story goes something like this.

One time there was a very poor family, a man, his wife and four children. It seems that nothing he ever tried ever amounted to anything, and the harder he worked, the less he had. Well, one night this man was sitting around the local store as they used to do in these days, and the other men got to talking about the pirate, Blue Beard, and how he would hijack ships in the high seas and kill all the crew and take the cargo for himself. They told how he was richer than anyone could imagine and that just before he was captured and killed he had buried all his treasure. And they said his spirit was still wandering to and fro trying to find someone to tell where his treasure was because his spirit couldn't rest until he had given his gold away. Well, this fella listened and he wished with all his heart that he could have some of the gold.

148

So on his way home, he had to pass an old deserted house, but before he got to that old house the wind began to blow and moan through the trees and a voice whispered in his ear, 'May I speak with you.' Well, this man was scared out of his wits and he started to hurry along that road, but the voice said again, 'Please, let me speak with you.'

So the man stopped in the road trembling, and he said, 'W-w-w-w-w-w-hat do you w-w-w-w-ant with me?'

And this voice said, 'I'm the spirit of Blue Beard and I want you to have my money. I want to tell you where it is so I can be at rest. I got my gold in the wrong way and now I must give it to someone before my soul can ever be easy. If you will come to this old deserted house at midnight Saturday, I will meet you here and you will never want for anything as long as you live.'

Well, that man ran all the way home as fast as his legs would carry him and he never told a soul about what he'd seen or heard, but every moment he thought about that midnight visit and kept asking himself, 'Can I ever do it? Yes, I must do it, just for the sake of my family.'

He thought Saturday would never come, but it did, and it was cloudy, cold, dismal, and dark. The family went to bed early because wood was scarce and the house was always cold. The man waited till everyone was asleep and he crept out of bed and put on his clothes, buttoned his ragged coat up around his chin, pulled his old felt hat down over his eyes and started out for that deserted house. Trembling in every limb, he got to the old house about five minutes before he was supposed to and he crouched down under an oak tree to wait for Blue Beard.

All of a sudden the sky became a black blur; he couldn't see his hand in front of him; every star disappeared in the sky; the wind began to howl and howl as it blew through the limbs of that tree. He just crouched there with his teeth chattering, almost paralysed with fear. And then he felt a hot breath on the back of his neck and his heart seemed to stop beating. With the last bit of strength he had, he gave a screech and jumped to his feet and took off for home, and the only thing he heard was a deep wailing among the trees in the woods as he passed. He got home and crept back into bed and no one ever knew about his visit.

Now one of the children in the family was a boy about twelve years old and he was retarded and he couldn't attend school, but he used to wander in the woods a lot. And almost everyday he would come home with all these gold pieces and throw them on the table and say, 'Look at the shiny things, aren't they pretty?'

And his father said, 'Where did you get this gold?'

The boy said, 'A big dark man with a blue beard down to his waist gave it to me and he told me to come back and he would always give me some every time I returned.'

And so that man knew that it was Blue Beard who was giving the boy that money that he was too frightened to take. (21)

Similar tales triggered speculation about Black Beard's treasure secreted away on Shank's Hammock above Tangier Island. A youth told his father one evening about his encounter with a strange man who promised him a pot of gold if he came down to the cow pond that night. When his father laughed at him for listening to too many ghost yarns, the lad tried to sneak out only to be returned to his room. The matter so upset him that he lost his mind that very night, and though he lived to be an old man, he never regained his sanity. From the abyss of his madness he was said to murmur over and over: "Old Black Beard and his pot of gold; old Black Beard and his pot of gold."

On Smith Island, Marmaduke Mister allegedly uncovered some of the pirate's gold:

Well, there was this man around here and he was supposed to have found a lot of pirate's gold. His name was Marmaduke Mister and he lived near Kizze's Point. And when he died, they said he told his family, 'I'm never going to tell you where that gold is because it will only bring you bad luck. And if anyone attempts to find it, he will never be able to get hold of it 'cause it will gradually slip away from his grasp.'

150

So Marmaduke Mister's ghost is supposed to be buried there with his gold. Now there was a family living on the island here and they were awfully poor. They had a large number of children and lived about a mile from Kizze's Point, and overnight they became wealthy, so everyone suspected he discovered the gold.

Now they say if you begin to look for this gold, you may find the chest but when you put your spade in to get it out, whoooosh, it will sink back into the muck and mire. Now that's the yarn they told. (25)

Others purport that Black Beard went up the Wicomico River as far as Tony Tank where he left behind some wealth which has yet to be uncovered, and in Jake's Hole, a ninety foot depression near the Choptank River, the pirate reputedly dropped a huge oaken chest overboard which the determined have fished for again and again without success.

Legendary accounts of this sort drew Eastern Shoremen forth to seek their luck, often with strange and varied results. Near Presqu'ile in Talbot County, a local midwife told a farm foreman where a cache of treasure lay buried. The foreman and his brother struck out after it the first full moon. They dug for a time at the spot when suddenly the rim of a chest appeared. "There it is," exclaimed the brother, and the cache subsided back into the earth without a trace.

Similarly, a Fruitland resident learned of treasure hidden near his home. The first convenient night he walked there, drew a large circle around the area, and began to dig. When he stopped to rest and unwittingly stepped over the line, a black bull with fiery eyes appeared and chased him 'round and 'round the circle until he fell dead from fear and exhaustion. Another Fruitland native sought buried gold in the brick fireplace of an old deserted house. He picked apart the bricks with great care, until the money lay visible before him. But before he could gather it up, the chimney collapsed with a loud clatter, burying everything. On his way home, a riderless white horse rushed by him, which he took to be a sign that the money was ill-begot.

Odd tales circulated about the bridge over Peachblossom Creek. A stage driver with a shipment of gold bound north approached the bridge one evening. As he did, the driver noticed the form of a headless man sitting on the railing. His horses shied, broke through the bridge supports and carried rider and cargo to a watery end. Treasure hunters combed the area for years, but claimed that just as they struck the gold and were about to remove it from the earth, a white horse and rider appeared from nowhere and the treasure sank back into Peachblossom Creek.

Two Hebron men got wind of money buried near a fork in the road. They began to dig but realized something was amiss when they turned around and spied an old man in a red shirt sitting in a rocking chair, cradling a shot gun in his arms and eyeing them intently. They threw down their shovels and fled. When they returned to the spot several hours later, all they found was a pool of blood with a red shirt lying next to it and no sign of any digging.

Three Rockawalking men heard that John Taylor's great-grandfather had concealed a large cash savings in the ground. They started for the Taylor farm and began digging. First a loud laugh interrupted their work. Then a vicious wind blew their hats off, and moments later a chain fell out of a nearby tree. When one of the diggers struck a tin box with his shovel, he called to the others, whereupon a fire-belching horse appeared and brought their treasure hunting to a long-term halt.

Dreams of treasure frequently helped locate the hoard. A Parsonsburg man claimed his grandmother dreamt that treasure lay at the corner post of the pasture, but her husband refused to go and look. When she told a neighbor, he raced to the spot and found a freshly dug hole with the imprint of a rusty pot clearly visible. The daughter of a family living at Snow's Turn had the same dream for a week. In it a woman told her to tap ten specific bricks on their barn floor and dig there if she wished a reward. But her father refused to let her tear up the barn. When another family moved in, they became wealthy overnight for no apparent reason. Captain Tom Bradshaw down near Oriole dreamed a man came to him while he was saying his prayers and advised him to take a certain route to the store the next day. When he followed the advice, he saw what he thought was a head of cabbage, but when he picked it up he discovered he had a roll of bills, all in large denominations.

In certain instances, strange lights provided assistance in leading the fortunate to a trove.

I've heard my grandmother tell that up there to Mount Vernon there was this house that was supposed to be haunted and nobody could stay there because they would hear things. But this one man come along and said he didn't care what the curses were, he was going to stay there. Somebody there even said they'd give him some money if he'd stay there overnight.

So he went over there into that house, and I guess he was half drunk or something, but he sat down in a chair and dozed off to sleep. Directly he heard something coming down the stairs, BUMP BUMP BUMP, and he woke up and saw this fiery light. It went right by him, right out the door and down into the cellar through the outside door. Well, he followed it down there and it went right over to the chimney and disappeared at a certain spot. This fella went over there and marked the spot with a knife, and the next morning he came back down there and dug there and found all kinds of money. (37)

But one had to follow the signs if treasure was to be uncovered. A couple in the same town of Mount Vernon moved into a "real old timey house" and the first day there the woman noticed a strange looking squirrel which sat on its haunches and beckoned to her. She told her husband about it, but he was skeptical. That night the wife dreamed that gold coins rained down off the roof, but the squirrel never appeared again to show her where they were.

The Devil

If Eastern Shoremen claimed "to raise 500 good crops of hell a year," the devil had to be behind it. And more often than not he was. That infamous figure did not leave the print of his cloven hoof at every historical marker as he did in New England, but there were those who had met him face to face and even contracted with him for supernatural powers. Best known for this feat was a Crisfield Negro named Skidmore whose allegiance with the powers of evil enabled him to perform tasks no mortal man could conceive of. He gained access to his powers through the usual channels.

> Now Skidmore, he went out to this special place for nine consecutive nights, and he waited and waited and on the last night the devil came to him. He wasn't frightened. And so the devil talked with him and gave him the power to do whatever he wanted to do, but none of it was motivated by a good spirit, just an evil spirit. From then on, if Skidmore wanted women, he could have women galore; if he wanted money, he could have all he wanted. That was why he was such a mystery. (38)

Skidmore took this power and he moved it in mysterious ways indeed. Two Crisfield watermen returning to port in their skipjack one afternoon encountered Skidmore out in the middle of the Bay sailing around in a tub. Both men found the spectacle of the black wizard in a tub highly amusing. But their mirth irritated Skidmore and he placed a curse on them. From that moment on, he told them, so long as he was still alive, this event would come to their minds, but they would never be able to convey it to anyone else. And, as predicted, the image of Skidmore in the tub did flit across the conscious memories of both men while they were out in their gardens or up in the bow of their boats, but by the time they had scurried into the house or rushed aft to tell someone, the memory had vanished. Not until Skidmore was dead did the entire story come to light.

Yet Skidmore is better known for his prowess as a possessed worker than a magician. His reputation flourished so widely in the Crisfield area that he became proverbial, and the expression "to work like Skidmore" still lingers on a number of tongues. Though the average man might "work like Skidmore," when the wizard himself worked, his help came from below. He merely summoned the devil's minions to aid him.

They used to say around here that you'd be going in the woods in the early morning where he'd been working and you'd hear more than a dozen axes going hard as they could. And when you got up to him, you didn't see a soul but Skidmore and he'd be sitting on a stump. But if you looked around you'd see any number of cords of wood, more than one hundred cord cut that very morning. But as soon as you'd leave, you'd hear all those axes going again. (38)

On the water as well as in the woods, Skidmore seemed able to secure more than the next man. In an afternoon he caught easily twelve times as many fish as the next man. Nor did he need power or sail to get him where he was going: "One time someone saw Skidmore going across this creek standing on a board. He didn't have a paddle or anything and it was a calm day and there he stood on that board, his hands in his pockets going right along. They say he was evading the law."

Apparently, the law got after him more than once.

Now another story I heard was that Skidmore had committed a crime. And in those days they used to have those old carriages. Well, this sheriff had him handcuffed in this carriage and he was taking him to jail. Well, he looked down the road in front of him and there was Skidmore in front of him calling, 'Look at me, here I go down the road.' And there wasn't any way he could have gotten out of there, and when the sheriff got to the jail, Skidmore was sitting right there and he said, 'O.K., lock me up.' (38)

No one knew whether or not the devil ever came to carry Skidmore off when he died, as he did with most victims who contracted with him. But with a man named Travis on Tangier Island there was no doubt about what happened to his soul:

Now my great grandmother told me this one. There was a man named Travis who lived over on Tangier Island and he never made enough money to even give his family the

155

bare necessities. It was a hand to mouth thing with him. And so one night when everyone had gone to bed, this old man was sitting by the fireplace smoking his pipe when there came this rap at the door. When the old man got up and opened the door, in walked this strange man. He said, 'Why is it that you can't get ahead in the world? If you will meet me at Job's Cove tomorrow night at midnight I will tell you how you can have everything you want.'

So he went to Job's Cove the next night, and that was the first time he realized he was meeting the devil. So the devil told him if he would bury two brown pennies, he would have a talk with him. When the man did the devil said, 'Now, my friend, you have sold your soul to me.'

The old man had communion with the devil several times later in his life, but he prospered beyond his wildest dreams. And when he came upon his sick bed to die, all his neighbors and friends were there in the room helping to care for him when in walked this strange man who had appeared before, and he picked that old man up right off of his bed and walked out of there. Everyone knew it was the devil, and there wasn't any funeral or anything. (21)

George Bender of Hebron sold his soul to Old Scratch to become a horse gambler. He never held much respect in the community as being a "believer," and when he bet on horses he always won. But people noticed that while he stood watching the races, two colored men always came and stood beside him, and when they did his horse immediately pulled out in front of the field. Bender's neighbor was a waterman and one time on a passage down the Bay he was startled to see George Bender at the reins of a carriage drawn by two black horses, scudding over the water. When he called to him, Bender's cry came back over the water: "I'm George Bender, I'm dead and I'm on my way to hell." And when he returned home he found Bender had died that very day.

Not many outsmarted the devil, but Molly Horn was one.

Now Molly Horn was supposed to be a very shrewd

156

and wicked person. She even made an agreement with him so they could farm together. Molly said she would farm and they would split the crop in half. They agreed that the first year Molly would take what grew in the ground and the Devil would have what grew on top.

So the first year Molly planted white potatoes and when they harvested the crop, Molly got the potatoes and the Devil got the roots. The next year the Devil wanted what grew in the ground and said Molly was to have what grew on top. So that year Molly planted peas and beans, and she picked the peas and gave the Devil the roots. And he had nothing again and he was disgusted.

So he and Molly met in the Northwest River in Dorchester County and they got into a terrible argument. Molly hit the Devil, and skidded him across the marsh to the edge of the water. Then the Devil stood up and shook the mud out of his shirttail and made Devil's Island, and div overboard and made Devil's Hole. (39)

An old Negro man near Cambridge needed his wife's help to get him out of a contract with the devil. When the devil bargained for the old man's soul, he grew afraid and ran to his wife crying. She said she would fix the old devil and she rolled herself in tar and feathers and went out to meet him. The devil appeared and walked around the creature muttering, "It sometimes looks like fowl, it sometimes looks like people," whereupon he became alarmed, climbed the nearest tree, and disappeared in a puff of smoke.

A man in the "Neck" district of Dorchester County did not get off so easily:

One time this man who lived down in the "Neck" wanted some gold, and he swore he would give his soul if he could have some. Well, that night a strange man appeared to him and told him to hang his boots upright against the wall and he would get the gold he wanted. So that night he would get the gold he wanted. So that night he hung up his boots like he'd been told, and the next morning he came downstairs and they were full of gold. And whenever he needed money he would just hang his boots up that way and he'd find them full in the morning.

But by and by he got greedy and decided he'd cut the toes out of those boots when he hung them up. And the next morning when he came down, there was gold all over the floor of his house. But that man disappeared; the devil came and carried him off. And they say that you can't hang boots up in that house that way, 'cause something will come along and throw them down off the wall. (39)

On the marshy islands north of Tangier the devil appeared to Miss Christy in the form of a bull.

Now, she had some cattle up there and she went out one evening after those cows to bring them in so she could milk them the next morning and right in front of her there riz up a little black bull. And there weren't a bull on all of Shanks then. She said, 'Go away, devil, I don't want nothing to do with you,' and it disappeared, and she never saw it no more. And she always said it was nothing more than a little devil a-trying her out. (3)

The devil tried Lloyd McCready out too:

One night I'd been over to Ward's Crossing and I was coming home about twelve o'clock and up the road here they used to have a little stand where they kept the confectionary, ice cream and whatnot, but of course it was closed down. I was coming along there and all at once I happened to look over on the opposite side from where that stand was and a fire illuminated up right in this ditch.

So I said to myself, 'My God, I'll be darned if I'm not going to make out what this is.' And I had one of these little .22 revolvers so I walked over towards the ditch and looked at all this fire and then I started to hear chains a-rattling and I said, 'My God, that's the devil,' and I didn't even have strength enough to pull the trigger on that gun.

I took off out of there and I run all the way home and as I came into the yard I hollered, 'Mother, open the door,' and when I told her what had happened, she said, 'That's probably some of your meanness coming out in you.'

But the next day, I went back up there to figure out what I had seen and there wasn't a darn thing in that ditch that you could see but a deck of cards that had been torn into a thousand pieces. So I guess that really was the devil I saw that night, 'cause they say he's in cards. (40)

Witchcraft

Witchcraft lives in the white culture of the Eastern Shore much as it does in other areas: more in memory and tale than in fact. And it almost seems from the stories one meets with below the Choptank River that the witch served a psychological function as her legends grew.

Men always need scapegoats to pin their bad luck or hard times on, and more often than not it was easier to hang one's misfortunes on the local witch than on one's own foolishness or ineptitude.

Watermen frequently became witches' victims. A reputed witch in Hopewell took a strong dislike to a local man, and one day when he was out on the water she drew a picture of him and placed it just above the low tide line. The water came up and covered the picture; he fell overboard and drowned. Another old hag brought nothing but misery to Jim Cannon when his altruism ran dry:

Now this woman I'm gonna tell you about lived down in Hunting Creek on the Eastern Shore of Virginia. My grandmother said this was a true story. There was this waterman and his name was Jim Cannon and one day he was tying up at the wharf and this woman who they said was a witch came down there just as he come in. Well, he had two baskets of hard 'jimmie' crabs and a basket of fish. She came up to him

159

and she wanted that mess of fish. He said, 'Lady, to tell you the truth, I just got enough for myself, but I got some hard crabs. Do you want them?' They were good lively ones, too.

Well, she put her hand down in that mess of crabs and they all dropped their claws and every one of them died. She put a spell on those crabs. So he got mad when he saw he'd lost all that money and he started for home, and she said, 'You'll be sorry of this. Won't give me that mess of fish.'

That night he went down to the local store and on his way home she overtook him and turned him into a beast of burden of some sort, a horse or mule or something, and she rode him all the way down to Cape Charles, some hundred miles, through the marsh and brambles and bushes just to get some fish which he'd refused to give her. So when he come home he was all cut up with briars and everything and all out of breath so that his wife called the doctor.

The next day he got a gun shell, and he took all the shot out and he put in some small pieces of silver and he wadded it back in and he drawed picture of that old woman as best he could and he put that on the wall and shot at it. And a day or so after that she got sick and died, and they say where the silver hit that picture is where it hit her, in the legs, breast and stomach. (5)

A Hopewell woman delivered the same treatment to a man she disliked. She loaded her gun with a disintegrated dime, drew his picture on the wall, and blasted away. At that very moment he fell dead in the Hopewell railroad station. Yet another man in Crisfield got word that his wife was a witch and he tried to alleviate the situation the same way. He hung a replica of her on the wall, loaded his gun with silver shot, and fired. The fragments carried through the picture and the wall and hit his wife who was sitting in the next room.

On Tangier Island a local crone maimed the wrong victim.

No one ever crossed her because they knew she'd put a spell on them. But this one old fella said he wasn't afraid of any devil or anything. When he come in off the water one

160

day she asked him for some fish and he refused. She said he'd regret it, but he still didn't give her any fish.

Well, between the wharf where his boat was and his house, there was this well. As she passed by that well, he heard her mumble some words, but he didn't know she had cast a spell near that spot. You see, she thought he would be the first one to walk by there. But it took him a while to clean up his boat and his wife saw him from the house and came down there to meet him. As she crossed that spot near the well, she started screaming and hollering, and from that day on she was never right again. She became an invalid. That's what they say. (24)

In the Mount Vernon vicinity a Negro woman named Henny Furr provided the local conjuring. On one occasion the old woman bewitched two coon dogs so they turned on their own master and refused to let him back in his house. When Ely Taylor and John Cullen began fussing over a piece of land that lay between them, Cullen told Henny that if she did away with Taylor she could have the best cow in his pasture. So Henny went to a friend and between them they concocted a potion which Henny plunked into old man Ely's coffee next morning. But Ely's granddaughter drank it instead. She became suddenly sick and began to vomit up snakes, and when she defecated she passed more snakes. The doctor's medicine failed to heal the girl, and her father ran down to another local conjurer. She told him that to figure out the mystery she needed an envelope, a pound of ten-penny nails and a pint of whiskey. When he returned with them, she took a meat platter, put the nails in the envelope and placed that on the platter, and then put the whiskey on top of everything and stuck a match to it. It all burned down, and there on the platter was the replica of John Cullen and Henny Furr.

"There," said the conjurer, "is the trouble with your daughter. Now take this whiskey bottle and bury it in Henny's yard and it will kill her cow and she won't bother you any more." It worked.

Another of Henny's neighbors fumed night after night about some animal eating his cabbage heads. After he took his gun and wounded the creature which stumbled off into the wood, it was rumored and later confirmed that Henny Furr was home in bed filled with shotgun pellets.

Unaccountable incidents also transpired at Head-of-the-Creek. Levin Robb's grandmother stood in her doorway one day as the lady next door came by. When the old woman shook her arms back and forth, Robb's grandmother found her own arms paralyzed. She immediately sent for the local "high john" who sprinkled dust around and uttered something incomprehensible, and that night her paralysis vanished.

Bokker Mills drove his two mules and wagon near the scene of a recent fatal accident. Strange voices issued from the side of the road and his mules halted. He backed up and tried again with no better luck. When he walked to the edge of the road and called the dead man's name, his mules moved on without hinderance.

Supposedly, after the Civil War, a Georgia witch chased a Maryland veteran all the way back to Head-of-the-Creek, cornered him one night, threw a saddle over him and rode him till she found a duck's nest. There she made him eat twelve rotten duck eggs while she raked him across the back with a bull briar, and he spent the next day picking the thorns out of his back.

Crisfield had its spate of witches. Older residents there still remember seeing the manes of horses plaited so the witches could use them for stirrups. Just south of town lived an old crone named Hanna Reedy. She tried to bewitch Harold Hammond's mother. The sorceress stuck a bottle of pins in the trash can and when the trash was illuminated the bottle exploded and the pins stuck into Mrs. Hammond.

Aunt Hanna also evoked suspicion with her miraculous traveling habits. A Crisfield couple in a horse and buggy passed the old woman walking twice while on the road to Pocomoke City. And when they finally arrived in town, they found Aunt Hanna, her shopping half accomplished. Likewise, no one could account for Hanna's remarkable productivity, until one morning several neighbors passed by her house and saw her sitting at her spinning wheel in the doorway of her cottage. When they returned several hours later, Hanna stood out in her garden picking tomatoes, but in the doorway stood the spinning wheel spinning away.

Midwives in Crisfield possessed occult powers and their

curses sometimes lasted a lifetime. Avalon Riggin's grandmother neglected to employ the usual midwife for one of her twelve children. She rued her decision, for though her other offspring lived robust healthy lives, this child was crippled for life. And years later the father was digging around in the brick of the chimney and he located a strange bag full of fingernail clippings, hairs and clothing patches, and these, they concluded, were the ingredients the midwife had used to bring about her spell.

A Venton woman suffered the spell of old Aunt Evelyn. When she stumbled and fell twice on her way to work one morning, she returned home and discovered a basket full of medicine bottles filled with a murky substance. After she emptied the bottles she had no further trouble. A Venton farmer's livestock suffered even worse from Aunt Evelyn's annoyance. His sow bore a litter and the witch demanded the pick. The farmer refused, whereupon one small pig died each day thereafter until only the sow remained and she turned senselessly round and round in her pen. The farmer, resigned to the events, thought he would put the pig out of its misery, so he struck her across the back with a fencepost. The pig immediately recovered and the farmer learned the following day that Aunt Evelyn lay at home, deathly ill with a broken back.

In similar fashion, a Hebron man awoke one night to find himself crushed face down in the bed by an invisible pressure. With all his energy he gave a violent heave and he heard something hit the floor and utter a long groan. The next morning he encountered Aunt Liza, long suspected as a witch, holding her back and conversing with his mother. When asked what the trouble was, Liza claimed she had fallen in her attic, but the story failed to hold up because her house had no attic.

A Salisbury family found something was worrying their meat out in the smoke house. When they found a black cat in the salt barrel, they struck off one of its claws, and a week later they learned that a neighbor had recently had her arm amputated. A Cambridge lady cut a black cat with her knife after it bothered her night after night, and shortly thereafter she noticed her neighbor, whom she had entertained qualms about, had a long scar on her leg.

Cambridge had other illustrious crones. Aunt Phoebe asked

Mrs. Parker for three of her Rhode Island Reds. Refused, she went away muttering, and the following day, Mrs. Parker noticed that three of her choice chickens had died during the night. Another Cambridge witch discovered stealing chickens brought uncomfortable reprisals. A farmer outside the town noticed that his chicken stock gradually diminished, and everytime he noticed a disappearance, he also spied a black cat in the vicinity. One morning he cornered the cat and threw her into a bonfire. Two days later he went to talk to one of his sharecropper's wives only to find she was indisposed. Suspicious, he entered her room, pulled back the covers, and there she lay without any skin on her at all, just raw flesh.

There were numerous ways of detecting and preventing witchcraft. In Princess Anne, a pan of cold water under the bed kept witches off. Fearful believers in the Salisbury region sprinkled salt around the house, or wore a lodestone in a Bull Durham tobacco bag over their heart to keep free from the occult. Around White Haven a broom across the door at night sufficed. By the time the witch finished counting all the straws it was morning. Out on Tangier Island the wary hung a flour sifter over the door. The witch balked at entering because she knew she must go through every hole in that sifter before she could depart. On Cash Corner outside of Crisfield, the de-witching process required more elaborate protocol. If bewitched, one took a nail and stuck it into a live tree, and went and tapped on that nail for nine straight mornings, finally driving it all the way in the last day. Then the spell would subside. Similarly, other Cash Corner residents placed a board with nails driven into to it, points up, on their chests at night to keep witches from riding them. A short tale from Cambridge confirms the efficacy of yet another procedure.

My mother told me about this woman who didn't like her when she was small. They said this woman was a witch and mother said she used to come in and ride her night after night, and she couldn't get any sleep. So my mother decided to fix her.

My grandmother told my mother what to do. She put a fork underneath the rocking chair, and when that woman came over my mother made sure she sat in that rocking

164

chair. She stayed there quite a while and when it came time for her to go home, she couldn't get out of that chair even though there was nothing holding her that anyone could see. Well, my mother got her to promise to stop making those nightly visits to the house and they would let her go, and when she promised, my grandmother took that fork away, and that old witch went home. (39)

Spectral Sights and Sounds

In rural communities long gaps often exist between houses. Roads are sometimes dirt and overhung with heavy foliage. Cemeteries intervene. There is a loneliness that pervades the lower Eastern Shore between towns and gives rise to legends and stories of supernatural occurrences. There is perhaps even a deeper loneliness that wraps itself around the island cloisters that huddle off the Crisfield shore, eight or ten miles to the west. It is a solitude born out of a maritime existence, for the Bay itself gives up strange sights and unaccountable sounds. The fog or the early morning mist of a false dawn makes known objects seem unreal; familiar landmarks loom hideously distorted; buoys look like men; land-formations look like ships; and even the crewman in his oilskins up in the forward part of the ship may resemble a figure from another world as he goes about his duties. Even the seasoned waterman admits there are things he has witnessed that offer no explanation. Tales that emanate from the life on the water reflect an uncertainty, and in the tale-teller's attempt to explain the unexplainable he draws heavily on traditional legendry.

On the East Coast of this country, no one legend so clings to the mariner's imagination as that of the phantom ship. Cotton Mather spoke of a phantom ship in New Haven Harbor as early as the 17th century, and since then every coastline state in New England has boasted one or more phantom vessels over the years. It is not surprising to find that Smith Island fosters such a legend.

Now Captain Lacey Tyler used to tell me this. He used

165

to live up there in an area called Sinner's Cove, that's near Foggs Point, and he said that there were certain times of the year, usually on pretty moonlit nights, a British man-of-war hove into sight near Foggs Point. And over the water you could hear the voice of the captain giving orders to his men. And just as plain would come the sound of a block and sheet rope and a traveler rod. After a while, when they went into the wind, the sailors started playing a martial air, one of the British Navy tunes, and that sounded just as clear, that's what he said. If you looked at that vessel, between the Bay and the moon, you could see—there was no doubt about it, she was a square rigged vessel. And he said, for a while it frightened the people when they saw that ship, but it came frequently enough that they just took it as part of their life. (25)

Other watermen encountered mysterious apparitions. A Tangierman went hook and line fishing one evening and a corpse drifted up against his boat. He pulled the man aboard, stripped him of his attractive coat, and when he finished for the evening, took the body ashore and buried it. Two nights later the image of the drowned man appeared to him asking for the coat. When this happened three nights in a row, the waterman threw the coat at the spectre saying, "Take your damned old coat, I don't want it."

Captain Will Dashnell was anchored in Teague Creek one night with no one else on board. While resting after supper, he distinctly heard a man come aboard, and the boat began to tremble all over. But when he went on deck, he found no one. When this happened three times, he pulled his anchor and headed back to Deal Island. Precisely the same thing happened to Clifton Webster and his father, Richard, while anchored in Stumpy Cove. Yet, again, no one on board could explain the puzzling circumstances.

Still another Deal Island crew confronted the same situation while in a New Jersey port, but they solved the problem:

These boys from here went up to New Jersey one time

and they were aboard the boat sleeping one night, anchored off the shore a ways so that you had to use the skiff to go in and out with. Well, there were about six or seven of them on board, and one of them had gone ashore and they were waiting for him. But it got late so they went to bed. They knew he'd be back soon.

So by and by they heard the rowboat a-coming, and it come right alongside and they heard the oars thrown up on the deck and heard him come aboard and come aft all the way to the cabin, and they even heard the handle turn, and that was that. Not a sound more. So a couple of them went up on deck and looked all around, but they couldn't find anything, and they come back down and went to bed again.

Pretty soon the same thing again; they heard the rowboat row right up alongside and the oars come over onto the deck and he come back to the cabin door. They heard him walk right across the deck. But when they went out, there was nothing at all. So the captain said, 'Boys, I think we've anchored over a drowned man's corpse, and I believe we'd better move this vessel if we want to get any sleep.'

So they all got out of bed and went up and they moved that boat, and they never had any more trouble that night, or the whole time they were in that harbor. (42)

Wherever maritime stories and beliefs have been gathered, folklorists have found that mariners believe implicitly in the existence of good vessels and bad vessels. Some ships, no matter where they go, what they freight, or what they fish, inevitably turn a profit. Other vessels, no matter how hard they are driven and no matter how precious their cargo, seem fated to bear only frustration for their owners and sometimes death to their crews. One of the worst omens a crew could encounter was a specter aboard their ship. Gorman Tull faced the situation twice. One time he and a young friend went to Baltimore to pick up a boat to oyster in.

We got up there and this old man, Tom Bacher, said, 'Boys, we got a nice boat for you. Her name's the *William B.*

167

Thomas. She'll catch you plenty of oysters, don't you worry about that.'

But when we got out of office this other fella said, 'Let me tell you something before you go and get drownded. I wouldn't go anywhere in that boat.' Well, we went down there and we overhauled her and she seemed all right, but her sails were busted out some.

So after we got her all ready to go, this same fella came down there and said, 'You're not going aboard of that boat, full of all those ghosts?'

I said, 'Hell, there's no ghost aboard of this boat.'

So we went on down the Bay, and she was a nice boat, didn't leak a drop. But the first night when we were anchored something funny happened. It was a slick calm and we were sitting down below, Smitty and I, everything in shape, and I said to Smitty, 'I don't find a damn wrinkle in her.'

Pretty soon that vessel began to roll like you've never seen, all around, from side to side. We could hardly stand up, and it was a calm night. Well, I went up on deck and looked around and I didn't see a thing. Nothing. Beautiful night the stars out and this vessel rolling around for no reason.

So when she calmed down I went below and started to go to bed. But she started to roll again and this time I got mad. I went up on deck and said, 'All right, whoever you are, let go of the anchor, throw your dredges overboard, pull them in; just be sure you got me a load of oyster in the morning, 'cause I'm going to bed. And you know, we never had any more trouble with the boat after that.

But afterwards we learned that before we got her she'd drownded the whole crew and they never told us that in Baltimore. (2)

Tull had equally bad luck aboard the *Fannie Daugherty*:

Now I'll tell you something else that happened. This was on the *Fannie Daugherty*. We lost a man overboard, a colored man, on Snake Rip, and all the crew that were

168

aboard that boat left me and went back to Baltimore, even one fellow I had with me for four years.

The reason that man went overboard wasn't really my fault. I told him to walk in the middle of the deck; we had oysters piled up on both sides, but he started to climb over them and the oysters slid and he went overboard. Well, all the crew left after that, but it wasn't long before one of them come back, John Miles, and he come aboard and said, 'Captain, I got to studying this whole matter and I don't think you were wrong. You told him to stay off those oysters and he didn't do it. If you want me to scrape up a crew, I think I can. They're a lot of fellows at home who ain't got nothing to do this winter.'

Well, after Christmas he come back and he brought a crew with him. So we went off oystering and we were doing fine for about three weeks when one morning this fella come back for breakfast and said, 'Captain, I seen a nigger jump overboard right here last night.'

I said, 'Why, man, you're crazy as the devil, you black boys always believe in ghosts.'

A couple of days later he come to me and said, 'Captain, I saw that man again, and this time he went over the stern.'

Well, I said, 'At least he's getting farther away, maybe next time you won't see him at all.'

He said, 'Captain, I know one thing, this boat ain't right, there's something wrong aboard here.'

Well, after that things calmed down and we didn't have anymore trouble, so that spring I sold the boat to Captain Walter Hard. I saw him about a year or so later after the oystering season was all through and I asked him, said, 'Captain, did you ever see any ghosts aboard the *Fannie Daugherty?*'

He said, 'No, I never seen a ghost, but one night four of my crew and I saw the biggest black snake on board that you ever saw in your life, When somebody yelled that there was a black snake on board, I got the hand spike to kill him but before I could get to him he disappeared down the blowhole.'

I said, 'Captain, are you sure that wasn't a sea serpent?'

He said, 'No sir, it was a black snake and it was just as big around as my arm, and when I come after him with that handspike, he went down the blowhole. But what I can't understand, is what a black snake was doing out there on deck in the middle of winter with a fourth inch of ice over that whole deck?' (2)

In general, ghosts assume different shapes when they return from the dead. They appear as shadowy wraiths or filmy forms that can pass through tangible objects without discomfort. Or they may return from the grave in more corporeal forms such as skeletons or semi-decayed corpses to work their malevolence. Most Eastern Shore specters fit the former description, though the ghosts are more often than not recognizable. Not infrequently the wraith returns on a mission of some sort. On Tangier Island, Miss Christy's son came back, it seems, simply to satisfy his mother. She prayed night after night to have her Tom appear, and finally one night after she retired, there came a knock at the door:
"If that's you, Tom, come in."
And with that the inner door opened rather slowly and Miss Christy pulled the covers up over her head in a fright and never prayed to see Tom again.

In Meekings Creek, near Cambridge, George Robbs' grandmother refused to return to the house where she lived with her first husband, because he invariably appeared to molest her. In Mount Vernon, Lelia Johnson's aunt died and left a small daughter. During a thunderstorm one afternoon the child was playing outside her grandmother's house. When she entered the house she said, "Grandmam, I seen Mom out there and she said she's going to take me with her." The following day the old woman went into the yard. There she found her daughter's grave open, the coffin visible. And in less than a month, the child was dead.

Not always was the ghost bent on such lethal purposes however:

Now back in the old days around Marion here, it used to be that when somebody died you always papered and painted their rooms over again. Well, old Lem's father-in-law died and they papered his room over again. They slept up-

170

stairs and that night after they went to bed they woke up and it sounded just like a fight was going on downstairs.

Well, Lem's wife called him and told him to go find out what was wrong. Lem said, 'Damned if I'm going down there, that's Cap'n Dave raising hell.' So the next morning they got up and went down to the room where he'd been staying and there was the paper, torn right off the walls and piled in the middle of the floor. Old Lem's always said that the old man just didn't like the paper he found on the wall and came back to change it. (21)

Strange and sometimes headless females inhabit the marshes of the Eastern Shore. Almost too well-known to bear repeating is the legend of Big Liz who has frightened visitors to Gum Briar Swamp for more than thirty years. The Big Liz legend turns on a buried treasure belief. According to Mary Pinkett, a slave owner hid his horde in the swamp and to insure its safety, cut off the head of one of his slaves and buried her with it. Her specter, head in hand, still haunts the swamp and guards the treasure, and the tradition has been kept active by teenagers who delight in driving to the DeCoursey Bridge at night to see Big Liz. They perform a ritual. The horn is sounded six times, the lights blinked three times, and with that Big Liz emerges from the swamp and approaches the car. Invariably the car fails to start the first try, and as the wraith nears the vehicle, the vehicle coughs into action and the occupants speed away to safety.

Smith Island storytellers also foster a tale about a headless woman:

One time way back when the island was being settled there was this man who for some reason cut off his wife's head. And ever since then she has been coming back from the dead to have him convicted. And every fall on a full moon, just once a year, that headless woman, dressed all in white appears by the coffin house in Ewell where they keep all the coffins, and she walks from the coffin house over the little footbridge there, and then turns around and goes back. Everyone was always afraid of that coffin house. No one wanted to go near it at night especially. (1)

At times there were ghosts who returned for benevolent purpose. Near the Catholic Church in Golden Hill the female apparition is a lovely woman dressed in black. Motorists affirm that if your car breaks down in the vicinity, she approaches carrying a lantern, taps you on the shoulder and refuses to depart until the car is repaired.

And in Crisfield, the ubiquitous tale of the ghostly hitchiker surfaces:

Now the fellow that told me this said it was a positive fact. I don't know exactly where it was, but there was this salesman who was driving from one town to another and it was dark and he wanted to get into town and get to a hotel. No motels in those days. Well, he come to this bend in the road and there was a guard wire stretched along there, and he saw this young woman stoop under that wire and flag him down. He stopped and asked her what she wanted and she asked for a ride into the town where he was going and she gave him the address of her home and then got in the back seat.

Well, this man began to talk to her, but he didn't get any answer at all and by and by he looked on the back seat and there was no one there. He stopped the car and got out and searched that car but nobody was there. He couldn't figure it out at all, how that woman could have got out of his car without his hearing her.

So then he got curious; he decided to go to that address that she had given him to see if he could find out anything. When he got there, he saw a little light on in the house. It was a dim light way upstairs. He shut off his motor and went up to the door and knocked and finally an old grey-headed man came down to the door with a light in his hand, and he said, 'What can I do for you?'

'Well,' this fella said, 'I've had a funny experience and it got on my nerves, and I don't know what to do about it. I was coming round this corner outside of town heading this way and a young woman got underneath of the guard wire on the road and flagged me down and asked me to bring her to this street number. I said I would and she got

172

in and I began to talk to her, and when I looked around, she was gone.'

'How was she dressed?' And the salesman told him. She had on such and such.

'Oh my God,' said the old man, 'that was my daughter and she was killed on that very spot one year ago tonight at this hour.' (26)

Between Langralls Island and Savanna, car lights appear but no car follows them. Several people have witnessed the strange sight. Driving along the marsh road where no turn-off exists, motorists suddenly see two headlights coming down the road. Motorists have even pulled off to the side of the road and waited, but no car appears and the lights gradually vanish.

A rash of haunted houses and strange noises afflict the Eastern Shore and spark the repetoires of local storytellers. In Tyaskin, Anette Hand's father moved into a house that had a long-standing reputation for being haunted. Families had moved in and out of it for years. After a few weeks strange noises issued from the attic. On successive nights the sounds got closer, coming down the attic steps. Finally one night, the father grabbed a lantern to seek the cause of the disturbance and he met a huge rat on the attic stairs. When he kicked at the creature, it vanished, but the following day he had to be treated for a broken foot. A week later the family vacated the house.

In Hoopersville, a local house carried an apparent curse with it as well as a poltergeist. For a number of years residents in the home complained of unaccountable sounds, thumping footsteps in the night, doors opening and closing for no reason at all. If every door were locked and barred before the family retired, they would be all swinging wide open in the morning. And a series of calamities furthered suspicion about the quarters. One man who lived there a short time lost his mind, a young girl died of tuberculosis and another resident perished when something went awry during his tonsillectomy. Two other occupants died mysteriously, one from an undiagnosed disease, the other from a terrible headache he contacted one night lying in bed. Later, when the home was vacant, two women came to look it over. When they entered the kitchen, they admired a splendid

173

pitcher that sat on the table next to a man's hat. When they returned from looking upstairs, the pitcher lay under the table, smashed in a thousand pieces, and the hat sat beside it, turned upside down. Not a sound had been heard while they were in the house.

Similarly, the Horsey place below Crisfield held the questionable distinction of being spooked. It was an old house and residents religiously claimed that there was a certain brass door that could not be kept shut under any circumstances. Out in back of the house was a huge willow tree and from time to time members of the family spied a strange man standing beside it. When a young boy took a shot at the elusive form, he found nothing when he inspected his results, and later received a firm lecture from his father on the inadvisability of shooting at ghosts.

A dwelling behind the Asbury Church cemetery near Crisfield was the home of the Parks family for a while and the family were firmly convinced that they shared it with spirits. One night when Mrs. Parks woke up, she distinctly saw a red-haired woman standing at the foot of her bed. When she pinched her husband, he woke up and hollered, "Oh for God's sake, Lizzie, what's the matter," and before she could tell him the specter evaporated. One Sunday morning Mrs. Parks heard a dreadful noise as if someone had struck the water tank outside. But when she looked she saw nothing. Presently, while she and her mother sat at the kitchen table talking, a terrible banging occurred at the stairway door accompanied by some hard panting. Again, investigation proved nothing. But it was not long after that that the Parks family readied another home.

Other strange sounds panicked rational people and made homelife generally unpleasant. For a long time a three story brick building on Shoal Creek used to be referred to by natives as the proverbial "haunted house." It was an old house with walls more than sixteen inches thick, but even through all that brick came the strange cries of someone in desperate pain. Occupants complained of the disturbances only to learn several conflicting explanations from the natives. Some said the old house was at one time a way-station for Patty Canon while she trafficed in slaves sent up and down the Eastern Seaboard. Others avowed that the screams issued from a young girl whose father

174

did not approve of the man she wished to marry, and so deposited her in a cupboard in the wall where she eventually perished. Neither explanation hushed the noises, and residents, up until a few years ago, still heard the fearful sounds.

Graveyard visits provoked inexplicable events. It was after a long hike near Fishing Creek that Randy Robbs' father and some friends found themselves in a graveyard surrounded by woods. They began to explore when a tombstone picked itself up out of the ground and came hurtling towards them, breaking trees and branches and everything in its path. They fled in terror.

In nearby Hoopersville, Hal Parker's sister lay deathly ill in bed while he tried to console her. To ease the situation, he told her that the first to die would make every effort to return from the dead an notify the other. A good while after the girl died Hal was walking home after an argument with his girl and he remembered his sister's promise. He walked to the family graveyard and sat on her vault and said, "O.K. if you're coming back, come on." With that a thunderous noise echoed from the vault and Hal sped for home. But ever after he wished he had stayed to see what his sister would say.

Spectral horses fused with human phantoms to produce wonder among witnesses. Just above Belle Haven, Virginia, a stream used to cut across the old stage road so if one came by on horseback he had to ford the stream. A highwayman attacked a man there one night, robbed him and cut off his head. And for a long time afterwards, even after a bridge was built, people approaching that spot claimed they encountered a headless horseman who followed them to the stream at full gallop and hurled his head at them.

When Ralph Potter was left alone in the family house near Princess Anne, he wandered out alone only to be chased back home by a headless horse pulling a cart with a man in it. Similarly, one misty morning a group of men started off from Dames Quarter to go tonging. As they stood on the wharf, down the road came a horse and carriage. It drove right out onto the wharf and plunged overboard, and every waterman watching agreed that the rider had no head at all. The omen was obvious and not a man went tonging that morning.

Out on Smith Island along the road between Ewell and

175

Rhodes Point a herd of headless horses has been seen. Islanders who have walked the road after dark tell of hearing the hooves of horses come crashing up behind them at a great speed, and just as they cross the bridge the herd thunders on before them. Some claim that when they reach home they have heard those horses grazing nearby.

Other Eastern Shoremen met spectral dogs. Near Dames Quarter, Daniel Messicks and his father were returning from an aunt's one evening when they encountered a huge dog in their path. When the boy went to pat the animal, his father pulled him off and kicked at it, but his foot went right through the dog as though it were air, and it vanished. With John Palin of Vienna the same experience resulted in a token. On his way to work one morning a strange dog followed him for about 500 yards and suddenly disappeared. When he arrived for work, he learned that his employer had died that very morning.

East New Market in Dorchester County, Maryland

Belief Tales and Popular Belief

With the belief tale the folklorist faces an even more fluid item of oral tradition than the legend. Belief tales, like legends, sometimes spring from folk motifs, but more often they appear as the narrative elaboration of a folk belief or superstition. It is a well-recorded belief among watermen on the Bay, for instance, that painting a boat blue will summon the worst kind of luck. If one were simply collecting Eastern Shore beliefs and practices and asked a waterman what would happen if he painted his boat blue, the response would doubtless be stated succinctly: "If you paint a boat blue, you're going to have nothing but bad luck." But among the watermen themselves, the belief usually appears in the context of short stories or memorates, such as these from a Deal Island informant:

Now this one time I started out the season and I painted my boat out of blue paint, fore and aft. And I went up the Bay oystering. Well, in the first week it happened: I tore my sail up. The second week, I had done, I broke my crank shaft on the winders. The third week, I carried my mast off. Now this is true. And so I said to Willie Thomas who was with me: 'Willie, there's something to this blue paint. I'll never, as long as I live, paint another boat out of blue paint.'

Now this other fella, John Webster, he sold his boat to a man, and he painted her blue before he left the harbor. The natives here said, 'You'll never get that boat to Baltimore. You're going to lose her before you get her there.' Well, he got halfway up the Bay and he got some water in her and so he headed for the western side of the Bay and he lost her before he got to Baltimore. (16)

These belief patterns work differently in different life styles. For this Deal Island waterman, his two accounts furnish proof positive of the inadvisability of striking out against tradition. Probably he would use his stories in a didactic way to admonish a younger man should the proper occasion arise, yet like most men he would never consider himself a superstitious person. On the other hand, there are people who proudly admit to being superstition prone. Carrie Boog, for example, has been written up in the Salisbury, Maryland papers as one who knows and practices a host of folk beliefs, and as students of mine who have collected from her have found, she is not in the least shy about admitting it.

More common, though, is the informant who has absorbed traditional folk beliefs without realizing it. A conversation with a Crisfield woman bears this out. She began our interview by stating categorically that the last thing she was, was superstitious. Then our talk took a rather interesting turn.

> Well, if you don't believe in that sort of thing, perhaps you remember some of the things the older people around here believed and practiced.
>
> Yes, that I do.
>
> Did you ever hear it said that if you heard an owl hoot it was a sign of death?
>
> Why yes, of course; now that's true. I know. There's a little owl that comes and sits in a tree outside my window and hoots at night, and every time he does that, I always hear in a week or so that someone in the family has died. That's the way it happens. Now that's a fact.

The Waterman's Way

One group who absorbed folk belief easily were the men who followed the water. Not surprisingly. When a sailor realized that only a plank lay between him and eternity he inevitably

178

sought ways of thwarting the fates, and what he turned to, to secure his safety were traditional practices. Blue water sailors of past centuries accumulated vast numbers of traditions which operated so imperceptibly but crucially in their lives that they often determined whether men lived or drowned. Sailors, for instance, convinced that a ship was a "bad" or unlucky vessel, would fatalistically despair more readily when the ship became endangered and begin praying rather than leaning on the pumps. And conversely, men aboard a lucky ship, knowing she was lucky, would not fear danger so immediately and attend more to the task of getting the vessel out of peril. Furthermore, the lucky ship would be more likely to attract the best sailors, while the unlucky one signed on seamen who could not get hire elsewhere, and thus her fate was sealed just that much more securely.

Today on the Bay, belief patterns still play a part in the everyday life of the watermen, but the old practices do not find so many ready converts among the younger generation as they once used to. A personal experience may serve to illustrate this.

In March, 1968, I went oystering for a day aboard a skipjack from Deal Island. At that time she was oystering out of Annapolis, taking her catch from the oyster rocks near the Bay Bridge. Aboard were a white captain, three white crew members and two black, all from Deal Island. Among the crew were the captain's older brother, a man in his early sixties, and the captain's youngest son who was obviously being groomed to take over the boat when the captain himself gave up the water.

About eleven o'clock that morning, as the boat eased across the top of an oyster rock, the starboard dredge struck something solid on the bottom and broke its frame. Replacing the dredge meant removing the forward hatch cover and bringing up another one from the hold. The captain's son turned to the task, took the hatch cover off and purposely turned it upside down on the deck, a practice that is widely known to draw bad luck. But no sooner had the boy done this than the captain's brother walked over and turned the hatch cover right side up, whereupon the youth scoffed at him roundly for believing "in all that nonsense."

Later in the afternoon the wind dropped out completely

and brought the dredging to a halt temporarily. As we lay there and rolled back and forth waiting for something to spring up, the captain's son again spoke to his uncle: "Go on, Lenwood, why don't you throw some money overboard so we can get a little wind. You believe in that sort of thing." Naturally, in the course of a shipboard conversation another widespread belief surfaced, but there was little doubt that the context in which it came up revealed a decided gap between generations, for the boy made his remarks in a teasing tone. Though conversant with the old belief patterns, he had come to suspect their efficacy.

To use this instance as typical of the breakdown of maritime beliefs on the Eastern Shore is not wholly fair. It supposes, in effect, that all old people are superstitious and that all young people are practical and rational; and this is just not so. I have encountered a number of young people from the lower Eastern Shore who, if they don't actually believe the supernatural yarns of their elders, have supplanted them with belief tales of their own. By the same token, older people may be conversant with a traditional practice, and yet have reservations about its efficacy. In talking to Captain Al Wheatley on Tangier Island, I inquired:

> Captain, have you ever heard about something they call "buying the wind" around here?
> Yes, I've heard people say if you throw a penny overboard there'd come a breeze. I don't know if it really works.
> Have you ever tried it?
> Yeah, I done it once over here in Pocomoke Sound and there come a nice little breeze. But that didn't have nothing to do with that.

This brief conversation not only tells us something about Al Wheatley's personal reaction to a traditional practice, but it also suggests the waterman's reliance on the forces of nature. Wind on the Bay has always been essential to the watermen's success. In another era they pushed their trade in schooners and pungy boats, bugeyes and skipjacks, all vessels of sail. Old men in Crisfield remember with a dash of nostalgia when the mouth of the Little Annamessex River was crowded with sails and the harbor itself so clogged with wind ships that one could literally walk across it stepping from deck to deck. As workboats, the pungies and schooners and bugeyes are all gone now, but unlike any other maritime area in this country, the Chesapeake Bay has oyster dredgers which are required by law to take their catch under sail at least three days a week, making the wind still an important factor.

Few watermen on the Bay have not heard of "buying the wind," and several anecdotes reveal that it was unwise to purchase too much. In one instance, when a Crisfield waterman found himself becalmed in Tangier Sound, he threw a dime over the side and called out, "Let me have a dime's worth." Immediately a gale sprang up and his boat was badly damaged trying to get back to the harbor. When he finally arrived a witness spied his craft: "My Lord, Captain, you've been out in a gale."

"Yes, and if I'd known the wind was that cheap, I'd never throwed that dime overboard."

An Elliott Island man was even more extravagant. He threw a quarter over the side and called for wind, whereupon a whirlwind tore out his mast.

Watermen knew other means for securing wind. Some drove a knife into the mast in the direction they wished the wind to blow. Others employed implements such as a pin:

Well, I don't know if this is a true story or not, but I've heard it told a couple of times. Bruce Baden was on the old bugeye *Triumph*—she was built around 1896—with old man Haney Warrick. They had been up the Bay to unload some wheat. Coming back from Annapolis, the Bay was calm as a dish, so old man Haney said, 'Let's see if we can get us a little wind.' So he stuck a pin in the mast. (Now I don't know what good that's supposed to do, but that's what they say.)

Bruce said, 'Scratch it a little bit.' Sure enough he scratched over where the pin was stuck in. That wind blew up as white as old Miss Higgerty's head. And it blew for three days without stopping. (24)

181

Another cycle of belief tales already mentioned surrounds watermen's superstitions concerning the color blue. Why blue has become associated with ill luck on the water is a question never definitively answered. One authority claims that vessels were never painted blue lest the ocean become jealous and exact retribution. Another source has speculated that since many of Britain's early seafaring enemies, such as the Spanish, frequently painted their ships blue, the color, when relative to things maritime, gradually became associated with ill omens; this tradition has carried down to the present day and is followed on the Eastern Shore and elsewhere along the Atlantic seaboard.

Apparently one did not have to paint his entire vessel blue to incur bad luck. Orin Talbot of Cambridge lent his boat to a man to sail to Baltimore. On his return, the boat sank, but Talbot wasn't at all surprised when he discovered that his friend had painted the bends blue. Similarly, a Western Shore waterman purchased a vessel, and no matter where he went he caught practically no fish. When he hauled her and scraped her down after the first season he discovered the reason: her bottom had been painted blue originally and some of the paint was still there. He took the boat down to the bare wood, repainted her and caught all the fish he could handle the following season.

With some watermen the suspicion of the color blue carried beyond just painting a boat. It affected the purchases they made. When Horace Webster showed Bing Tyler some brand new shirts that had just come into the store in Wenona, Bing wanted them in the worst way. "I want them sure; and I sure need them bad enough; but I just can't buy them 'cause they've got blue labels in them."

Ron Purnell witnessed a similar incident in Crisfield. Purnell for a number of years has run a machine shop, and among other things he turns out oyster tongs. He used to paint them blue until one day he was in a nearby hardware store when a waterman came in to make a purchase. He looked over Purnell's tongs which were on sale there: "Christ, these are just right." Then he examined a competitor's brand: "Now these cramp your hands; I can hardly use them they're so stiff, but I'm going to take them anyway. I don't take nothing aboard my boat that's painted blue." From that day on Purnell painted his oyster tongs with aluminum paint.

Another waterman in Crisfield simply asked that the color be changed.

> There was this fella from the island that came into a shop here on the street a few days ago and he wanted a wheelbarrow, one of these big heavy jobs. They're pretty expensive, but it was painted blue. Fella said, 'Damned if I'd have that to take aboard my boat or home for gift. I wouldn't expect to get home to the island. I'd twist the shaft off or throw a piston through the head or something. I don't want it. But I'll tell you what I'll do, I'll give you five dollars if you'll paint that red and I'll pick it up tomorrow when it's dry.' Now that was a pretty expensive wheelbarrow and he give him another five dollars to paint it red. 'Course the blue paint was still on it, but it was covered up with red. (4)

A comparable taboo observed by many watermen concerned taking black luggage aboard ship. Mamie Changer's father used to ferry people back and forth from Smith Island to the mainland. On one passage when he encountered violent weather, he went below and discovered a black satchel. He immediately purchased it from its owner, dumped the contents and threw it overboard. Pretty soon the sea subsided and they continued their voyage to Crisfield without mishap.

A black satchel in the hold might hamper fishing as well as spawn storms:

> Now there used to be a man by the name of Edmund Busell and he was fishing a big boat. It was a steamer, and he couldn't catch no fish. So he stepped up on deck one time and said, 'Every man that's got a black satchel down there in that forepeake, bring it on deck.' So they brought them on deck. 'Now,' he said, 'I'll give you a dollar a-piece to throw them overboard, everyone of them.' And that's what they did. He said, 'There ain't a man in this world can catch fish with all them black things down in the forepeake.'

183

Now when he did that, they commenced to catch some fish. (3)

For Otis Evans of Crisfield, the experience with black luggage was a personal one and suggests in part the way an individual might come to accept popular belief.

Well, now, nobody likes blue on the water, and they don't like black suitcases either. When I was living on Smith Island running to Washington, there was a lady whose folks lived on the western shore of Virginia, and at that season of the year we were buying our fish out of Reedsville, that's in the Great Wicomico River, about twenty-five miles from Smith Island as the crow flies.

Anyhow, she went down to my brother-in-law's early one morning with a black suitcase and he said to her, 'You're welcome to come across the Bay with me, but I'll be damned if I can carry a black suitcase aboard this boat.' (He'd had a lot of trouble with his boat. She'd been burned and he'd almost drowned.)

So she said, 'I can't go without my suitcase.' And she went back home and the following Sunday he asked me if she could go with me, and I said, 'Yes, certainly she can.' And when she come down Monday morning, I never knew anything about it, but I noticed she had a beautiful handbag. All these fancy creations. I didn't know that black suitcase was underneath it. But it was. She had simply covered it up. But nothing happened that time. Everything went along fine.

But later I did have one experience I didn't like. It was on a Monday and I was going to Reedsville to pick up some fish. And they were plentiful then. But I had to come back to Crisfield that night before I went to Washington, and on the way I looked over the side and there was this black suitcase and it was brand new and the buckles were sparkling. 'Well,' I thought, 'I can't pass that by; I'll stop and get it.' Well, to make a long story short, that was the worst run I ever had in the fish business. We couldn't sell nothing. I lost my shirt that time, and I said then that I'd never stop to pick up another black bag, no matter how many I came across. (4)

Certain watermen fear reprisal when other objects came aboard their boat. Black walnuts, for instance. Harry Webster's grandfather took his family out for the day on his boat. When they stopped to picnic, the children gathered walnuts, but their father made them throw then overboard before he started the short trip back to Deal Island.

Poor Harold Reedy suffered no little anguish because of his belief about walnuts.

This old waterman, Harold Reedy from over on Smith Island was having all the luck in the world crabbing one summer. He was having good luck and then all of a sudden that luck he was having was cut off, until some youngster over there told him some walnuts were aboard of his boat. These other watermen knew how Harold felt about walnuts and they planted some under his ceiling just as a joke. Well sir, Mr. Reedy practically tore his boat apart until he found those things, and until he found them, he couldn't catch one thing, not one thing. (24)

For Jonas Taylor of Rhodes Point, black-eyed peas were taboo on the water. One day he brought his wife over to the mainland to do some shopping and when she returned to the boat with a bag of them Taylor stopped her: "Those things will never go back aboard this boat. They're bad luck. If you want those black-eyed peas, the only way you'll get them to the island is put them on the mailboat."

Animals and birds also prognosticated good or bad fortune. Cats invariably triggered bad luck when brought aboard ship, and watermen avoided their presence when possible. Though undesirable on boats, cats on shore helped tell the tides. When their pupils enlarged, the tide was flooding, when they narrowed it was ebbing. And watermen might also determine which way the wind would blow if they noted the direction which a cat looked after it washed its face.

The actions of rats likewise indicated certain things to observant watermen. While Ed Parks' father was examining a bateau he planned to buy, he noticed a rat swimming away from her. "She don't leave this place," he told his son, and several weeks later when he saw the boat again she had opened up badly just above her waterline.

Crisfield watermen believed the number of crows that flew across the bow somehow determined the kind of luck one would have that day. If it was only one bird, there was really no need to continue, but if there were two crows, the boat would be full of seafood by sundown. The actions of seagulls likewise predicted what might befall a man on the water, as was the case with John father's porch and the colored fellow wouldn't go on board that boat. My grandfather said he was so scared he almost that point. Right near it, the kerosene lantern fell over and fellow to go with him and one day a seagull flew into my grand-Mile's grandfather who lived near Cambridge: he used to haul grain to Baltimore. He would hire a colored

Now the old man used to have a big three master, and turned white. And so the old man hired another fellow. But that colored fellow told them not to go out in the Bay. Not to go out past the point. My grandfather never did get past wreck of her out there. (36) that boat burnt right down to the water. You can still see the

A variety of other practices help Eastern Shoremen ward off bad luck on the water. Some watermen never venture out in their boat unless they have a flag flying from the craft. Elliott Islanders throw a cup of fresh water overboard into the salt water to insure a large catch. In the Cambridge area, one good way to produce ill tidings on a boat is to point the boat hook or the bristles on a broom towards the stern. And Crisfield crabbers aver that if you sweep your boat out after sundown you'll sweep all your luck away.

Out on Smith Island there were those who would never tie their boats up at night with the bow pointing towards the land, for to do so meant you would have to back out of your slip in

186

the morning, and surely, that would make things go backwards for you all day. Similarly, there were a great many watermen who, when they went out on the water in the false gray light of dawn, never turned back no matter what they had forgotten. Returning could only invite disaster. Still others who drew their living from the Bay insured the long-term luck of their boat by providing a wet launching or secreting a lucky coin in a particular part of the ship. In 1966, Charlie Little of Easton bought the *Shadow Walker*. She had been built on Hooper's Island forty-one years before. When he stripped her down and began to fix her up he discovered a two and a half dollar gold piece under her sampson post. Just for safe-keeping, he left it there when he restored the vessel.

Tokens

Unquestionably one of the most prevalent types of belief tale on the Eastern Shore deals with death omens. Known in the northeastern United States as "forerunners" and in the south as "tokens," these stories spring easily to storytellers' lips and are uttered most commonly as personal experiences or as accounts heard from very reliable sources. Not surprisingly, watermen's yarns included token narratives. Aboard ship in thick foggy weather, or in the dead of night, a man's eyes can play tricks on him and a wisp of mist can easily acquire the proportions of a man. Yet in some cases the coincidence of the apparition and the death of an individual defied a rational explanation. Miss Elizabeth Hall of Crisfield recalled an incident she had heard her grandfather, Captain Len Tawes, recount many times:

Well, this was one of his favorite stories and he used to tell it over and over. He was on a trip to Demerara and he had a Maryland crew on board at the time, and the mate was from around here somewhere, and he [the captain] noticed that the mate wasn't feeling well, and from the description it sounded like he might have had typhoid. It was a gradual thing. But he couldn't get him to a doctor after they left Baltimore. And on the way to Demerara he became more and more ill. And before reaching there he stayed in his cabin the whole time, and when they reached port, grandfather was so concerned he took him up to the hospital there.

Now this was in the summer in the rainy season and you couldn't leave the boat for hardly a minute and so he didn't go up to see him until he had to go. And when he went back he thought the man was so much better. He had all the faith in medicine you could have and as if by magic, this man who had felt so badly was so much better. And so he was very surprised when the English doctor there told him that the man was in no condition to make the trip. That he was a very sick man. And grandfather felt a great hurt and pain to have to leave him there in that strange place. It was a very upsetting and hard thing to do, even though he knew that he would be all right with the American Consul there for they would take care of him and get him back home.

From Demerara grandfather went to Barbadoes and from Barbadoes he came home and it was a hard trip for the weather was bad and he didn't have a mate, so he was having troubles and so were the whole crew and everyone was working more hours and grandfather was standing watch. And one night it was so stormy that when the other watch came on, he told them to call him if anything was needed.

He was asleep in his cabin when he heard someone coming down the companionway and it was one of the two men he had left on watch. And the man knocked and knocked and grandfather got up and said, 'What's the trouble?'

He said, 'Captain, the mate's aboard.'

He said, 'What do you mean, the mate's aboard? We left him in Demerara.'

He said, 'I know we left him there, but he's on this ship. He was on the poop deck first and then he went over and looked at the binnacle. And if you don't believe it, you go up and look for yourself.'

And so grandfather went up and he talked to the helmsman and both men were frightened. Not only was it a rough night, but they were both sure they had seen him, seen his face and they had spoke to him and called him by name and he didn't reply. So grandfather tried to calm them down and said that it was the wind or the night or something, but he knew they didn't believe him. And so he went down below and wrote all this down in the log book recording the hour and everything.

It was quite a time before they went back to Demerara again, and he had never heard of this mate again on any other ship or anything, and when he did go back, he went immediately to the hospital to inquire when this mate had been discharged and what had happened to him. And when they looked in the hospital directory, they found he had died on the day and at the very hour that grandfather had recorded it in his log. (34)

Frequently, those most able to predict the future or interpret signs or witness tokens were born with a veil over their face. The veil, or caul as it is sometimes termed, is a slender covering of skin which hangs over the child's face at birth. If preserved, it endows the person with special powers. Avalon Riggin's grandfather, Seth Blades, had the power. He had come into the world "with this thing before him." Later in life his grandson, Fred Forbes, and another man were lost in the Bay when their small boat sank in a gale. Though the companion's body washed ashore after a few days, Forbes' body could not be found. Then one evening Captain Blades had a dream in which he crawled along a particular creek to the young man's body. And the following day when he re-enacted his dream, edging through the weeds to the same place on all fours, he came upon his grandson's corpse, tangled in the water bushes.

Earlier in his life, Captain Blades had an equally remarkable experience:

Pop used to talk about this, too. They used to have excursions and this particular one ran from Baltimore to Tolchester and this one time there were a great many people on board this excursion and a heavy storm came up. Finally

189

that boat began to sink and everyone jumped off that boat and a lot of people were drowned.

Now Grandpa Blades was going up the Bay in his boat at the same time this happened, but he was a long way from this sinking ship. Suddenly he said he saw a sign of death. He looked up there and he saw all these bodies all over the deck of his boat. Well, if you see one of these signs you're not supposed to speak to anyone, otherwise it will disappear. So he tried to get another crew member to look up near the cabin. He just beckoned or pointed in that direction. He knew something awful had happened.

Well, he went on up the Bay, and he seemed to know right where he'd find this ship sinking. And when he got there he loaded up his boat with people, some were drowned and some were still alive. And those corpses lay across his deck just like it had been in his vision. And he said the death sign that he'd seen was in the form of a skull. He really did see it. (24)

Other tokens came without actual visions. They might prefigure the event simply with the sound of a voice or the actions of an unseen presence as was the case with Zach Wall who lived below Crisfield:

Now this happened in 1899, and the day was the 29th of March if I'm not mistaken. Well, Zach Wall's father was building a boat and Zach and his brother was helping him, and they got up one morning to go down and work on their boat and Zach said, 'Pop, I'm not going down to work on the boat this morning, 'cause Jimmy Brice has been drowned.'

'Well,' his father said, 'Zach, you've had a nightmare and a wild dream, you know there's nothing like that happened; nobody's told you about it.' (Of course then there was no communication, no ship to shore phones or radios or nothing like that.)

But he said, 'I know what I'm talking about. Jimmy Brice has been drowned and he was a very close friend of mine. I'm going downtown and see if I can hear any news.'

190

And the old man said, 'You know you're not going to hear any news 'cause nothing like that has happened.'

Now this all happened at the last of the drudging season and boats were all getting ready to come home and were coming home, some going to Baltimore, some going to this point and that point, most of them coming to Crisfield.

But anyway, Zach went down to town, and the day went by and no news, and finally along about the edge of night a boat come in and told the yarn about Jimmy Brice had sunk the boat, capsized her under full sail, loaded with oysters. Well, when Zach saw his father, the old man said, 'Zach, how did you know all this?'

'Well,' he said, 'I'll tell you how I know it. I come home last night from seeing my girl, and it was very cold. It was exactly midnight and I jumped into bed and pulled the covers up over my head to get warm. And I had no more than pulled the covers over my head before something tore them off. Now I never saw no man or nothing, but I heard Jimmy Brice's voice and he said, "Zach, I have just lost my boat, capsized and drowned all hands on board."'

Well, the old man said, 'You're crazy, you never saw no such thing. There's nobody never told you nothing. It's just a wild dream.' But he said it wasn't a dream, but an actual fact.

And a long time after Zach always said that the worst part of it was that nobody would ever believe him and they thought he had fallen asleep or been drinking or something but he said that that quilt actually come right off of his face and he heard the voice of Jimmy Brice speaking to him.

And the funny thing about all of this was when they brought the boat up from the bottom—and she had full sail, all hands and a load of oysters still aboard—the clock had stopped at exactly five minutes after midnight. And later, when the men got to talking about it they said that Jimmy Brice had sailed by them that night—it was blowing a gale and cold too—on his way home, and one of the captains on another boat said as he went by, 'You're not going to carry that set of sails to Crisfield tonight, you'll never make it.'

191

And this is what they said Captain Brice said: 'Oh yeah,' he said, 'I'm going to eat breakfast in Crisfield tomorrow or I'm going to eat it in hell.' (26)

In another token narrative told by a retired Crisfield school teacher, the actual death warning did not become clear until interpreted by a fortune teller many years later.

Now Mrs. Wallace, who used to live out this way, her husband followed the water, and one time while he was away she was staying with her mother. And the family used to have an old slave named Jake. He'd lived with them all through the years and his duty was to keep the fireplace wood well supplied, and do the handy work around the house. And on this particular night Mrs. Wallace and her mother were quilting and Jake brought in the wood and Mrs. Wallace said to him, 'Jake, close the door.' And he closed the door and sat down by the fireplace. Shortly after that the door opened again and Mrs. Wallace told him, 'Jake, close that door.'

He said, 'I did, M'am.'

She said, 'Well, close it.' And he closed it and just as he sat down it opened again. And so Mrs. Wallace got up herself and went and closed it and latched it and it came open a third time. She never thought anything of it at the time, and it wasn't long after that that she learned that her husband had been drowned.

Now it was about thirty years after that that Mrs. Wallace went to visit her uncle in Annapolis with Mrs. Sterling and Mrs. McCready. And one day after dinner they decided to go up to Baltimore to have their fortunes told. Now Mrs. McCready was very well known to this spiritualist. Her name was Miss Childs. She had been an organist in one of those Baltimore churches but on this one particular night that she was to play, she couldn't turn a tune. She went absolutely blank and she said she was damned and she never played anymore. But she was able to read the future. And so these ladies went up there to see her.

Now Mrs. Wallace said, 'I'm going to be the first to have my fortune told 'cause I'm not going to allow you to go in there and tell her a lot of stuff about me and then have her tell it right back to me.' So in the afternoon they went to Miss Childs' and when they were sitting in an adjoining room she came out and spoke to them.

She said, 'I'm going to speak to this lady here first.' That was Mrs. Wallace. And she went in with Miss Childs and she said, 'I ought not ever to talk with you. Today at noon you made fun of me and ridiculed me seriously, and I resent that. But since you've come all the way over here I will talk with you.' And she took Mrs. Wallace's hand and she looked at it a minute or two and she said, 'I see water everywhere and I see a man coming up and going down three times and I see a door opening and it opens three times.'

Mrs. Wallace said, 'Miss Childs, don't tell me anything more; I don't want to hear it.' And she went out into the reception room. (42)

Other Eastern Shore residents underwent comparably unnerving token experiences. Dot Stallings of Quantico sat outside her kitchen door one afternoon when presently she heard the door to the refrigerator open and, after a short pause, close. When she went inside the room was empty. An hour later she received a call that her youngest son had drowned, and as she thought back on it she recalled that whenever he came home the first place he ever went was to the icebox. In Hopewell, Nancy Neilsen's mother was born with a veil. She pressed it and saved it so she would retain the power to see the future. One winter afternoon at five o'clock she glanced out of her window and there over the tops of the trees came a ship with all sails set. Several hours later she learned that her husband had drowned— at exactly five o'clock. More incredible still, on November 2nd, at 7:25, an elderly Byrdtown woman passed away and both a cuckoo clock and an alarm clock stopped at the same minute. Precisely one year later, to the very minute, the clocks started again, fully wound. In Crisfield, Alice Denn's great aunt noticed the cradle of her sick child rocking itself late one night. When she tried to settle it, the pressure of an invisible hand was too great and the cradle continued to sway back and forth. Two days later the child perished.

In folk belief birds and animals acquired a kind of animation which allowed them to prescribe future events. And often their actions, if interpreted correctly, can warn an observer of an approaching death. To Eastern Shoremen, the howl of a dog betokened a soul that has departed. Likewise the cry of a whippoorwill at night indicated a death, as did the sight of a turtle dove in the yard with its head under its wing. Owls hooting, birds pecking at window panes, or buzzards winging past the house foreshadowed the end for someone in the family. And the actions of roosters at times made them the harbingers of death:

> Well, this person was papering to this lady's home and they had ate their lunch, and she went to the bathroom, or outside toilet, I guess you call it. Well, this family had chickens and this big old rooster run right up to the door and crowed right in her face. And Mary Toms, she was with her, and this woman turned round and said to her, 'Mary, what would you do if that happened to you?'
>
> She said, 'Well, I'd kill the rooster.' But no one did. Well, they went right in the house and before that woman got one piece of paper hung, she died. She had a cerebral hemorrhage, and when they got her to the hospital, she was dead. (37)

On Tangier Island it was the unaccountable disappearance of three ducks which foretold a disaster:

> Now Richard Spence, he was a-gunning up there [the northern end of the island] one time. I don't know whether it was in the spring or the fall, but it was warm. He had his coys out in a deep hole. And there wasn't any breech loading guns then, just old big muskets. You had to pour the powder in them and put a wad on them and ram it down, and put in the shot and put a cap on the tube. Well, he was laying there with his coys out, kinda warm, and he fell in a little doze of

194

sleep, and when he waked up he looked in his coys and there was three flock fowl ducks in there. He said he laid as flat as he could and he got to his gun and when he got his gun he put up and he shot right in. He said, in one shot he killed them all. What it was like: one stayed in the coys, and one jumped up and fell over in back of the blind and the other fell over in front of the blind. 'Well,' he said, 'I'll go round and get this one first.' And he went around and he couldn't find anyone. And when he came round here to the foot of the blind, he couldn't find anyone. And when he looked out in his coys, that one was gone. And three days after that, there come three drownded men up agin that shore at that same place. Three drownded men; and they buried them there at Long Tump. (3)

Another Tangierman likewise experienced a strange duck hunting incident which, though he didn't realize it at the time, prefigured his own death. While hunting at a place called Sedges one night, George Davis encountered a strange presence which he shot at. Suddenly the specter turned on him and chased him all the way home. Two weeks later when returning from Washington his boat went aground near Sedges. He made it to shore, all right, but before help arrived he froze to death at the same spot where he shot at the specter.

For some reason pictures hung on the wall possess an animate quality which enables them to warn of an imminent death. Delmar inhabitants contend that if the glass in a person's portrait cracks, his days are numbered. More common perhaps is belief that if a picture falls from the wall, someone will die. Nan Eller of Delmar recalled that six hours before her father died, a picture fell off her wall down behind the sofa and cracked. And to this day she has never replaced it.

A similar incident converted a Marion woman to the belief:

Last August when I went to pick up my father to take him to visit my brother, I found him in bed unconscious. He had a stroke and when we got him to the hospital they didn't give him much of a chance. But the fifth day he was doing much better when I left the hospital and I thought he

195

would certainly know me the next day. When we got home and started watching television, a large picture that Mother and Daddy had given us for Christmas about ten years ago crashed to the floor behind the sofa. My husband and I looked at one another but we didn't say anything, and I couldn't move to pick up the picture. Next day before we ever got to the hospital we got this call saying to come in a hurry, and before we left the house, we got a second call saying that Daddy was dead. (24)

At times the token took shape in a mysterious appearance of the one who was to die. Such was the case with a Hoopersville man who had been taking care of his bedridden father for some weeks. One evening he walked out to the backhouse and opened the door: his father walked out. Flabbergasted, he raced back into the house only to find his father lying in bed, still critically ill. But the next morning when he entered the old man's room, he was dead.

Similarly, a Hopewell woman was so startled by the likeness of her uncle standing in her back yard in his tall silk hat, that when she saw him she grabbed her husband by the shoulder in such a grip that it drew blood. Yet look as he might, her husband never saw a thing. But the following day word arrived that, indeed, the uncle had passed away at exactly that moment.

Unaccountable sounds also could mean that death was close at hand. The night before a Lawsonia woman's grandfather died, thunderous sounds of coal being poured down a chute into the cellar broke the evening stillness. But subsequent investigation showed that nothing of the kind had ever taken place. There was no coal and no tracks of any vehicle. The following day, the old man perished. On Hooper Island it was the loud strains of heavenly music heard outside the stable that predicted the owner's demise. And at Rhodes Point, over on Smith Island, there was an event that recalled the Passover. One night outside a number of houses, a dreadful noise occurred. It resembled the crashing of tin cans and the pounding of drums combined. Captain Griff Hoffman actually ran out in his underwear and tried to find out what it was, to no avail. Yet within each household

196

where the noise had been heard, a member of the family died within the next week.

There were occasions when signs could be favorable. A Salisbury man recalled an astonishing event which occurred to him when he was living in West Virginia.

Several years ago when my father was being operated on for cancer, Mother and I were keeping house, and though I lived on a farm for eighteen years I still wasn't able to milk a cow worth a pickaroon. So a neighborly lady had been coming up to do the milking for us.

The doctors had said that if Dad lived for the next forty-eight hours he had a chance of pulling through. So that morning I got up rather early—Mother with me—to get breakfast 'cause I had to take a group of men in that morning to give blood in case of a blood transfusion. So it was about six o'clock in the morning and Mother and I were seated in the kitchen eating breakfast.

Now there was an outside gate to what we call the lower lot and that had a steel bar that fell over into a steel notch. And then there was the gate to the yard itself that had a button to hold it shut. Then there was a board walk, in probably ten to fifteen feet, that went from there to about four steps that came up on to the screened porch. Then the screen porch opened into the kitchen.

So that morning while seated there eating our breakfast I heard the lower gate to the lot. I didn't hear it open but I heard the metal bar lift into place. And given the normal amount of time, I heard the gate to the yard open, and somebody walk on the board walk up to the steps, step up the three or four steps onto the screened porch. There the sound ended.

So we waited and my mother looked across the table at me and she said, 'Edna certainly has been good while Dad's been sick, hasn't she?'

I said, 'She certainly has.' So I knew then that Mother had heard the sound, too.

So we waited and waited and Edna didn't come in. So

197

I got up from the table and went out on the porch to see what was wrong with Edna. Edna wasn't out there. There wasn't anybody out there. There is a small stream that runs along in front of the house and on the other side of the stream, over the bridge that goes across it, there's a country road. So I went to the front and looked up and down the road and there was no one there. I looked under the house; there was nothing there. There was no one else in the yard. It couldn't have been chickens 'cause the chickens were still in the chicken house. So I came back in and I said, 'Mom, there's nobody out there.'

She said, 'Of course there's not. That was a token. If the sounds had been walking away it would have meant Dad was much worse. But because it was coming towards us, he's probably a lot better.'

So at nine o'clock that morning I took the men to the hospital up there in Clarksburg. One of the nurses on duty was a former classmate of mine and she saw me and said, 'Vernon, do you want to go up and see your dad?'

'At this time of day?'

'Yes, I can take you up.'

'Well,' I said, 'how is he?'

'Oh, he's fine.'

And so help me, I went up there and they had Dad half-way sitting up there in bed eating breakfast. So what we heard I have no explanation for except it was possible a change of temperature taking place in that board walk. But how can I describe the sound of the metal bar falling in place at the lower gate? And how can I explain hearing the screen door open and close on the screened porch? I can't do it. (43)

Strange Occurrences

In an area where people respect religious zeal beyond almost anything else, it is hardly startling to uncover stories in which great faith is rewarded and lurking skepticism punished or ridiculed. On Deal Island, for example, there lived a woman rich in the faith known to residents simply as "Aunt Darky." A huge tree grew in her front yard, and for years it had leaned menacingly over the roof of her home. When a neighbor politely suggested that she have the tree removed simply to insure her own safety, the old woman silenced him: "No, I'm not a bit worried about that. My Lord has promised me that this tree would never blow on my house." And sure enough, two weeks later a violent thunderstorm sent the tree crashing to the ground in the other direction.

Captain George Anders who lived on the same island also seemed to sense that the Lord was on his side. One particular winter the weather turned desperately cold and Captain Anders and his large family began to wonder where the next meal was going to come from, for everything was frozen up tight and commerce with the outside world had virtually stopped. When everything in his house was totally depleted, he prayed to God for deliverance and in his reverence he received a message that the Lord would look after him. Indeed, the very next morning a wagon drawn by four horses pulled up to his house and unloaded flour, lard, yeast, and beans, more than enough to last him through the freeze. And to this very day, no one knows where that food came from.

Out near Smith Island, another bad freeze placed a young widow in a comparable situation. She and her husband had for a number of years lived out by themselves on one of the "tumps" or smaller islands adjacent to Smith Island. With three children to care for, her husband drowned one winter, and as if to add insult to injury, the weather turned bitterly cold. Ice choked the waterways and impeded intercourse with the mainland. The family's supplies dwindled to nothing. After several days with no sustenance at all, the woman took a pot from the cupboard and put it on the stove.

"Mama, why heat an empty pot?" asked one of her children.

"Don't worry," she countered, "there'll be something in it before this day is over."

And at midday, salvation arrived in the form of an ice sled loaded with supplies.

Another Smith Island woman's strength of faith and prayer brought deliverance to a group of endangered watermen caught in an ice jam. Many on the island thought Aunt Caroline a saint. Her humility and generosity coupled with strong religious fervor lent credence to the thought. And an event that occurred one winter afternoon left little room for doubt. The oystering fleet had been working on the western side of the island that day, and when they noticed the sky turn dark and the wind begin to pipe up from the northwest, they turned towards the island only to find the harbor entrance blocked by an ice flow. People gathered on the shore to watch what looked like a full scaled disaster. Suddenly, Aunt Caroline dropped to her knees and prayed for the Lord to spare the fleet. Miraculously, a rent in the ice opened up and every boat squeezed through to safety.

And for the atheist, there was equally miraculous proof of the existence of God.

One time preacher Wilson told this tale about a local man who died. I forget his name, but no matter. He didn't believe in God and one day while they were out in a boat, he got mad because they weren't catching any fish, and the weather didn't suit him none too well either. Well, in a fit of temper he took his diamond ring and threw it overboard and said, 'If I never see that ring again as long as I live, it's my proof that there is no God.' Now I wasn't there, but I heard Preacher Wilson say that the next line that man threw over he caught a fish, and when he opened the fish to clean him he found his diamond ring. (24)

Indeed, the hand of God moved in strange ways. In Ewell, on Smith Island, He gave parishioners a lesson in humility when He intervened providentially to burn their church.

A while ago they built a church on the camp grounds in Ewell, and it was a fine church. But the people got to boasting about what a wonderful church it was and how it was better than any other churches on the island. Well, after a while that church caught fire and it burned to the ground.

200

The whole works burned: the church, the parsonage, and everything connected with it. And it didn't bother anything else. If that fire had got out of hand it would have taken the whole town. But it didn't; it just burned the church. (1)

Unaccountable events also surrounded the burial of the dead on the lower Eastern Shore. The region has its water table very near the surface of the ground and interment frequently presents a problem. In most cases the dead are put in small vaults which protrude six inches to a foot above the ground. On Tangier Island, one sees these white vaults with their simple headstones right in the front yards of the houses, as it was long the practice to bury family members on the property of their earthly home. With such ground level interment, it was not always possible to keep the dead contained in the earth when the waters rose. In one instance on Deal Island the casket floated out of the cemetery and back home much to the widow's dismay:

Willa Green, an old colored lady living on the island, lost her husband. You could hear her in the morning or late at night at sunset crying, 'Oh Lord, send him back to me, send him back to me.' After several weeks there was a terrible hurricane—real high tides on the island, and his coffin washed up to her doorstep. She heard this bump, bump, bump against the door. She looked out the window and she saw his casket lying there. Then she screamed out and said: 'Oh Lord, I don't want him. I didn't mean it. Take him back. I don't want him.' (16)

Similarly, two young Smith Island boys discovered a corpse along the shore which they courteously buried. The next day it had freed itself and was floating along the shore again. They put it in the earth once more. But after the body freed itself for five straight days, the boys decided that it probably didn't want to be buried, and let the corpse float out into the Bay.

The appearance of strange lights along the Bay likewise provoked wonder and concern, particularly among watermen. Older men termed these small whisps of flame "jack-ma-jugs" or "jack-ma-lanterns" and claimed that they often appeared over floating corpses. Other watermen avowed that the strange, candle-like fires possessed mesmerizing powers and warned others against following them on the water. "Now these jack-ma-lanterns," declared Captain Al Wheatley on Tangier Island, "when it got foggy, they come and get close to your boat, and then they'd carry you out into deep water, and then they'd leave you lost."

Apparently the lights worked much the same way on the land as a Tangier woman learned:

A woman over to Tangier went visiting one evening at a friend's house. The two ladies were busy sewing. I think they were making dresses. Well, anyhow, the time went by quickly and after saying goodnight, this old lady headed home. She lived up in Kenton, which is the upper part of the island. And to get home she had to walk over some marsh-land. When she came to this two plank bridge, this light appeared in front of her. It had such a magical pull that she followed it and just wandered and wandered following that light. Some people call them jack-o-lanterns. Well, that woman walked and walked till she was so tired she said, 'In the name of the Lord, where am I?' It was as if the spell had been broken because she came to her senses and heard cackling laughter. She looked all around and found out she was way out in the marsh far away from Kenton. But that poor woman couldn't help herself, following that light I mean. Jack-o-lanterns would do that to you anyhow. (24)

Malevolent as these lights might be, methods did exist for breaking their spells. Some broke the charm simply by turning their pockets inside out. Watermen, however, used more elaborate means. Gorman Tull of Crisfield explained: "Now the old head [people] used to say that if you wanted to get rid of them jack-o-lanterns, take a jack-knife and stick it in the deck, and the flame will come over and burn itself out on the handle of that knife. It will take the handle with it. And they say those jack-o-lanterns come either just before or just after a storm."

Certain of these mysterious illuminations appeared often enough to warrant names. Along the western shore of Tangier and Smith Islands a good many people witnessed from time to time a bright light which appeared for no apparent reason and moved with incredible velocity along the shoreline. No story ever explained its existence, but its presence frightened those bold enough to approach it.

Sometimes men would go big gunning. They would lash a big gun to a skiff and they would lay around the sand dunes waiting for wild geese and ducks. They would gather there at night and a light would come out of one of the sand dunes and start flying up and down and circling around. They saw it so much, the old people, that they gave it the name of "The Striker."

At first they wouldn't get too close to watch it, but one night five of them got real brave and were going to go up close to it. They said that thing come out and hovered over the tops of them and finally burst into a million pieces. They got up and really flew, they were so scared. Now I don't know what happened to it. The old people talked about it for a long time but none of them ever found out what it was. I know this happened. I heard it talked. (3)

In Dorchester County "Cal's Light" has, over the years, gained notoriety as a death omen. Reputedly, on first sighting, the light popped up beside a waterman's boat and when he passed his hand through the flame it disappeared. Somewhat later, the same light appeared outside his home during the evening, and the following day he perished. Since that time, the light has appeared outside other nearby homes, and on each occasion some-one within has died in the next several days.

Below Crisfield in a marshy region, now deserted except for the shells of several old homes, another light appears from time to time. Local residents call it "Elsie's Light."

Now our ancestors owned all of that land down there; it was called Emmessex. They had that grant of land and there were a lot of big houses out there. But there was one small house and that house caught fire and Elsie herself caught on fire and she burned up. And the people that come by that night saw that ball of fire roll down to the wharf. That went on for years and years and they called it 'Old Elsie's Light,' and that's what it was: it was her running down into the water all afire. (44)

In small communities the art of fortune telling commands notable respect. At times the feats of these seers pass into oral narrative and linger in the repetoires of raconteurs. Jesse Evans, who lives just outside Crisfield, recalled hearing Mrs. Sterling tell of her visit to Miss Childs in Baltimore.

She said she went in there and Miss Childs took her by the hand and said, 'I see running water and I see something that's choking. Mrs. Sterling, you have an enemy. Her name is Kay; she's stopped the water there and she's trying to choke you.'

And Mrs. Sterling, when she came home to her surprise her strawberries were very much damaged by this water and when they searched for the trouble, they found under the bridge across the ditch, a dike, a crude dike and bags and rags and shells and grass and everything so that the water couldn't get through. And they discovered the lady who lived next to the field had stopped it up and ruined Mrs. Sterling's strawberries. Now that actually happened. (42)

In Marion, Al Johnson recalled that his father encountered a fortune teller near Mount Vernon one day who, for fifty cents, told his future with a deck of cards. She informed him that he would soon lose two neighbors; one would die, the other move away. When the prophecy proved true, the client became sorely agitated. Both neighbors owed him money.

On the other hand, for a Lawsonia man, the forecast of a fortune-teller brought him some money, but at the sacrifice of a shattered kneecap.

Now this local woman round here could tell a fortune with cards. If you looked at her she looked like a witch, though she's a very good friend of mine and I love her to death. And her daughter, she's the cutest thing in the world; she could also tell fortunes.

One night we were up there at her house, three couples of us, and this woman said, 'Let's have some fun. Let's play some cards. Let's tell some fortunes.'

I said, 'Good.'

She said, 'Well, I'll take you first.' And she took this ordinary deck of playing cards and she ruffled them and shuffled them and told me to make three piles out of them. So I did, and she picked up a card and it was the ace of spades. 'Well,' she said, 'I hate to tell you this, but you're going to be involved in an accident.'

I said, 'When is it going to be?' (Skeptical, you know.)

She said, 'I don't know, but it's going to be within one day, one week, one month, or one year, but you're going to have an accident and you're going to get a lot of money out of it.'

Now if this is not the truth, may God paralyze my tongue in my head. I was walking out of church one beautiful summer's night and I was walking along facing the traffic and this guy—I didn't know he was drunk—pulled off the road and run right into me and hit me in the kneecap and knocked me end over end. Tore that kneecap all up and I had to go to the hospital. And a little while after that, the adjuster came from Baltimore and I got $300.00, and that was a lot of money then.

Another time, this same woman—her husband came home one night, and he believed everything she said—he had a little paper bag in his hand and she said, 'What have you got in the bag, John?'

He said, 'I've got a cat in there.'

She said, 'I'll bet it's yellow.'

He said, 'How in the world do you know it's yellow?'

One other time when he come home she said, 'John, give me that $10.00 you collected today.'

205

He said, 'You're a damn fool, I never collected no $10.00 today.'

She said, 'Yes you did; there was somebody owed you $10.00 and he paid you today, and I want it.' And she got it, too. (24)

Courtship, Marriage, Pregnancy and Birth

Future prediction also found its way into the realm of everyday folk belief. One could consult a seer to discover whom he would marry, but it was just as easy to stay at home and carry out a traditional practice or look for a particular sign. Cambridge girls, for instance, claimed that if your eyebrows grew together when you were a teenager, you had already met your future husband.

But how did one determine who the future husband was? Methods varied. Hoopersville women remembered placing a snail in a tray of soft, powdery soil to watch him etch out the initials of the prospective mate. Other Eastern Shore females hung a wishbone over the door and waited for the first eligible male to walk beneath it. A Salisbury woman recalled peeling an apple in a continuous spiral, throwing the peeling over her shoulder, and then reading the future intended's initial on the ground. For some there was an even more complex process.

Now, we used to do this on May Day. You got up before the sun came up and you went downstairs backwards, looking into a mirror, and you went to the well—we all had shallow wells around here then—and you bent over until you almost fell in the well, and then you were supposed to see whoever you were going to marry in the mirror.

And also, there were ways to tell what he was going to do. You'd break an egg in a glass of water and put it somewheres in the sun and let it stay there until midday, and then go and get it and something would be forming. Well, almost always it looked like a boat, 'cause the yolk would sink and the white would sort of sit out on the top and come to a point, and so you'd marry a waterman. (24)

206

·Boys on Elliott Island followed a similar procedure to discover their future wives. On Halloween they went to a deserted house, built a fire and each placed an egg in front of it. At midnight the door would supposedly blow open and the spirit of the prospective wife would enter and turn over the egg of one particular boy. But among the boys there seemed to be more the spirit of adventure involved than any real belief in spirits.

The traditional Dumb Supper as practiced by Eastern Shore girls likewise provoked some frights, and doubtless a good deal of amusement:

> Now when we were young girls, they used to set Dumb Suppers. We had an old kitchen like this one, but there were two doors and a hallway from the kitchen into the dining room. And we were sitting in there one night after we'd set that Dumb Supper. Now that Dumb Supper is like an old saying that you put two eggs and put pepper and salt and cut them open just like you're going to open them, and set them on the table, and the man that you're going to marry will come in and eat that egg. Always at midnight. And after you've set it you're not supposed to say anything. We did everything with oil at that time, no electricity, and all the lights were low and we set there by ourselves, nobody but me and this girl, just waiting for people to come in. Just at twelve o'clock, the wind commenced to blow and it blew a gale, and the lights were flickering, and we were both scared expecting something to come in, and Pap had an old horse that he used and she come and poked her head in that door, and I swear, we like to tore that house down getting out of there. We like to broke the door down. (37)

When Virginia Russell tried the same thing in Crisfield as a young girl, a black cat came through the door at the appointed time, and the eager watchers fled in terror. Similar, too, was the "ghost table" which was placed before the fire on Halloween. Each person then deposited an egg on it. If all went according to plan, at midnight a black cat would come through the door, then a coffin, and finally the figure of the future mate who would walk to the table and overturn the appropriate egg. When a group of girls tried it in one Crisfield home, the wind blew the door open and in came a black cat, after that a coffin, but nobody stayed to see the rest of the ceremony.

According to one Marion woman, however, these episodes for divining one's husband did not always provide one with the most propitious mate.

> Well, I'm going to tell you a joke. My grandmother told me this and she said it was the truth because it happened to her family. In olden times you'd bring a shirt—you know, we used to wear these undershirts—and you'd wash that and wring it out and hang it up to the fireplace—we always had fireplaces at that time—and you'd let it dry out and the man you're supposed to marry will come in and turn that shirt over. Some of my grandmother's friends done that and a man come in and stuck a knife in that shirt. They said she kept the knife and later she married that man and he killed her. They found the knife and said he'd killed her with the same knife he stuck in that shirt. (37)

To determine your future husband was one thing, to get married to him was another. Certain signs intervened which forecast postponement. If a woman stumbled and fell upstairs, she would not be married that year. Or if she reached for the door knob at the wrong side of the door it meant she would have to wait at least another twelve months. And if a single girl were unwitting enough to take the last portion of food on the plate or fail to lift her feet when crossing a railroad in a car, she might anticipate a lifetime as an old maid. Yet if four people crossed their hand shakes in greeting, one of them would soon take the marriage vows. And a sneeze at the table meant either an imminent marriage or an imminent death in the family.

Once married, the question of bearing and raising children invariably confronted the parents. Popular belief helped determine if the woman was pregnant. If her apron strings became untied, she would soon have something to fill out the apron. To dream of fish, or to dream that your best friend is pregnant denoted the dreamer was probably pregnant herself. And for the potentially barren: "Place a new baby on the bed of a married woman who seems unable to conceive, and she will soon become pregnant." There were likewise methods for discovering the future child's sex. Round shaped women will bear boys, pointed shaped women will bear girls. According to a male informant from Marion, "You don't measure a woman's pregnancy by months; you measure it by days, like a cow. A girl is carried 283 days and low, while a boy is carried high for 285 days." Crisfield women employed a well known practice to determine a child's gender. They threaded a needle and held it by a knot in the thread over the hand of the pregnant woman. If the needle swung in an oval motion the child would be female; if the needle swung back and forth or pointed straight down, the woman might expect a male.

One of the most common causes for concern among Eastern Shore women centered on the belief that some act or experience undergone during pregnancy might in some manner affect the baby, or mark it in some way. In a recent article on pregnancy folklore in California, Lucile Newman commented that, "The verbal communication of beliefs concerning pregnancy seemed to be designed to effect social separation of the pregnant woman from the group of non-mothers and to identify the social relationship of mother to fetus."* In essence, Miss Newman sees this communication as symbolic of pregnancy status, that is, carving out a role for the pregnant woman within her group situation. The beliefs, she finds, offer no "useful instructions" to the expectant mother.

Clearly, these ideas apply to Eastern Shore belief patterns about pregnancy. And the beliefs or short anecdotes in which these beliefs appear reveal several conditions: those in which the individual is a helpless victim, and those in which the pregnant woman has some control over her situation and that of her fetus. For example, deriding a deformed or retarded person while pregnant will result in similar defects to the fetus. When a Crisfield woman from a very wealthy family laughed at a feeble-minded

*See "Folklore of Pregnancy: Wive's Tales in Contra Costa County, California," *Western Folklore, XXVII* (1969), p. 115.

child during her pregnancy, her own child was born badly retarded, which simply went to prove that "the wrongs you do one by one, you pay for two by two." In another Crisfield family it was the father who sealed his child's destiny:

Now there was this woman around here and she had a peculiar, ugly laugh. Oh, it was frightful. You know, you've seen people that way. It was really a frightful sight to look at her when she laughed. Well, this man who used to be the storekeeper over here—he's been dead now eight or ten years—when his mother was pregnant, his father laughed and made fun of this other woman who was frightful to look at, and when that child was born—it was a male child—it used to cover up its mouth with its hand, like that. It was exactly like the laugh of the woman they had made fun of. You could put those two beside one another and if they laughed, they look exactly alike. Now that's a fact. (26)

If children could be disfigured through arrogant acts on the part of their parents, so too could they be marked if the mother craved certain foods or was frightened by something. With a Princess Anne woman, for example, all three of her children were somehow marked. With the first she craved strawberries, with the second beef, and with the third she was frightened by lightning. The first baby had strawberry marks all over its body, the second had an emblem in the form of a steer on its arm. The third child was normal, except during thunderstorms when it became terrified and actual streaks of lightning appeared on its forehead.

Another woman from Hoopersville had a deep craving for beets during her "time" But no market carried them at that season. When the baby arrived, it had a big blotch on its toe, and every beet season, the blotch turned a deep red, identical to the vegetable. A Delmar, Delaware female was twice marked when her mother was carrying her. The mother was frightened by a snake while picking strawberries, and to this day her daughter carries a snaky line on her thigh, a strawberry mole on her hip, and harbors a strong aversion for snakes.

For a Marion woman, it was a longing for oysters which marked her son:

> Well now, there's a girl down here with a strawberry right across her eyebrow and in strawberry time that's just as red as anything can be. And I got a son down here on the way to Crisfield, he's got an oyster right on his side. We went over to a neighbors and we had just had supper and we didn't have oysters, and they had fried oysters. Well, I thought I'd die for one of them fried oysters but I wouldn't ask for one, and when that baby was born there was that oyster, and it's still there. (37)

Certain actions on the part of the woman might affect the fetus. If a pregnant woman looked upon a corpse, her child would be born pallid or blind. Or if she were foolish enough to raise her hands above her head, she would choke the baby with its own umbilical cord. A Venton woman put her hand to her face so often while she was bearing one of her sons, that the child was born with a hand print on its face, so plain that he presently wears a beard to cover it up.

But more often than not, the woman had little control over the events that marked the child. If she had heartburn, for instance, she could expect a hairy offspring. If she was frightened by an animal, she would doubtless be able to find the mark of that animal somewhere on her baby. Another Venton mother, scared twice by snakes during her nine months, bore a child whose shriveled arm contained no conventional hand, but a lump which greatly resembled a snake's head.

On Hooper Island, it was the sight of disease which induced disorders in the child:

> One day during the spring of the year while my mother was pregnant, she had to work in the field planting sweet potatoes. My mother looked up and saw an old woman working in the patch. Her eyes were filled with infection. She said that infection was just dripping from them. My mother got so sick she vomited. And when I was born, my

eyes were weak and sore, and every spring my eyelids became infected when I was young. Mother always said it was a birthmark because she had seen that old woman. (24)

Some women believed that when the child was finally born, one of the best ways to ease the labor pains was to place a knife beneath the bed. Moreover, one could predict an offspring's future sometimes, simply by knowing the birth day:

Sunday, good luck;
Monday, health;
Tuesday, wealth;
Wednesday, best day of all;
Thursday, losses;
Friday, crosses;
Saturday, no day at all.

There were other signs. If a girl favors her father, she is born for good luck. Likewise, if the male child favors the mother. If the baby keeps its hand clenched tightly, it will be a stingy person. And the seventh child would always be gifted. Yet, at the same time, the family can, if willing, control the future of their infant, either through a positive act or by preventive action. "When a baby is born, take it upstairs or hold it up high so that it will be high-minded." "When an infant loses the naval cord, it must be burned. If it is thrown away, the child will wet the bed as he grows older." "Placing bread in a baby's crib will ward off disease." "If you let a baby's face get sprinkled with rain before it is a year old, the child will have freckles." "If you tickle a baby's foot, it will make the child stammer." "If a baby sees his image in a mirror before he cuts his teeth, he will have a difficult time with teething." "Never turn a baby upside down or it will turn its liver up."

Home and Domestic Pursuits

From the home spring a great many popular beliefs. It depends on the particular home and the individuals involved, but

212

belief patterns not infrequently become so important that the entire lifestyle of the family relies on rituals connected with superstition. As we have seen a Crisfield resident actually paid a Negro male to come to his house immediately after midnight on New Year's Eve to avoid bad luck. In another instance, a Fairmount waterman called all superstitions "a lot of crap," but these same superstitions so moulded his wife's life that he was indirectly influenced too.

Now, [he complained,] with my wife I've had to turn my car around and go back because a black cat run across the road. Now I don't think there was anything to that. What's a black cat got to do with me? Another time this man come in the back door. I knowed him. I hadn't seen him in a while, and his family were waiting at the front door, so I went and called him in. And when he left he went out the front door. Nothing ever happened to him; there ain't no bad luck in that. That's happened often. If a woman would come to the door on New Year's Day, my wife would see her and she wouldn't let her in. A man had to come first. (9)

A Lawsonia woman who described growing up in a family where popular belief practices were common, recalled with an ease of memory many which she knew as a child. Though she firmly maintained she was not a superstitious person, she admitted to always carrying a Saint Christopher's medal and never · sweeping the house after dark. She, like other white female informants, rationalizes her own belief patterns by discoursing at length about the strange practices of black women who come to work in her house. She expressed great amusement when recalling tales of idiosyncratic blacks who balked at stepping across a broom or who detoured around lines drawn across the road in front of them. Or if it wasn't the blacks, it was the neighbor down the lane who was superstitious, not the informant, as this conversation bears out:

I'd like to know just how you picked up some of these stories and sayings. Would people just be sitting round the

213

room and something would happen and your grandmother would say something?

Now I've been born in the era of the horse and buggy and I remember all of that. I lived out on a farm and naturally in the evenings people would go around to various houses and sit around for a couple of hours, and then go home. And they'd sit around and I don't know about telling stories; it would just be things that would come up, but they would just talk about it and it would be fascinating.

Well, for instance, the beliefs, how might they come up?

Well, I can tell you one for instance. Now of course our family didn't believe in it or anything like it, but there was a family that lived across the road, not too far away, and they were very superstitious. And they were, let us say, uneducated, and they believed in tokens, and if a person were to die, well, they'd say it was on the stroke of midnight or something like that, and a picture falling off the wall, that would mean a death in the family, and the stove lids lifting and all that, you know. They believed it just happened and it was a token of death and perhaps somebody had just died, and this would be the thing that would bring it on, this token.

And they would come over and tell you these things?

Yes, they would say these things, just sitting in normal conversation. (45)

And the household beliefs that issued from these "normal conversations" turned on innumerable things. Such things, for instance, as house pets: "To keep a dog or cat from straying, measure their tail, pluck out one hair from their tail, and nail it to the doorsill." "If you feed asparagus to a cat, it will go wild." Or clothing: "If you happen to put your clothes on inside out, don't change or you will have bad luck." "If the hem of your dress is turned up, spit on it and you'll get a new one." "If you bite off the head of a butterfly, you'll get a new dress the same color." "Never patch a garment with a new piece of cloth." "Don't kill crickets; they'll come back and eat the clothes." "Never wear new clothes to a funeral; it's bad luck."

There were also a host of ways to predict the arrival of

company. If your nose itched, you would have company in your house by sundown; right side a man, left side a woman. Clumsy handling of kitchenware also foretold visitors. Drop a dishcloth and a stranger would soon appear, drop a fork and it would be a woman, a knife, a man, and a spoon, either a child or a fool would soon keep you company. If one dropped a pair of scissors, they would point in the direction from which the visitor would come.

Animals, birds and insects likewise possessed determining roles in predicting company. A cat washing himself on the doorstep meant an unexpected arrival. And a rooster crowing in the doorway inevitably crowed up guests. By watching spiders in their webs, one could ascertain the kind of visitor. If the spider descended to the bottom of the web, a waterman would make a visit. Reciting the alphabet as the spider descended and stopping on a letter when it stopped, gave the host the initial of his imminent visitor. Or checking the color of the insect would give the observer the color of clothing his guest would wear. If you didn't like the intruder, all you had to do was throw some salt after him when he departed, and he would never return.

If there were ways to predict company, there were also methods for interpreting bodily sensations. When your ears burned or rang, someone was talking about you, left a woman, right a man. If applying spittle stopped the sensation, the talk was favorable, if not, it was derogatory. To stop the talk, all one had to do was to cross his arms over his chest and pinch them gently. Similarly, the right ear itching meant one would hear good news presently, the left ear bad news. The same thing went to the left and right eye, itching or twitching. If the foot itched on the bottom, the person would soon walk on strange ground. And if the left foot was stumped, a disappointment was in store, the right foot a pleasant surprise. Placing someone's shoes on the table would make his feet burn, brushing beneath his feet would send the victim to jail. A small white spot on the fingernail indicated the individual had a friend or else he would receive some money.

Carrying out certain procedures of bodily hygiene correctly was a necessity if one wished to avoid trouble. Cutting fingernails on the wrong day might result in problems. If you cut them on Sunday, you'd be embarrassed before the sun went down; if you pared them on Monday, you'd be sick all week. Pulling teeth also demanded precaution. If you neglected to bury a pulled tooth immediately, and a dog happened to find it first, a dog's tooth would grow in its place. Similar aberrations occurred with the hair: "When you comb your hair, or cut it, burn the combings at once. If a bird gets them and builds a nest, you'll have a headache." Moreover, cutting the hair in March brought on a headache for the entire month, but cutting it on a full moon made it grow thick and full. And there were some who held that it was unwise to cut a baby's hair before the child was a year old, lest it grow up a weakling.

Common, everyday activities and objects also required signs and rituals. Getting out of bed on the side opposite that you slept on invariably set the stage for a bad day. Telling a dream before breakfast brought ill consequences. Dreaming of snakes meant you had enemies. To acquire curly hair, you might eat the crusts of bread. If you helped yourself to food when there was already some on your plate, someone hungry was coming soon. Certain combinations of food, some said, would kill you: whiskey and watermelon, and ice cream on crabs. It was unwise to thank someone for a gift of flowers, lest the gift dry up and die. And a knife given in gift always cut a friendship. Stepping over a person on the floor, particularly a child, halted his growth. Beliefs about such inconsequential things as pins cropped up so frequently that they were often mouthed in rhyme:

> See a pin, pick it up,
> All the day you'll have good luck.
> See a pin, let it lay,
> Bad luck will come all the day.

As did the concern over whistling women:

> Whistling women and crowing hens,
> Are neither fit for God nor man.

Ill planned indeed was the day when the woman left her sweeping of the house till after sundown. But once the slip had been made

216

she might curtail bad luck by waiting until the following morning to scoop up the dirt. Folk belief also embraced shoes: "If your new shoes squeak, they haven't been paid for." "Shoes placed in a coming or going position will prevent nightmares." "If you sleep with shoes under the bed you'll have a restless night." "If you put your left shoe on first, you'll have bad luck all day."

To insure well-being around the house one could observe established taboos or carry out prescribed traditions on particular days of the year. On New Year's Day: allow a man or a boy to be the first person in the house; eat pickled fish, black-eyed peas, hog jowls, sauerkraut, or ham and cabbage; never allow a woman to talk; never hang out clothes (to prevent lice during the year); never take out ashes (unless you wish your house to burn during the year); cut a garment and finish sewing it; pay all your bills; wear clean underdrawers (to guarantee cleanliness all year).

A Salisbury woman recounted how luck might be transferred on New Year's Day:

> One New Year's Day, Eva Dillsworth's mother called to ask my cousin Ann to tell Eva that she had finished some sewing for her. Ann walked over to deliver the message right away. Eva listened to what she had to say, but followed Ann out of the house. Then she broke off a cedar branch and swept the ground behind Ann right to her doorstep. And when she left she said, 'Now the bad luck will come to your house, not mine.' (46)

Friday was habitually an ominous day. No project started on that day of the week was ever finished. And most journeys begun then were ill-fated. A dress sewed on Friday lasted longer than the wearer. Moving furniture into a house on a Friday affirmed only one thing: the owners of the furniture would never live there. A Mardela woman testified how the day affected her husband's working habits:

> I've known John to go out on a Thursday afternoon and plant two rows of corn so he wouldn't have to be starting something new when he planted the field the next day.

217

You know it's bad luck to start anything new on a Friday. And if that happened to be the 13th, he just messes around and won't do much of anything at all. (47)

Animal Husbandry, Planting, and Weather

In much Eastern Shore folk belief the phases of the moon play a determining role. To get rich one could shake a purse at an increasing moon. Then, too, some watermen felt that there will be more pealers shedding their shells during a full moon. If one observed a new moon over the right shoulder, troubles were on the way. But if one glanced at it over the left shoulder and wished, the wish would be granted that month. The moon even affected such inanimate matter as dirt: "If you dig a hole on the decrease of the moon, you'll never have enough dirt to fill it up. But dig that same hole on the increase of the moon, and there will be too much dirt for the hole." And soap likewise came out better when made on the increase of the moon. According to a Vienna woman, "You always make soap on the increase of the moon 'cause if you don't that soap will draw up. You know it will shrivel or shrink and you won't have as much soap. I've seen this myself; it's really true."

For many Eastern Shore farmers, the phases of the moon also prescribed when animals should be slaughtered and crops planted. Hog meat from hogs killed on the waste of the moon would, they affirmed, shrink or turn to grease. Smart men always killed on the increase. They also planted all crops that yielded on top of the ground on the increase, but waited till the dark of the moon to plant the crops that yielded beneath the earth. A butter bean crop produced best, however, when planted on a full moon, or on a Twin Day (the Gemini).

Other indications signaled also the most propitious time to plant. When the oak leaves were as big as a squirrel's ears or when the whippoorwill sounded, it was time to plant corn. White potatoes grew best if they went in the ground on St. Patrick's Day, and string beans thrived if seeded on Good Friday. But it was foolish to plant anything with a vine in a northeast wind lest the vine become dreadfully tangled. If one planted butter

218

beans in a northeast wind, they created too much wind after being eaten. And a sure way to provide a wretched yield of corn was to burn the corn cobs from seed corn.

In a region where people depend for their livelihood on either the land or the water, the prediction of weather becomes a paramount consideration. Few wish to make a passage or even go out fishing if bad weather is going to interrupt the venture and endanger the life of the crew. Nor does the farmer want to plant seeds only to have them flushed away by a torrential downpour of rain. On the water even a sensible yachtsman knows better than to listen to the inanities provided by the marine forecast. If he has any wisdom at all he looks for signs. So do many farmers and watermen such as this Deal Island captain:

> Now a lot of people asks us questions about how we can tell the weather and that sort of thing. Well, we have signs that lead to that. For instance, in the evening, we always look up to the north and see if we see a bank up there that forms like a rim, a black rim. Then we'll say (and you know we're captains that go on the water and we've got to be careful), and we'll say, 'Well, boys, it's gonna blow a gale tomorrow, we'd better not move.' And that's the way we mostly tell if it's going to blow a storm the next day.
>
> My own boys got to believe me about the weather. They asked me if it was going to be calm tomorrow and so I looked up in the sky and I saw just a few stars and they were flickering like they was jumping and I said, 'Well, it's gonna blow tomorrow.'
>
> And they said, 'How do you know it's going to blow?' And I told them.
>
> And the next day we got up and it was blowing a storm and the boys said, 'Daddy, it must be something to that.' (16)

Animals and plants frequently provided signs for forthcoming seasons. If the fur on a squirrel's tail was short, fall would come early. Likewise, if he packed his nuts away early in large quantity the winter would be hard. Heavy coats of fur on caterpillars or dogs foretold severe winter months ahead. So did a cat with its back to the fire, a wasp's nest high in a bush,

219

fish swimming deep in the fall, and a dark breast bone in the Thanksgiving turkey. Those who watched nature closely predicted a foul winter season if the corn husks were thicker than usual, if flowers bloomed late in the fall, or if the holly tree bore an abundance of berries. Yet if the onion skins were thin or the fruit was scarce, the winter would be mild. To determine winter weather, one might also observe the first three days of December, for some thought they foreshadowed the weather pattern for the next three months. Further, local weather prophets declared that if New Year's Day brought northeast winds two-thirds of the year would be wet, but if it blew from the northwest quarter, two-thirds of the year would be dry.

Short range predictions seem more viable and appear to function more immediately in the lives of the Eastern Shoremen. Only a fool fails to recognize the omen of a ring around the moon, or the sun setting in a thick bank of clouds. And the waterman will keep a keen watch for the northwest day when puffy clouds begin to appear early in the morning; it will be blowing hard by afternoon. Men who followed the water sometimes became weather prophets on shore, as this ex-waterman from Mount Vernon:

I'll tell you something about the weather. There's rain seeds that you can tell eight to ten hours before it rains. There aren't many people that knows that. It's like a big black cloud with a lot of little dots around it. Dark clouds are off from this big cloud. Well, it will rain in eight to ten hours. Don't know how much, but it will rain. I was up to the store one time and it was beautiful. It was as pretty a time as you ever did see. A man asked me, 'What's it going to do?'

I said, 'Rain.'

They thought I was a nut. Next day it nearly rained a flood. Next time I saw him after that he wanted a weather forecast for tomorrow. You see, I used to watch for rain seed when I worked on the water. (16)

Innumerable other signs presaged the coming of rain. "If

there is a circle around the moon, count the number of stars in the circle and that will be the number of days until it rains." "The position of the new moon indicates whether or not we'll have dry weather. If it lies on its back, it's a dry moon. But if it's in a position so water would flow from it, then it's going to rain." Other signs, if heeded might provide rain indicators: fish swimming near the surface; bees near their hive; the big dipper pouring into the little dipper; cows huddled together lying down; a rooster crowing at night; a turkey buzzard sitting on a fence with his wings spread out. If it started raining on low water, some watermen said it would rain all day. Also a clear sunset on Friday denoted rain within twenty-four hours. Rain on Monday inevitably meant rain three days that week. One might even fashion the weather by following traditional procedures. When you killed a snake you could bring on clear weather by burying it, rain by hanging it over the fence or in a tree.

Wind controlled the waterman' daily routine even more than rain, and wind indicators naturally became part of their daily weather forecast. The signs invariably marked either the strength of the blow, or where it would come from. Skippers could look for heavy weather and wind if they saw seagulls flying inland or if a high red rim appeared in the east at sunrise. A light streak beneath a dark cloud told watermen to seek a lee as soon as possible if they wished protection from a line squall. And "when the skies get black or sort of purple and dark blue, skippers around here [Oxford] say, 'Look out, a flock of Jinny Wrens'll come through shortly.' That means there's going to be a real blow."

Easterly weather usually betokened unpleasant sailing. The sight of land looming in the distance or porpoises swimming near the shore forecast wind from that quarter. At night, one might look for the bright end of "the milk maid's path." The bright end revealed where the wind would blow from the next day. Others, on shore, watched the activities of cats to determine wind direction. These creatures always scratched the side of a tree, or after washing their faces, looked in the direction the wind would blow.

There were some indications which predicted general weather changes. Several signs meant falling weather: blackbirds near

221

the house, hens rolling in the dust, the sight of a sundog, or silent grasshoppers. A flock of birds settling in a field meant snow would fall soon. Smoke ascending from the chimney guaranteed good weather; smoke falling to the ground prefigured a storm of some kind. Fog in the morning meant a clear day. So did a heavy dew, crows perched on the top of trees, or chickens sitting on a fence picking their feathers. And some Eastern Shoremen insisted that if there was enough blue in the sky to make a pair of kitten's britches, it would stop raining. Older informants recalled that when it was raining and the sun was shining, the devil was beating his wife, and to hear her cry they put a fork into the ground and placed their ear next to it.

Yet more well-known weather prophesies appeared in jingles, and were thus more easily remembered:

> Ring around the moon,
> Bad weather follows soon.

> Rain before seven,
> Clear before eleven.

> Evening red and morning gray
> Will set the traveler on his way.
> But even gray and morning red
> Will bring down rain upon his head.

> When the sheep collect and huddle,
> Tomorrow there will be a puddle.

> A sunshiny shower
> Won't last an hour.

> When a spring gets low,
> It's bound to rain or snow.

> Rainbow at night, sailor's delight.
> Rainbow in the morning, sailors take warning.

Luck, Good and Bad, and Conversion

If one begins to examine folk belief in any detail, certain

222

structural elements become apparent. Most superstitions contain either a sign and a result, or a cause and a result. Many beliefs on the Eastern Shore which concern death fall into the first category. "If a picture falls off the wall (sign), someone is going to die (result)." "If you see a falling star (sign), a loved one will die (result)." "To dream of a birth is a sign of death." "To dream of a nude woman is a sign of death." "If you dream of a boat on land, that is a sign of death." "To dream of fire, meat, teeth falling out or snakes is a sign of death," and so forth. In most of these instances, the individual who experiences the sign clearly has little to no control over the events that will succeed it. But with causes and results, the human can prevent bad luck. To wit: "When two look in a mirror at the same time (cause), the younger will die (result)." "To hang a tea towel on a doornob (cause), is a sure sign of death (result)." "If you wear new clothes to a funeral (cause), someone in your family will be the next to die (result)." Obviously, in these examples, the ominous results can be avoided if the person chooses to hang his clothes on a hook in the closet or selects a modest habit to attend the funeral in. Man has more of a chance here.

Good and bad luck superstitions on the Eastern Shore exhibit the same structural pattern, though with good luck beliefs the emphasis is more on sign than cause. "A bird defecating on your clothing is good luck." "When you crack a double-yolk egg, you'll have good luck." "If you find a pin and it points towards you, you'll have good luck." "A white cat following you is a sign of good luck." When, however, the luck signs do become causes, that is, when the human element becomes the catalyst for the luck, the suggestion of magic is apparent. For example, "Wrap a spare key in tin foil and bury it near the house (cause); you'll never be locked out again and it will always give you good luck provided you remember where the key is (result)." "When your baby is nine days old, take a thimble of water and pour it on the ground. This will bring the baby good luck." "If you carry a bent coin in your pocket, you'll always have good luck." "A horseshoe placed horns up on the back of the Sampson post will bring the boat good luck."

According to folk superstitions, most bad luck stemmed

from human causes. Though it was deemed auspicious if a black cat or a crow or blacksnake crossed your path, or if a picture on the wall became crooked, more often an individual's action caused the ill fortune that followed. At times the beliefs were stated succinctly: "Never place a hat on the bed," but implied was a result (or you'll have bad luck). A plethora of other actions presaged misfortune: climbing through a window, giving an empty pocketbook, lighting three on a match, whistling in the home, bringing a hoe into the house, rocking an empty chair, hanging clothes on the doorknob. It was likewise considered unfortunate to have all the family in one photograph, to walk in someone's footsteps or shadow, to seat thirteen people at the table, to sing before breakfast, in bed, or at the table, to have two Christmas trees in one year, to lay a baby on the table, to kill a cricket on the hearth, or to wear new shoes out of the store.

If some magical or mystical connection is suggested in the cause and result that one finds in folk belief, that magical expression becomes even more pronounced when the belief is expanded to include conversion. That is, suggested in many folk beliefs is the notion that by following a prescribed ritual, one can convert bad luck into good luck. For example, "If you spill salt (cause), you will get a beating (result), unless you throw some of it over your shoulder (conversion)." "If you give a pair of shoes to a friend (cause), he will have bad luck (result), unless you sprinkle salt inside them (conversion)."

A number of other superstitions follow the same pattern. Certainly one of the most common beliefs on the Eastern Shore and elsewhere turns on the suspicion of evil connected with the black cat. If one crosses your path, bad luck undoubtedly will harry you. But a series of rituals allow one to avoid pending bad luck: "to break the spell, go back sit down, and cross your legs six times before going on"; "throw away something good to keep bad luck away"; "turn around three times to break the spell." There were even some wary individuals who went out abroad prepared for encounters with black cats. A Hebron woman recalled: "In order to break the spell when a black cat crosses your path, spit in a hat. Now my uncle carried a hat in his car for this very purpose and I've seen him use it several times."

On the Eastern Shore, human spittle, long associated with positive magical powers, also conquered potential bad luck. It was bad luck to hear an owl hoot, but you could silence it by spitting in your hand and putting your hand tight under your arm. Similarly, if you urinated in a path and someone stepped in it before you spit in it, you could anticipate a spate of bad luck. And the sight of a cross-eyed woman likewise signaled misfortune, unless you spit in your hat to curb her charm. Spittle might also work as a determinant, converting as it were, ignorance into knowledge. "If your ear burns, someone is talking about you. If you put spit on it and it stops burning, it is something good; if it continues to burn, it is something bad."

If one dealt correctly with common household items, he could stem the flow of bad luck. If a dog howled or an owl hooted it meant "someone dead was visiting around"; but if you turned your shoes upside down or threw one in a corner, the sound would cease and the spirit would stop bothering you. Also, if giving someone a pointed or sharp object severed a friendship, one might mend the breech by offering a penny as an afterthought.

But it was actions more than objects that served to insure a conversion to good luck. "If you and a friend are approaching a post or a pole, or some other object, and you go around one side and he goes around the other, each of you should say 'bread and butter,' or bad luck will follow." Some believers locked little fingers and put their thumbs in their mouths before uttering the magical words. For young females, there was an elaborate exercise that prevented spinsterhood. "When crossing a railroad in a car, do the following or you will become an old maid: lift your feet from the car floor, hold your breath, cross your fingers and touch them to the top of the car." Some other conversions demanded incredible dexterity. "If you stump your toe, turn around three times holding your foot in your hand and make a wish. You'll have good luck." "If you have a crowing hen, catch her, bring her into the kitchen, turn her over and over from one corner of the kitchen to the far corner. If the tail comes to the corner, save her. If the head comes to the corner, cut it off— she's bad luck."

Conversion also plays a salient part in the area of folk medicine. Presumably, all folk cures suggest ways of turning sickness of some sort into health. In some instances, the people who propose these cures swear to their efficacy citing chapter and verse of cases where the patient has been miraculously brought back to health. "Now," reported a Crisfield man,

> there was this girl and she was burned real bad, third degree burns and the flesh just running right off of her and so they said you'd better go and see Miss Emmy. So they took her down and she didn't use any ointment or anything. Just rubbed her hands along those burns and when that girl healed, there wasn't one scar on her anywhere. (26)

Inevitably, women like Miss Emmy became accepted in the community as people with special powers. In some parts of the Eastern Shore, they became known as "high women," and their male counterparts were "high men." Their cures were many and varied, and though the white healers seem to be in less evidence than they were a century ago, black healers still provide medicine for believers, both black and white. Annie Carter of Perryhawkin is a good example.

> You could probably describe Annie as a sweet old colored lady who would help anyone she could. She's in her late sixties and a hard worker—one of the best farm hands you can find to pick tomatoes, beans, cucumbers or anything like that. She lives on her social security check but she can't work in the factory during the summer because of her pension check. She raised seven boys and seven girls and some of them went to college. Everyone thinks she's one of the best people around. And if you have some minor ailment, a skin disease or mild sickness, you can just dial Annie and she'll give you a remedy. (16)

Here clearly we have a fine instance of traditional folklife patterns fitting themselves to modern conventions. Seventy-five years ago, one would have gone to the folk practitioner's house to receive the cure, and probably have her prepare and apply it. But modern communications have changed all this. Today one can dial a folk remedy as simply as one can dial a prayer or the weather. But even though the methods for acquiring cures may be updated in a way, the medicine that Annie Carter dispenses is very old and very traditional. For boils, she tells us: take the lining of a raw egg, place it on the boil, smooth around the edges and it will draw the boil to a head. For nosebleeds: drop cold keys on a string down the person's back. For piles: always carry an Irish potato in your pocket. To reduce fevers: make a poultice of crushed onions and place it on the chest; if it is a child tie crushed onions to the wrist and the fever will be reduced. For asthma: find some field mullet and make a tea from the dry leaves; boil it, steep it, and add cream and sugar if you want; smoke the field mullet and smell or inhale the fumes. To get rid of warts: go to your neighbor's and steal a dishcloth, but don't tell anyone; rub it on the warts and they will go away before the rag rots.

A practical base often underlies much of folk medicine. Crude or unappetizing as some of the cures may sound, time and tradition have proven them effective. When prescribed medicine is not easily come by because there may be no one to prescribe it, people fall back on traditional prescriptions. Many of the cures for colds, coughs, and croup, for instance, involve inhaling a strong smelling substance. Whereas a doctor might prescribe a croup kettle filled with water and benzine, Eastern Shoremen wear a piece of flannel soaked in kerosene, and surely the smell from this garment would act probably more effectively to open up breathing passages than a croup kettle. Likewise, goose grease applied to the chest, as is done on the Eastern Shore for a chest cold, would certainly help to lessen the chance of chill on the chest.

The origin of much of the folk medicine practiced today on the Eastern Shore derives in part from the large pharmacopeas published several hundred years ago. In these thick volumes appeared long lists of cures, then accepted as medical fact. But with the advancement of scientific knowledge, physicians dropped many of these remedies from their practice. Still the folk con-

227

tinued to use them, and through the binding factor or oral tradition, many of the cures have persisted in time and are administered today much as they were two hundred years ago. Then, too, there is the simple fact that many of these folk remedies may have more efficacy than the calculating scientists of the American Medical Association are willing to admit. Indeed, one licensed Crisfield doctor actually deferred to his folk counterpart for the treatment of warts:

> Now there used to be some 'doctors' in this area who could cure your warts. There was a time when I had grown a big horn wart on the end of my nose and I went to a regular doctor in the village and he wouldn't touch it. He told me to go see George Stevenson. Said he could fix me up. My regular doctor said all he used was spit and all he did was rub a little spit around on the wart and it went away. But in the end I didn't go; I went to Baltimore instead and had it burned off. (26)

Because of the quixotic nature of warts they provided a variety of folk cures and drew in a great deal of business for the unlicensed healer. According to the same Crisfield informant:

> There was another fellow who used to live around here and he used to use some sort of leaf or something to do the same sort of thing. There was one man who came to him who had warts all over his hand, and one in particular that bled. This 'doctor' told him to come back the next day because he had to go and get some special kind of herb to fix the warts. So this fellow come back the next day and this 'doctor' put this medicine on it and he come to me a couple of weeks later and showed me his hands and there weren't a wart on them, and I said, 'They're gone.'
> And he said, 'Yes, but I still don't believe it.' (26)

Some healers miraculously removed warts by absorbing them onto their own skin. A huge blood wart rose on the back of a Mount Vernon man and he went to the local "doctor" who simply stared at the wart. Two days later the patient met the healer

228

at the store, remembered his wart, felt for it, and found it was gone. Later when another wart rose on his hand, he knew where to go. This time the doctor took a look at his patient's wart, rolled up his own sleeve and displayed an arm covered with warts. "I guess I've got room for one more," he said, and proceeded to stare the man's wart off. At the same time he revealed to his patient that he had inherited his powers, and that before he died he would pass them on to someone else.

Some healers had the power to induce warts as well as remove them. A white man in Dames Quarter bargained with a black "doctor": one bag of candy for the removal of one wart. When the wart vanished in a week, the Negro approached his client in the local store and asked for the fee. The white man demurred until threatened with the return of the wart, whereupon he quickly paid his debt.

If a medicinal reason can be offered for some traditional cures, there is little rationale that can be applied to the magic suggested in most of the cures provided for warts. There appears, for example, little logic in this belief: "To get rid of warts, go out in the woods and drive a nail in a tree. File on the nail the number of warts you have. Then walk away and never look back, and your warts will disappear." Yet there is a good deal of sympathetic magic suggested in the process that folklorists call "plugging away." The assumption is that somehow the nail becomes an extension of the warts when the number is etched on it, and thereby the warts are transferred into the tree. Once the spell is cast, it would be loss of faith to look back, and if one did the spell would be broken. Other obvious transfers occur in the process called "selling away." "You want to get rid of warts? Just rub a penny over them and throw it over your left shoulder. Don't ever look at that penny again and your warts will go away." Sometimes the transfer becomes complete as in this example of what is called "counting away." "To remove warts cut a hole in a stick for each wart. Throw it away. When someone picks up that stick he'll get your warts." Frequently the warts are transferred and then buried away. "If you want to cure warts, steal a dishrag, wipe it over the warts, and bury it under a rock. When the dish rag rots, the warts will be gone." "Now if you want to get rid of warts, tie a knot in a rope. Rub the knot on the wart and then bury it under the water drain. In five days the wart will be gone." "On a real cold night, go down to the river and get a whole lot of seaweed. Wrap it around your hand and then put the seaweed in a bag and bury it and your warts will go away." Similar burying rituals worked with bacon rind, peas, pork, and a stolen bean.

Water frequently worked as a cleansing agent in wart cures. Presumably, by burying a wart transferred to a dishrag beneath the water drain, it would be washed away. Another belief suggests that water actually carries the wart away. "To get rid of warts, just rub a grain of corn on the wart, throw the corn in a running stream of water and forget about it. The wart will disappear. But you have to completely forget about it." Others who wished to lose their warts simply found a hollow tree in the woods and bathed their warts in the water it contained. An Upper Fairmount healer employed fish in her method:

> One time my father had a large wart on the side of his face. He'd always remind the barber every time he went for a shave to be sure not to cut it off. Well, this day he was down to his place of business and an old colored woman came in and noticed the wart. She said she'd take it off for him. He didn't quite believe her, but he went along with her anyway. Now she went and caught a minnow and rubbed it on the wart and told him that the next time she saw him the wart would be gone. And after she'd rubbed the minnow on the wart she let it swim away.
>
> A week or ten days later, my father went back to the barber for a shave and reminded the barber about that wart. But when the barber looked in the whiskers, it was gone. He couldn't find any wart at all. It had just disappeared. (16)

Clearly, with folk medicine, the more common the malady, the more varied the traditional means of healing it. With a cold for instance, one could concoct a brew of kerosene and sugar, or rub mutton tallow on the chest, or prepare a pine shat [needle] tea, or grease the temples and bottoms of feet with beef suet,

230

or cover the chest with a rag soaked in turpentine and tallow, or simply wear a tar rope around the neck. But if one were really clever, he didn't get sick. He prevented colds by carrying an onion around in his pocket all winter, or hanging an asefetida bag around his neck. Other safeguards were more elaborate: "To ward off colds: rub down in goose oil; take a fresh muskrat skin and sew the bloody side to a red flannel vest; put the red flannel next to the skin with the fur side out and wear until it falls off."

Eastern Shoremen eased sore throats by taking off a dirty sock, sprinkling it with salt, and wearing it around the neck to bed. Some used a rag wrung out in child's urine around the throat. Urine also worked as a beautifying agent. Pimples disappeared if the face was swabbed with a wet baby's diaper. Fevers subsided when beaten horseradish was bound to the pulse or an onion poultice lashed to the head and feet. Some women reduced fevers by attaching salt fish or cucumbers to the feet while others made the patient swallow cobwebs that had been rolled up. Cobwebs could also be applied to cuts to stem the bleeding. A combination of sulphur and molasses replaced geritol for tire blood in folk cures. A great number of people drank a brew of sassafras tea to thin the blood in the spring, and a dosage of hog's liver improved low blood pressure.

Common everyday aches, pains, and discomfort likewise found relief in folk remedies. An axe under the bed prevented sweating, while children were fed chicken gizzard tea to cur bedwetting. A wad of chewed tobacco on bee stings drew the pain out, and placed on cuts it brought the wound together faster. A mixture of fresh lard and tar helped rid the hair of dandruff. Diarrhea, referred to by some as "downards" (vomiting was "upards"), improved if one ate a mess of browned apple scrapings. For constipation, boiled "physic grass" roots or poke salad tea brought results. Flax seed in the eye removed foreign matter. A drop of urine, or smoke blown gently into the ear brought relief from an ear ache, and ear wax helped cure a fever blister. Hemorrhoids improved if one sat on a warm pine board or mashed twelve red bed bugs in lard and applied it as a poultice. A shark's tooth hung down the back of the neck prevented nose-

231

bleeds. If one occurred, however, the victim could either chew a piece of brown paper vigorously or apply a piece of brown paper with the word STOP written on it to the roof of the mouth and hold the head back. Toothaches subsided if a fried egg were bound to the ear or if the face were bathed in water boiled with a hog jowl bone. Backaches abated if a tarred string were tied around the waist. And nutmeg carried in the pocket rid the system of boils. Corn remedies required magic. "To remove a corn on your toe, spit on your finger and rub your finger over the corn every morning for nine mornings before you speak to anyone."

Children's ailments naturally demanded the attention of the folk practitioner. A mole's foot dangled from the child's neck alleviated teething. So did a thimble rubbed over the gums. For weak infants, some bathed their heads in whiskey to make them gain strength faster. Children recovered from chicken pox if placed in front of the hen house so the chickens could fly over them. Catnip tea soothed the colic in the very young. Mumps subsided when the swelling was rubbed with the marrow of a hog's jawbone, or if the soot from a wood stove was smeared from one side of the face to the other. The disappearance of chronic croup demanded a complex ritual. "If a child has the croup, bore a hole in a door facing, and put some of the child's hair in it. Put in a plug and saw the end off even with the facing. When he grows over that height, he won't have the croup anymore."

Less well-known human afflictions also developed traditional cures. If a person contracted worms, pumpkin seeds were the answer, or else he could wear a ball of garlic around the neck and say a prayer. The smell of garlic suffocated the worms. But if the patient vomited, it was a sign that the worms had already gone to the heart. One avoided sunstroke by placing horseradish leaves inside the hat, or foot cramps at night by turning the bottom of the shoes upwards. And a piece of copper worn around the wrist removed the acid from the stomach. Eastern Shore tradition even included a cure for love ills: "If a woman takes a drop of blood from her menses and puts it into a man's drink, he will be hooked on her for life, sexually."

Minor Genres

Folk Speech and Naming

At least one folklorist has successfully launched a collection project on the supposition that in areas where relic words have turned up, traditional narratives and songs would also persist. Relic words are archaisms that have been held over by a folk group and if they are listed at all in modern dictionaries they are invariably cited as obsolete. Poets, like Robert Frost, for instance, sensitive to local folk idiom, often draw these words into their verse. In his widely read poem, "Mending Wall," Frost speaks of using "a spell" to make the rocks of the wall balance. Most readers conjure up the idea of magic, but Vermont farmers will tell you that a spell is simply a sliver of small rock used as a wedge for holding larger boulders in place.

Though folklorists seldom go into the field just to collect traditional words or idioms (this is more the job of the linguist), they frequently find local patterns of speech in the texts of narratives or songs, proverbs or riddles. These speech patterns appear in what the schoolteacher might consider grammatical deviations, though the person who utters them does so out of force of tradition with no thought as to whether they are "right" or "wrong". Eastern Shoremen, for example, say "div" for dove—"he div overboard and was gone."—and "drownded" instead of drowned. And their pronunciation is likewise traditional and deeply set in the dialect. Bay watermen sail 'drudge' (dredge) boats when they go "austerin" (oystering). When their boats are hauled out of the water once a year they are "corked" (caulked) before they are "lanched" (launched) again. Weather is never calm, always "kam" and the watermen usually embellish their phraseology with images, referring to the Bay as "slick kam" or "kam as a dish." In Eastern Shore lingo, one "heists" (hoists) his sail, heads his vessel towards a "pint" (point) of land, and then drives it up or down a "thurfer" (thoroughfare). And a waterman goes either to the "northerd, sutherd, easterd or westerd."

Other traditional variations occur in syntax. "How come I to know this" replaces "The way I learned this" on the lower Eastern Shore. 'Either' frequently means any. "I have lunch for you, but I don't have either biscuit." To be "up and down with somebody" refers not to a hot and cold relationship as one might suppose, but rather to the fact that the person can't be found. Hard working people never get tired, they simply "give out". Similar traditional alterations reveal deep-seated roots: "I heard tell of; He overed his cold; When I listen at the preacher say, 'Love one or nother . . . ; I'd like for you to do this for me; It belongs to be that way; Shut the door to."

Still more striking are the actual words and sayings, some of which are highly localized. Alex Kellam recalled that in the old days on Smith Island in the village of Rhodes Point there was something the watermen referred to as a 'Rhodes Pointer'. The term did not designate a person from the village, but rather a perfect mooring made under sail. To bring a small skipjack without engine to a perfect mooring demanded a good deal of skill. Sailing well below the mooring, the helmsman then shot up into the wind so that the boat glided gently to the mooring float enabling the crew to pick it up without difficulty. If one overshot the mark the headway of the vessel would make it almost impossible to secure the float, while undershooting resulted in the boat falling back off to leeward before the float could be gathered in. Rhodes Point watermen apparently became so adept at making their moorings, no matter what the weather, that Rhodes Pointer became proverbial folk speech for a perfect mooring.

And of course, [concluded Kellam] there was this old fellow from Tylerton who came over there one time and tried to come up to one of those moorings. Well, the first time he brought her up but he didn't give her enough and she fell off. So he tried her again, and the same thing happened. She fell right off. He brought her up a third time, but he got her too close and he overshot; went right on by. So he just stood up there in the bow of his boat and waved. (Gesticulated as though beckoning the mooring to come to him). You see he wasn't from Rhodes Pint. (1)

Smith Islanders have a battery of expressions that smack of traditional speech patterns and add considerable spice to daily conversation. When one expels gas, he "poots" and he "gaps" when he yawns. Something that is prone or flat is "spreeted out". Someone is not badly burned, but "burnt up alive". A "snapper rig" is a makshift arrangement which might lead one into a "kelter" or a "pretty time" (bad situation) and bring on a "duck fit" (unpleasant reaction). When a waterman has the engine of his boat at a high pitch, he "has really got it on her." Not surprisingly several expressions suggest seafaring language. A mother chastizes her wayward child with, "If you do that again, I'll flinder your stern" (whip you). One "battens down" the home as well as the boat for a severe storm. Gear is "stowed away," and when a girl faints she "keels over." One doesn't get ready and leave, but "rigs up and goes."

The weather, so immediate to the waterman's way of life, likewise lends itself colorful phrases. A Tylerton man recalled that the threat of a clearing front and a northwest gale hastened his grandmother's remark, "It looks like the wind's going to come down to Aunt Judy's." But who Aunt Judy was, or what she had to do with the weather, he couldn't say. On Tangier Island when ominous thunderheads gathered in the west neighbors yelled across the way, "My good Lord, it looks like we're going to have a Fuzz Cod." But on quiet nights Tangiermen commented, "Why it's so still tonight you could hear a fart on Watts Island" (four miles from Tangier). On the Chesapeake when it "breezed up" into a "reverend gale" the wind was "really a-caukin out there" and the "white bellied sou'wester" quickly turned the Bay a "feather white."

Some Eastern Shore storytellers recognize different speech patterns. Crisfield residents who have moved ashore get much mileage and a good deal of mirth out of tales that depict islander's naivete and traditional language. Islanders pronounce the word 'here' as 'year' and one is informed of the old waterman closeted in a small noisy room who could stand it no longer and cried out, "It's so damn loud you can't year your years in year" (hear your ears in here). One is also told of the two island women who came ashore and confronted a steam engine for the first time:

"My good Lord, what's that?"
"I certainly don't know, but it looks for all the world like a cookstove on wheels."

And in another account two Tangier ladies are humorously ridiculed for their diction:

There were these two women from over to Tangier, and they come over here on the steamboat. They didn't have much education, you know, but they wanted to act like they did, so this one said to the other, 'Now we've got to say everything just the right way while we're there.'

Well, in those days, the steamboat would blow its whistle when it got ready to go, so as to let people know. So these two women they went into town, shopping, you know. And so after a while that steamboat blew her whistle. One of them turned to the other, said, 'Well, we've got to gew.'
'How did ye knew?'
'I heard it blew.' (18)

Alex Kellam, always sensitive to old ways and speech, recalled the Smith Island expression 'sigh', a contraction of 'says I,' which several generations ago cluttered the watermen's conversation:

Now for instance, if we were kicking up, my grandfather's uncle would say, 'Sigh, boy, sigh, you let me speak to you just one more time.' They always said, 'sigh'. They never said 'says I' to you. Said, "Sigh, boy, sigh, what are you doing?" And they used that all the time. They would mean, "says I" but they cut it down to "sigh", and I've heard them all, all my uncles use that. Grandfather too. I remember it very well now. The women didn't use it but the men did. (1)

Kellam remembered other terms. The word "jubrous", he allowed, designated skepticism. One might say, "I'm jubrous of that" when he had real doubts about it. Or for an event highly out of the ordinary, a Smith Islander might remark, "Well Mags, I've just heard the champus." Tippy boats were not tender, but "cranky" or "wally." Clumps of grass or seaweed were "tumps" and the gnarled roots of a tree stump "sprangled" out of the ground. A hunting experience brought another Crisfield man into contact with the expression, "They've toomed her."

> I went duckin' on Smith Island once. There's a boy over there; he was very witty. He and I were in the blind one day and he had a call goose. And that goose was as human as humanly possible for a dumb fowl to be. He could talk to that goose and he'd do anything he told him to.
>
> For instance, we saw a flock of geese flying some distance off and this fella says, 'Bob, pull down your lever and blow.' [Imitates goose call] And that goose started in a honking and two or three times he brought them in that way. A call goose, they don't permit them now, but a call goose was most effective in ducking in the early days.
>
> Well, we were in the same blind and he says, 'Clem, get down low. Here they come. They're just sweeping the water, a whole raft of them.' He stopped and says, 'They've toomed her.' I don't know ever how to spell it, and they still use it over there; I found out what it meant was that they had lighted or pitched on the water. But he said, 'They toomed her, so get yourself ready.' (24)

Eastern Shoremen also flavor their speech with proverbial comparisons which fit neatly into daily conversation. Again the weather provides a number of traditional examples. It's not just hot or cold to Eastern Shoremen, but "as hot as hell-o-pete," or "so damn hot you melt and run together," or "as cold as a well digger's ass," "a stepmother's breath", or "as cold as pewter." Nor does it simply rain on the Shore; "it rains so hard it sounds

237

like a cow pissing on a flat rock." Niggardliness, never an admired trait, furnishes several variations. One is so close with his possessions "he'd skin a louse for its hide and tallow" or "he'd chase his carcass through hell for the cracklings." One can also be simply, "so tight he squeaks." General attractiveness or unattractiveness yield a spate of comparisons. "She's as ugly as a mud fence," "looking like she'd been drug through a knot hole," "as ugly as mashed mud." If she's really terrifying, "she's so ugly she has to sneak up on a glass to get a drink of water," or "she has a face that only a mother could love." By the same token a comely girl could be "as pretty as a steamboat," or "as pretty as a robin in a rosebush."

Other human traits besides looks lend themselves to proverbial expressions. A person with a dearth of brains can be "as dumb as a meat axe," "as dumb as an ox," or "as dumb as Baalum's ass." If he's truly stupid, he doesn't "have sense enough to carry guts to the tub," or so foolish "he can't pour piss out of a boot with the directions written on the heel." A person can also be "as *grouchie* as an old bear," "mad enough to chew nails and spit bullets," or "so poor when I was born we had to get the neighbors to have me." If a man is worthless he's "not worth his salt" or "as worthless as the teats on a boar hog." He may even "lack a dollar and a half of being worth a damn." At the same time a hard working individual can be "as busy as a bee in a tar bucket," "a cat with diarrhea," or "a one eyed dog in a meat market." Hunger draws some familiar comparative hyperboles: "I haven't eaten in so long, my stomach called up to see if my throat was cut." "It's been so long since I last ate that my stomach thinks my mouth's gone on vacation." "It's been so long since I've had any food, my stomach thinks my ribs have taken in washing." But after a hearty feed, the same men could be "full as a tick", "as full as a frog full of flies," "or so full it makes you poor to carry it." One could also be "worn to a grummit" "as happy as a clam at high tide," "as mean as Guybroth," "as polite as a dog pissing on a briar," "as old as Methusela" "as silly as a goose," "as queer as Dick's hatband," "as awkward as a cow," "as fat as a pig," or "so thin he had to drink muddy water to cast a shadow."

The entire realm of description takes on new image patterns

when placed in folk speech. Colors are placed in a new context. Something is "as green as gore" "blue as a robin's egg" "black as a crow," "or white as a hound's tooth." Common objects also take on another dimension. A thing can be "as hard as lightered knots," "as tough as whit leather," "as scarce as hens' teeth," "as sharp as a hounds tooth," "as smart as a briar," "as thick as hops," "as slick as a mole," "as slippery as an eel." An item can be "no bigger than a killdee" "a beer taller than a drudge boat's mast," "as big as a barn door," or "all outdoors," and "as broad as a box car." Something gawdy or out of place is spoke of as being "as awkward as a breast pin on a hog." But one who appears in fancy clothes is "dressed up like Astor's pet goat." And anyone with a large hat on "looks like a snow bird under a sifter."

For the most part, proverbial comparisons found on the Eastern Shore express their similies as they do in other areas: with a terse traditional statement that adds spice to an object's or a personal shortcoming. On occasion, though, Shoremen turn ironic with their comments. Instead of something being "as clear as a bell" or "as clear as glass", it becomes "as clear as mud." A bald man is humorously referred to as being "as hairy as a doornob," and an individual whose percentage of success is low, "has about as much chance as a snowball in hell." Other comparisons suggest something beyond sheer bliss when one is "grinning like a skunk eating briars" or "sweating like a nigger at a lynching" though to be sure, the irony is less apparent.

Colorful speech carries over into the realm of folk naming as well. On the lower Eastern Shore, especially in such small communities as Lawsonia and Jenkins Creek, just below Crisfield, the process of nicknaming is a way of life. In semi-isolated regions where there is little influx from the outside, a good deal of inbreeding takes place and dominant names emerge. South of Crisfield, one can hardly knock on a door without turning up a Ward or a Lawson, a Nelson or a Byrd. So prominent are some names in a particular location that the clustering of that clan in one place lends a name to the place. Thus we find Lawsonia and Byrdtown and on Smith Island, where Tyler is a common surname, Tylerton. Tylerton also provides a host of Marshalls: and Ewells and Rhodes Point, the other island settlements, furnish plenty of Evanses and Bradshaws. On Tangier Island the key name is Crockett.

Intermarriage on the Eastern Shore has been going on for quite a while, in some places since the seventeenth century when certain of these communities were first settled. A lot of George Lawsons or William Bradshaws or George Sterlings can build up in a small area over ten or more generations. And when you have more than seven or eight George Lawsons living within a radius of less than five miles, it becomes difficult to designate whom you mean when you say, George Lawson. But the folk solve the problem by pinning a nickname on everyone. After a time the nickname becomes so much a part of the person, he sometimes forgets what his real name is. Edmund 'Ham' Tull—he cannot recall how his own nickname was conferred—carried the mail in Lawsonia for many years and claimed that all letters were invariably directed to an individual via his nickname. Humorous situations often arose when an outsider did not know the nickname code:

> This fellow come down here one time from Salisbury. He was delivering something to him (Pony) or something like that. I don't really remember. But anyway this fellow come up and knocked on the door. Pony comes to the door, says, 'Yes, what can I do for you?'
> Man said, 'I'm looking for a Mr. George Lawson.'
> He said, 'I'm sorry, nobody by that name lives here.'
> So that fellow turned around and started back for his car, and Pony, he started back to go into the house. And all of a sudden he realized that the fellow was after him. 'That's me, I'm George Lawson.' He didn't even know his real name, just that name, 'Pony'. (10)

Few people could come up with the etymology of their own nickname, but "Bluebird" Nelson was one. He remembered his family telling him that as a young child they had dressed him up one Sunday morning in a brand new suit, and on the way to church an old black man remarked, "Well, will you look, here comes a bluebird." The name obviously held. Similarly Ligea Nelson was dubbed 'Ducky' because as a child he used to run down to the duck pen and try to twist the heads off of the family ducks. Others, like "Snubber" Bennett acquired their nicknames later in life:

> Ed and Norm Bennett were bringing a little old bugeye loaded with oysters up to Cambridge. They couldn't get her around, so they squared her off and took her up where the big ships was. Finally they nosed her in under a high clay bank. Norman was letting out the anchor chain when Ed called, 'Snub her.'
>
> Norman answered, 'Snub her, hell! It's all gone. Three hundred foot of chain and the whole works.' Well, she nose right into that clay bank and stuck there. They went up a couple of days later and pulled and tugged until they got her out. People herebouts used to call out to him after that whenever he came in the store, 'Here comes Snubber Bennett.' (36)

Christian names at times stemmed directly from the maritime culture, Avalon Riggin's grandfather followed the water and that had a great deal to do with her name:

> Now this was when I was born and grandpop was coming down the Bay on his boat. There used to be these side-wheelers that some firm had built to go from the Western Shore to the Eastern Shore, and their names were the *Piankitank* and the *Rappahannock* and the *Avalon* and I don't know what the other was. But anyway, he was coming down the Bay that morning and he went right by the *Avalon,* and he come on home and I had just been born. Well, my parents had no name and so he said, "Let me name her," and he named me Avalon. And, of course, my middle name is Pearl from the oyster, and I'm married to a Riggin, which is a boat's trimming, and it seems funny that I have all these things. And now I'm living on Chesapeake Avenue, and that's the Bay. No wonder I like the water. But, I've always been real thankful that that morning when grandpop came down the Bay that the *Piankitank* didn't go in front of him. (24)

241

Place naming also belongs in part to the folk. Place name anecdotes, or legends if you will, spring from the people's attempt to give a rational explanation to something that on the surface may seem odd. Apes Hole Creek, for instance, or Crapo, or Dames Quarter, or Chance, or Bloody Point unquestionably snag the imagination and almost plead for some sort of explication. And the folk usually provide it, though the stories may not always be consistent. Clearly an entire book could be devoted to place names on the Shore, and here I shall only suggest the kind of thing one might encounter in collecting this genre of folklore.

Eastern Shore names issue from several sources. Indians supplied the rivers, among other things, with titles—the Choptank, the Nanticoke, the Manokin, the Pokomoke. Along the shore, the naming process suggests land formations (Flatcap Point, Broad Creek, Half Moon Island, Long Point and Penknife Point) or recalls, presumably, the name of the person who lent his name to the spot simply by living there or by performing some memorable act. (Jones Creek, Jenkins Creek) According to one informant, Crisfield, previously named Somers Cove, derived from John Crisfield, an important figure in the railroad business. He came to town when they were building the railroad that presently runs along one of the major thoroughfares through to town. When the townspeople took Crisfield for a spin around the harbor on a boat, he accidentally fell overboard, and to appease him, they promised to name the town after him fearful he might not finish the railroad. That is the folk etymology. A more precise account appeared in a letter to *the Crisfield Times:*

Your last issue carries a request for correct historical knowledge of the naming of the Post Offices, as well as a story (somewhat distorted) concerning the name or naming of the city of Crisfield. The facts are:

Honorable John Woodland Crisfield, twice member of Congress, and otherwise outstanding Somerset Countain [sic] of Princess Anne, was the attorney for the principle landowners, viz: Benjamin F. Somers, Thomas Dixon, William Roach, and Michael Somers of this area, when a branch

242

line of the old Maryland railroad went from Salisbury to Michael Somer's store at the mouth of the Little Annemessex River. The Somers store was the transfer point for good [sic] coming to this area by water traffic.

Mr. Crisfield had maintained an interest in promoting the Eastern Shore Railroad, authorized by an Act of the Maryland Legislature in 1835, but which had not materialized at the time a new town was being laid out at the close of the war between the states. Finally, in 1866, the railroad was completed . . . .

When the railroad got the mail contract, and the first mail left the area by railroad, it bore the Crisfield post mark. That was in 1866. The promoters had honored Mr. Crisfield in naming the new city for him . . . .

One day in October, 1874, eight years after the name Crisfield had appeared on the post mark, Mr. Crisfield, with several of the promoters, was walking the wooden ramp to the steamboat wharf. He happened to step on a rotten plank and fell into about twelve feet of water. He might have drowned, except for the timely and quick dive of Mr. William Chelton, a man of towering proportions and stalwart build. He rescued Mr. Crisfield who had had a real dunking. When the crowd gathered because of the excitement, one of the men in the group, Mr. John Carman, the railroad station agent, remarked, "Well, Crisfield's been baptized now, and the name is official."

In the passing of time, events have been so telescroped that the naming of the town and the fall of Mr. Crisfield have been brought together in the somewhat falacious story, "How Crisfield got its name . . . . "

I trust the above will aid in setting the record straight. . . .

Respectfully,
Joseph S. McGarth
Historian Laureate of Crisfield

Other Eastern Shore areas along the Bay acquire their nomenclature from the ecology (Herring Island, Drum Point, Persimmon Point), and often it is the ecology of a bygone era, not that of today. Take, for instance, Hog Neck at the lower end of Smith Island. No one lives on that waste of marsh today, but there was a time when the land was not only habitable, but also arable and capable of supporting livestock as the oral history makes clear.

Esso roadmaps and geodetic charts seldom carry place names known to the long-term residents. Older Tangier Islanders speak of such esoteric parts of the island as King's Ridge (the people who lived there thought they were above everybody else) and Meatsoup ("that was about the only thing they ever ate there"), or they recall the people who used to live at a place north of the main settlement on the island, termed simply Upwards. Government charts understandably lump everything together under the town of Tangier.

Inland the process works much the same way. One could spend a long time searching on a roadmap for a place near Quantico, Maryland locally referred to as Catch Penny. Yet local inhabitants know it well. Accounts of its naming differ. According to several informants, people passing through spent so little money at the store there, that the site gradually gained the name of Catch Penny. But a Quantico man explained it another way:

> There was an old man that always sat on the hill by the the branch that runs up to the river road, that went to the river. There a road that went round to Quantico Town, you know. Well, there used to be an old man sat on the hill and asked for pennies. He'd ask anybody for a penny. Any time you went by there he'd be out there asking for pennies. The folk would say, 'There's old catch penny man, Dink West.' So they called that section, Catch Penny. (31)

Similar folk naming occurs in the Deal Island area. Old maps and charts reveal that Deal Island was previously called Devil's Island, and the nearby section on the road to Princess Anne, now Dames Quarter was once 'Dam' Quarter. A map dated 1832 still lists the community as "Devil's Island" but by 1841 it had been changed to Deil's Island. A local resident suggested why:

In the early days of Deals Island, it was known as Devil's Island. There was a ship bound for Virginia Shore, off course and wrecked on the lower end of the island. The survivors looked out and when they saw nothing but marshes and wilderness, said, "This is Purgatory, the land of the Devil." And so it was known as this until the time of revivals of Joshua Thomas. The people on the island thought they would like a more dignified name, and so this visiting minister suggested that they change the name to Deil's Island. Deil, that's a Greek word meaning Devil. (16)

As late as 1896 government charts still carried it as Deils Island. In the 20th century, the name gradually became standardized to Deal's and then to Deal. According to one source, the 's disappeared when the wooden postmark stamp that the postmaster used got old, split, and lost the final letter and the apostrophe.

The progression of Damn Quarter to Dames Quarter is less easily explained. Most folk etymologies for the original name stick closely to the same theme. A man walking along the road (sometimes he is fishing from a bridge) drops a quarter which he cannot retrieve. "Damn that Quarter," he reputedly mutters, and so the name. One informant however tied the naming to Indians:

So far as I know, this is how Dames Quarter received its name: in the early days there were a couple of white settlers on the marsh and they met some Indians. The Indians were very friendly and helped to show them the muskrat leads and several other places to hunt. These settlers appreciated this and when they left they gave the Indians a quarter and told them to divide it between themselves. So the Indians took their hatchets and tried to cut into it. But they didn't know much about the silver of the day. That's why they tried to cut it with their hatchets. They thought that would be the proper thing. After they cut at that quarter for a long time, they sort of lost patience and they threw that quarter away. They said, 'Damn that white man's quarter, it's no good.' And so they called that place Damn Quarter for a while. (16)

245

Early maps and charts are by no means consistent chronologically with the change in the name of Dames Quarter. In 1775 cartographers list it as Damned Quarter, but almost twenty years later it is mentioned on a map of the lower Chesapeake as Dames Quarter. In 1832, the Quarter goes by the same name, whereas ten years before, it is marked down as a single word: Damquarter. After 1862 it conformed to its present name.

Though no specific reason exists for the evolution of the name Dames Quarter, the different listing on various early charts clearly suggests a misunderstanding on the part of early cartographers. As other students of place names have discovered, this misunderstanding often results either from a simple misconstruing of the intended name, or from failure to decipher the local pronunciation. Along the Maine coast, for instance, geodetic charts site a number of Bear Islands which, because they lack any sign of vegetation, were obviously meant to be Bare Islands. Likewise, present day Tenants Harbor, on that same coastline, appeared on earlier maps variously as Tallants and Tarrants Harbor. Anyone familiar with Maine dialect knows the difficulties an early cartographer doubtless faced when he asked a local inhabitant the name for this or that place.

Much the same sort of thing probably occurred on the Eastern Shore, particularly with a place like Dames Quarter. Older pronunciations of dame rhymed more with 'bomb' than they did with 'aim', and I have frequently heard old Smith Island residents (or younger ones trying to imitate the old way of speech) say 'dahm' instead of 'damn'. Thus folk speech and articulation may well explain why the names of Dames Quarter vacillated from Dame to Damned until 1862.

When supernatural incidents mingle with place naming, the pattern of stories becomes still more complex. Ghost Light Road near Hebron provides a good example. Accounts of strange lights appearing along the road became so common that numbers of people visited the spot in 1952 to witness the apparition. Local newspapers even drew attention to Ghost Light Road by publicizing the appearance of the inexplicable light. The mystery needed some rational and the folk obliged with varied accounts. A Rockawalkin man explained it this way:

246

About seventy-five years ago there was an old man named Joe who lived near here and had a lot of money. He buried this money, so they say, somewhere in them woods. They say that light is old Joe's ghost that comes back every twenty years to see if his money is still there. When he sees it's all right, his ghost goes away. (31)

Stories about the ghost light circulated so widely in the area that the folklore began to shape itself to other purposes. Teenagers picked up the story. One college student from Salisbury recalled driving over to Ghost Light Road when she was in high school, just to test fate. The ritual, as she described it, was to park the car on a secluded spot along the road and wait for the light to appear. When it did, the teenagers sped away in the car, but the light always followed them until they turned off Ghost Light Road. Such dare-devil pranks frequently led to frightening experiences as another Salisbury informant reported:

> Several of us boys rode over to Hebron to the Ghost Light Road one night. While we were sitting there a light about the size of a soccer ball appeared through the woods. It came straight for the windshield. Charles who was out sitting on the hood of the car screamed, 'It's coming; the ghost with its light's coming.'
>
> As he screamed he ran around to the car door and wanted to get in, but we had locked the doors. Then we started up and left him on the outside. He grabbed onto the trunk of the car and clung there just like an eel. He was so scared he couldn't move much less fall off. And he kept screaming as we rode off, 'Let me in.' (31)

If the ghost light could become an object for terrifying adults in a kind of indoctrination rite, so too could it function as a kind of 'boggie man' tale for youngsters. A Sharptown woman remembered her father employing the tale as such:

> Poppa used to tell me when I was little the light came from an old woman sitting in a rocking chair with a lantern

247

in her hand. She always sat in the middle of the road so she could hear all the children who didn't mind their parents. Poppa said if I didn't take my medicine, or do what he said, the old woman would come and get me.

I have never heard anyone else tell this story about the light and I think he just made it up so I would be scared into taking some bad medicine, or doing something I didn't want to do. (15)

Other place names mix elements of folk rational with humor. A Mt. Vernon man explained away Kedges Strait (listed on early charts as Cagis Strait) as a sluice of water, at one time so shoal that vessels had to "kedge" their way across it by throwing the anchor out ahead of them and then pulling the boat up to it. With Hebron, at one time a railroad station, mispronunciation gave the village its name. When a group of passengers arrived at the stop, a well-wisher greeted them: "Well, you're in Heaven now," but it came out "Hebron," and so the place was named. Similarly with Fairmount: "Well, there was a time when they had these land grants and they give this fella this fare and he looks it over and he says, "Well, that's a fair amount," and they named it Fairmount." A stranger christened Ape's Hole Creek, just below Crisfield. After he had surveyed the surroundings briefly, he remarked, "This looks just like an ape's hole," and the name stuck. And Negroes around Nanticoke ascribe etymology to what is obviously an Indian name, Tyaskin. Apparently, farmers and merchants met in the area to do their business. Altercations frequently erupted and to settle the disputes the men "tied asses" or fought.

All too frequently historians slight folk naming, passing it off as sheer whimsy. Not long ago I spoke with an ex-professor from the University of Maryland who has grown up on the lower Eastern Shore, near Snow Hill. He spoke at length about a recent history book by a Princeton professor which argued that no facts existed to prove that the now famous Chincoteague ponies came from a Spanish vessel wrecked there in the 17th century. Yet my Maryland acquaintance remembered vividly as a boy playing on a sand spit along the shore locally called Spanish Bar. Certainly this fact does not disprove the Princeton

248

historian's thesis, but it would seem that behind this particular place name lies a reason that may still linger in local tradition and deserve some sort of investigation.

Folk Verse and Riddles

Traditional white folksinging, if indeed it ever existed, has completely lapsed on the Eastern Shore; however, folk verse still has a place. Those who recite the verse seldom recall where they heard it, and usually they remember only the poem in fragments. But certain lines stick in their minds and surface in the course of a conversation. Milton Fitzhugh, a retired waterman from Cambridge, spoke of one fellow who went oystering on a Sunday. When he learned that the church was going to put an end to it, he reputedly responded in verse:

> They think they'll convert us
> An throw all our rum away,
> But they're gonna be mistaken
> On the drudge boat down the bay. (48)

Fitzhugh recited another snatch of verse which depicted the times "when the old drudgers fought and stuff like that":

> After drudging all day,
> The Captain picked up the spyglass,
> And seeing the police boat far away, . . . [?]
> Then in sail the gallant pungy flew
> In forbidden waters to steal a jag or two.
> We hadn't been there over an hour at night,
> Before the police boat pulled in sight.
> He said, "Haul down your jib with good command,
> But we begin to fight. (48)

The poetry that appeals to the folk frequently hinges on homey philosophy or turns to moralizing at the end. One encounters such a simple, though sound observation in:

249

As a rule a man's a fool.
When it's hot, he wants it cool.
When it's cool, he wants it hot.
He always wants what he ain't got. (1)

Or from a longer piece on "The Indispensible Man" which ends didactically:

The moral of this story is:
Be proud of yourself; do the best you possibly can.
But remember, there's no such thing,
As an indispensible man. (1)

Some fragments of verse treat the inevitable onslaught of age where the body "with age is bent" and the once affluent pocket now contains "not a cent." From another rhyme, the fate of man's virility is humorously disclosed.

When you're young and in your prime,
You can get a little baby in one night's time.
But when you're old and your stone gets cold,
You can't get a little baby to save your soul. (48)

Delmas Shores, a Dames Quarter waterman, claimed that a generation ago crew members on drudge boats often created satiric verse to heckle their shipmates. The purpose of the verse was to incorporate as many people by name as possible, as in this bit of rhyme.

Jack Dabbage stole a rotten head of cabbage.
Jim Hewett saw him do it.
Hen Doan says, "Let it alone."
Joshua Thomas made a promise
With Jim Elliot never to tell it. (49)

Shores himself dabbled in verse and recited an extended text which he said he'd made up twenty or more years ago when he was following the water, working for Captain Johnny White.

250

One Thursday morning when the weather was thick,
Captain Johnny White sailed down to Crab Crick.
He was tonging hard and culling fast,
While Elmer Shores sat on his—the engine box, smoking
    cigarettes.
He thought in his mind, if he'd drive them like me,
We'll have a big jag by half past three.
To his surprise, come Insley and Winterbottom,
And culled through his pile, clear down through to the bottom.
Now Captain John, you're in a mess,
For the rest of the winter, you'll have no rest.
You lost your record with Randolph White,
A man who will always treat you right.
You lost your record with Insley too,
You'll get a fine before you're through.
You just as well put her in Fanny's Gut,
And get a berth and tong with Mutt,
For he's the best tonger on the Eastern Shore,
(A good looking man and very bold.)
And put Elmer Shore right back on the shore,
So he can sit out at Delmas's Store. (49)

Shores explained his ironic creation as something he never wrote
down, but rather thought up to recite to his friends and ridicule
Captain White. Crab Crick, he indicated, was the oyster rock
they were working at the time, and Insley, Winterbottom and
Randolph White were all members of the Bay Police force. No
proof exists to suggest Shore's poem ever passed into oral tradition, yet a number of people in the area had heard him recite
his verse at the local store and elsewhere. If nothing else,
Shore's attempt at satiric verse would seem to reveal a pattern of
folk creativity, which could be legitimately studied were more
material available.

    Riddling has long been an active tradition among the folk.
If often works in an educational vein, stimulating the minds
and wits of children and adults alike. We know that old watermen
on Smith Island often tried to stump their friends at the local
store with problems drummed up out of the Bible. On the

Eastern Shore one finds old and very traditional riddles such as this from Oriole:

> As I was going across London Bridge,
> I met my sister Ann.
> I cut her throat and sucked her blood
> And let her body stand.
>
> (A bottle of wine)

In a region where the oyster is king, it is hardly surprising to discover the above riddle altered to this:

> As I was going cross London Bridge,
> I met old old Daddy Gray.
> I ate his meat and drank his blood
> And threw his bones away.
> Now, just who was Daddy Gray?
>
> (An oyster)

Or reshaped altogether into a riddle which suggests an obscene answer, but returns an innocuous one:

> It's thin, long, stiff and slender.
> You stick it in and wiggle it about
> And then the juice comes running out.
> What is it?
>
> (Shucking an oyster)

Rhyme frequently occurs in the older forms of riddle, thus facilitating memory:

> Long legs, crooked thighs,
> Little head, no eyes.
>
> (Fire tongs)
>
> Long, slim, slick fellow,
> Pull the trigger and hear him bellow.
>
> (Gun)
>
> Round as a doughnut,
> Busy as a bee,

Prettiest little thing
You ever did see.
(Watch)
Twenty white horses on a red hill,
Now they're dancing, now they're prancing,
Now they're standing still.
(Your teeth)
I hide in many secret places,
I scarcely ever show my face,
I keep my house upon my back,
And roll along a silver track.
(Snail)
Riddle me, riddle me,
What is that?
Over your head
And under your hat?
(Hair)
Black without,
Red within;
Pick up your foot,
And stick it in.
(Boot)
I have eyes but cannot see;
A skin but not a face;
When farmers dig up ground for me
They find my hiding place.
(Irish potato)
I have legs but cannot walk;
A leaf, yet I'm no tree.
I may be square or round or long,
Sometime you sit on me
(A table)

At times riddles suggest entire scenes:

As I was going through the world's wisdom, I met Heldom-Beldom. I send for Scriglum-Scraglum to drive Heldom-Beldom out of the world's wisdom.
(Bull got out in the woods and I sent for the dog)

253

Two Legs sat on Three Legs by Four Legs.
One Leg knocked Two Legs off Three Legs.
Two Legs hit Four Legs with Three Legs.
(Old man sat down on a three-legged stool to milk
his cow. The cow kicked him and he hit her with the stool)

But more often they are simple and demand a single thing for an
answer:

On the outside is a stonewall; on the inside a small
golden lady?
(An egg)
What is it a poor man puts on the ground that a rich
man puts in his pocket?
(Snot)
What do you cut off at both ends to make longer?
(Ditch)
What goes from door to door but never comes in?
(Path)
What has eyes but cannot see?
(Potato)
What has ears but cannot hear?
(Corn)

Certainly riddling as an active tradition which employed
puzzles relating to such common everyday things as brooms and
shoes and eggs and andirons has noticeably declined on the
Eastern Shore. As the culture becomes irretreivably more sub-
urban many of these rural items and objects are no longer as
paramount in the home as they once were. The vacuum cleaner
has supplanted the broom, the oil furnace diminished the ultimate
need for andirons. From recent studies it appears that the school
children of today on the Eastern Shore and elsewhere incline
more towards the *reductio ad absurdum* of the sham riddle as
found in the "moron joke" (Why did the little Moron bury his
mother under the step? He wanted a stepmother) or the ubiquitous and more recent "Eelephant Jokes" (Why do elephants
drink? To forget) or those riddles which turn on word play and
suggest a more sophisticated form than the older folk genres
254

(What did the bald-headed man say when he got a comb for Christmas? I'll never part with this; Why are fish so smart? They go around in schools; Was it the apple on the tree that caused all the trouble in the Garden of Eden? No, it was the pair under the tree.) Some riddles reveal their age, or youth as the case may be, by the slogans they employ (What did the Pepsi Cola say to the graveyard? "Come alive, you're in the Pepsi generation.)

Perhaps the change in riddling is emblematic of the entire change in folklore and folklife that will irrevocably occur on the Eastern Shore. Many of the stories and traditions included here, though still active in some quarters, doubtless will find fewer and fewer narrators and adherents as modernization homogenizes the culture. But the old forms of folklore will be replaced by newer ones, and this book will someday stand as a memento to the way Eastern Shore folklore used to be.

Informants and Collections

1. Alex Kellam
   Crisfield, Maryland

2. Gorman Tull
   Crisfield, Maryland

3. George Alan Wheatley
   Tangier Island, Va.

4. Otis Evans
   Crisfield, Maryland

5. Allen Parks
   Crisfield, Maryland

6. Clifton Webster
   Wenona, Maryland

7. Reginald Truitt
   Stevensville, Maryland

8. Rob Williams
   Crisfield, Maryland

9. Will Holland
   Fairmont, Maryland

10. Ham Tull
    Lawsonia, Maryland

11. Bain Bradshaw
    Rhodes Point, Maryland
12. Dewey Landon
    Crisfield, Maryland
13. Link Ward
    Lawsonia, Maryland
14. Harold Hinman
    Lawsonia, Maryland
15. (ES 69-10)
16. (ES 68-48)
17. Fred Cullen
    Crisfield, Maryland
18. Charleton Marshall
    Crisfield, Maryland
19. Winfred Evans
    Rhodes Point, Maryland
20. Alfred Johnson
    Marion, Maryland
21. (ES 68-34)
22. (ES 68-19)
23. Ronald Purnell
    Crisfield, Maryland
24. (ES 68-1)
25. Alice Middleton
    Ewell, Maryland
26. Steve Ward
    Lawsonia, Maryland
27. (ES 68-33)
28. (ES 69-4)
29. George Glenn
    Annapolis, Maryland
30. Avalon Hill
    Crisfield, Maryland
31. (ES 69-39)
32. Thomas Tyler
    Tylerton, Maryland
33. Harry Hall
    Fairmount, Maryland
34. Elizabeth Hall
    Crisfield, Maryland
35. (ES 68-2)
36. (ES 68-12)
37. Lelia Johnson
    Marion, Maryland
38. Cleo Johnson
    Hopewell, Maryland
39. (ES 68-5)
40. Lloyd McCready
    Crisfield, Maryland
41. Daniel Messicks
    Dames Quarter, Maryland
42. Jessie Evans
    Crisfield, Maryland
43. (ES 68-30)
44. Rachael Cox
    Crisfield, Maryland
45. Virginia Russell
    Lawsonia, Maryland
46. (ES 68-4)
47. (ES 68-17)
48. Milton Fitzhugh
    Cambridge, Maryland
49. Delmas Shores
    Dames Quarter, Maryland

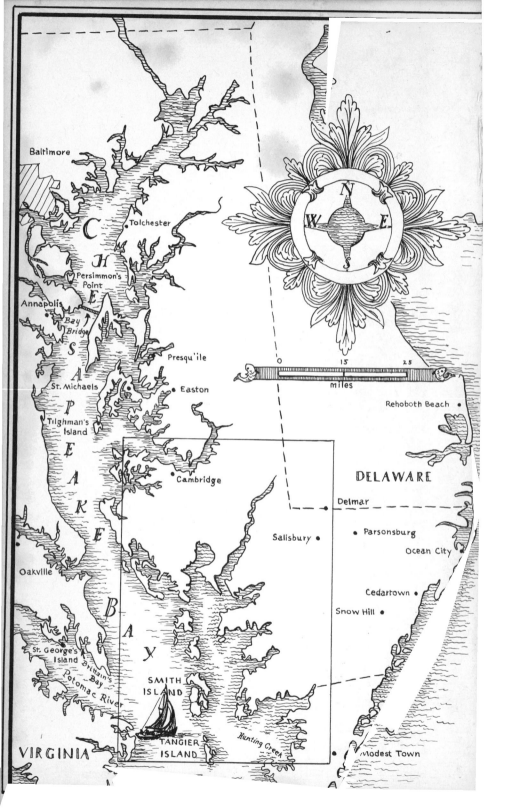